STRATEGIES FOR THE HUNTER

DURWOOD HOLLIS

Published by

**krause
publications**

700 East State St., Iola, WI 54990-0001
715-445-2214
www.krause.com

Please, call or write us for our free catalog.
To place an order or receive our free catalog, call 800-258-0929. For editorial comment and further information,
use our regular business telephone at (715) 445-2214

Library of Congress Catalog Number: 00-107845
ISBN: 0-87341-908-1

Printed in the United States of America

Acknowledgments

There are many who have had an influence on this work. Among these luminaries are outdoor writers, Jim Matthews and Bob Robb. Both men freely provided extensive research and photographic support to these pages. Thanks for your friendship, your encouragement, and your unselfishness.

My wife, Anita, was a source of endless inspiration during the course of this project. She served as my copy editor and her critical eye caught many of the mistakes that would have otherwise escaped my attention.

I am also grateful to professional outfitters and guides, Duwane Adams, Tim Doud, and John Winter for allowing me to share their campfires. Each trip was a learning experience that I will always cherish. And to all the others with whom I've shared elk camp—friends like Al Kavalauskas, Jacob and Zieb Stetler, and Thad Young, as well all the other guides, cooks, and horse wranglers—the debt is mine alone.

Finally, my appreciation is extended to the staff of Krause Publications, Book Division, for providing this opportunity to share my love of elk hunting.

Dedication:

For my father, Hubert Hollis
I can still feel his hand on my shoulder, and hear his voice on the wind

Table of Contents

About The Author

Durwood Hollis was born and reared in Los Angeles, California, just about the time World War II was beginning. In those days, southern California was still rural enough to afford a taste of the outdoors. Absent the freeways, concrete and asphalt, one could find plenty of dove, quail, rabbits and even deer in the outskirts of the city. While other boys were playing baseball, catching waves on their surfboards, and building hotrods, Durwood was learning about hunting, fishing, and fly tying.

During his college years, Durwood was introduced to big game hunting by a close friend. All it took was one deer hunt to set his feet on the path. Over the last three decades, he has pursued this interest on three continents, and throughout the United States.

Durwood's freelance writing career began more than 20 years ago. His writing and several of his photographs have appeared in most major outdoor magazines and several books. He has served as a columnist for Petersen's *Hunting Magazine, Blackpowder Hunting,* and as a contributing editor for *Shooting Sports Retailer.* His work has been regularly published in *Gun World, Guns & Ammo, Bow & Arrow, Blade Magazine,* and many other publications.

Whether it's in Wyoming's Bridger-Teton Wilderness, Utah's Book Cliffs, or Oregon's coastal rain forest, no one brings any more intensity to elk hunting. When he's not in some remote hunting camp, Durwood still makes his home in southern California with his wife, teenage son, and newborn daughter.

Author Hollis with a fine 6x6 bull, taken more than 30 miles from the nearest roadhead.

Preface

There are a lot of prolific outdoor writers in the industry these days, but very few who possess the amount of knowledge that Durwood Hollis has gleaned from decades of hunting in a wide variety of settings. He know what it takes to become an elk hunter, how to plan the hunt, what you need for different situations, how to prepare yourself and your gear, and how to hunt whether it's hot and dry or cold and wet. On the technical side, he's as close to being an expert as anyone I know on optics, knives, and rifles, all of which he's written about extensively, and more importantly, used personally in the field.

I've known Durwood Hollis for a number of years and long ago recognized his enthusiasm for the hunt. To say that he's an energetic companion is putting it mildly. He'll hunt with you, help you pack your elk, and should there be any doubt that elk venison is some of the best wild game meat, he'll conjure up a recipe and cook it for you. He'll even do the dishes, unless you beat him to the sink on purpose!

Durwood has hunted elk all over the West, and along the way he's taken some fine bulls and experienced elk hunting in all of its many forms. He's hunted on public land and private ranches, and he's been surprisingly successful no matter what the circumstances. It's September, the elk bugle is in full swing, and it's hot and dry in Wyoming's Bridger-Teton Wilderness. No problem, Durwood will be there. It's November in the Rockies, the elk are on the move and there's snow everywhere. No problem, Durwood will be there.

I've hunted with Durwood on several occasions and I've learned from each experience. I've walked the wild places with him and I can tell you from personal experience, that he has, as they say, "the right stuff." He has his priorities in order and will head for the door to hunt with a friend at the drop of a hint.

Durwood Hollis is from the old school of outdoor writing, the school of personal experience. In other words, he knows whereof he speaks. By the time you finish reading this book you'll know it was written, and written well, by someone who knows the ropes like few others do these days.

Somewhere the elk season is open and Durwood is probably there, or he will be soon. Let these pages be your guide to elk season and you, too, will be on your way to enjoying years of memorable hunting no matter where you live.

John Higley, Freelance Writer
Palo Cedro, California

Outdoor writer John Higley is no stranger to elk camp.

Foreword

Most elk hunters begin their tutelage in their teens, under the direction of a parent, a relative, or a close friend. Unfortunately, my dad was a shotgunner, not a big game hunter. It wasn't until I was an adult and living away from home that big game hunting, and specifically elk hunting, became a reality. That's not to say that I hadn't *wanted* to hunt elk early on, but the actual in-the-field experience just wasn't part of my early upbringing.

My interest in elk did receive a *jump-start* while I was still a teenager. During summer vacation from school, I had the opportunity to work in Yellowstone National Park. On my first day off, I hitchhiked to an area where the Yellowstone River meandered through a broad open valley. Unlimbering the fly rod that was my constant companion in those days, I spent the afternoon tempting cutthroat trout to the hook.

Just at sunset, the din of an eerie bugle reverberated throughout the valley. Punctuated at its conclusion by several guttural coughs, the sound was unnerving to say the least. Seconds later, the silence was once again shattered by a similar jarring dissonance. Totally unfamiliar with elk, I wondered *what* had produced such a disconcerting sound.

The answer to my question didn't take long to materialized. Across the river, a band of elk slowly drifted out of the trees. One of those animals, a huge bull, stopped just as he came into the open. Declaring his dominance over creatures large and small, he issued another roaring challenge that echoed from one side of the river to the other.

For years, the sight and sound of that Yellowstone bull haunted me. However, it wasn't until early adulthood that I entered the arena of big game hunting. My first step was to learn the basics. After that, a number of successful deer hunts provided some badly needed seasoning. However, it was clear to me that an elk hunt would take more than a few forays for deer and some theoretical knowledge. That cognizance would come in the form of my first elk hunt.

No elk hunter ever forgets his first bull. That seminal experience came for me on a remote section of Ruby Mountain, near Butte, Montana. Friends Kelly Hemmert and Bob Justice joined me on my first elk hunt. I do recall that it was so cold on opening morning that the 3:30 a.m. breakfast nearly froze before it hit our stomachs. Stepping off in the darkness, we hiked straight uphill for an unrelenting two hours. Without the benefit of a trail, that effort extracted its toll on little used leg muscles. By the time we reached the top, to a man, we were exhausted. Even so, opening day adrenaline kept us going. By the time I found a stand, the first rays of the newborn sun were already rebuffing the night. Despite my best efforts, I didn't see anything even closely resembling an elk that entire day.

The next couple of days, we hunted high and low, but continued to draw a complete blank. On the third evening, while hunting through some dark timber, I ran right into a bull at point-blank range. Both the elk and I were equally surprised. However, that *old boy* didn't waste any time assessing the situation. In an instant, he whirled around and disappeared. I tried my best to get on the fleeing animal, but to no avail. Even if somehow I could have, the trees were so dense a clear shot was totally unmanageable. No, I didn't shoot an elk on that trip. In fact, it would be several years before my bullet would take a bull. No matter, that Montana elk was my first, and so he will remain.

There have been many bulls between then and now, each one a learning experience. Some have come after just a few hours into the hunt. Others have taken days of bone-weary pursuit. There have been occasions when the discovery of a solitary elk track was the totality of the hunt, and other times when the animals were seemingly everywhere. The pursuit of these magnificent *cervids* has left me cold, wet, and so tired that every muscle in my body cried for relief. I've torn up good gear, dislocated a shoulder, and severely strained a marriage—all in the name of elk hunting.

If you're already an elk hunter, or are interested in become a member of this age-old fraternity, then in the pages ahead you'll find lots of valuable information about what it takes to hunt these majestic animals. You'll read about the life cycle of elk, what they look like, and where to find them. Information on how to get your rifle, your bow, your gear, your vehicle, even your body in shape for the hunt, is explained in detail. So you'll have plenty of fodder for campfire arguments, there are chapters that cover elk calling, ballistics, optics, knives, and game care. Since no one wants to be uncomfortable in elk camp, there is commentary on what to wear, what to take, and how to pack it. Finally, there's a look into the mysteries of saddle stock, how to draw an out-of-state elk license, where to hunt and new hunting strategies.

Whether it's your first elk hunt, or just one more in a string of memorable hunts, there's no substitute for elk hunting. Exciting, intoxicating, and at times—exhausting beyond imagination, it is what big game hunting was *meant* to be. Hopefully, it will always be that way.

Durwood Hollis, Rancho Cucamonga, California

Author's Note

Fire season changes the face of elk habitat in the American West

The manuscript for this book was sent to the publisher long before the devastating fire season of 2000. Neither the author nor the Rocky Mountain Elk Foundation could have anticipated such an event. See the comments in Chapter 19 regarding the importance of fire to the health of the forest ecosystem, and elk. The scale of the fires was so large, some 73,000 different fires had been reported between Montana and New Mexico by the end of August, that few people can understand the gravity of it all. Fires burned 6.3 million acres across the West. Nearly 2 million acres were consumed in Idaho and Montana alone. Government officials called it the worst fire season in 50 years and estimated it would cost more than $1 billion to battle the flames.

The effects of these fires on the elk population has yet to be determined. But if the Yellowstone fire of the late 1980s is any indicator, the removal of old timber will allow a proliferation of new growth, including the graze that elk depend on. Many parts of the West will look charred and barren to the average viewer. But soon grass will appear. New brush will sprout and tree seedlings will take hold. These types of things are a free buffet for elk and deer. While fire can have a disastrous effect on human habitation, commerce and recreation, it is part of a natural cycle that is usually beneficial to wildlife. Over the next three years, I expect elk populations throughout the West to explode.

Durwood Hollis

Chapter 1

A Family Affair

It's all in the genes

Not long ago, I attended a family reunion. That event, held in a regional park included branches of the family that had no knowledge of each other. Looking at the participants, one could see considerable disparity in size, hair color, even ethnicity. Taken as a group, however, there was a certain manifest commonality among all reunion attendees.

Biologists group living organisms together that have either common ancestral origin, or manifest similar features. Consequently, several closely related individual species make up a genus, and when these groups are combined, they are consid-

ered a family. All of the attendees at my family reunion, whether tall or short, blond or redhead, and regardless of ethnic makeup, shared my surname and were part of my family.

Likewise, in the non-human part of the animal kingdom, related species are grouped together in family units. The nomenclature, Cervidae (from the Latin root, Cervus, meaning stag or deer), is the scientific designation for the deer family. Originating about 40 million years ago in the Old World, this lineage contains a number of members, including: moose, caribou, reindeer, all the various species of

With bulls weighing up to 1,300 pounds, the Roosevelt elk is the largest of all North American elk. Photo Credit: J. Mark Higley

By the mid-1800s, only eight tule elk could be found living in isolation in California's central valley. From this handful of animals, a thriving population of over 3,000 elk now inhabit many parts of the Golden State. Photo Credit: Jim Matthews

deer, and elk. Segments of this family tree can be found worldwide.

In The Beginning: Possibly as early as 120,000 years ago, Asiatic red deer moved across the Bering Land Bridge into North America. Finding a welcome habitat, they quickly spread and diversified. Through time, this genetic adaptation produced the various subspecies of what we now know as "elk." Thus, an elk is nothing more than a cousin to the red deer of the British Isles, Iberian Peninsula, northern Europe, and Asia. Likewise, where red deer have been transplanted, in regions as far flung as Argentina, New Zealand, and South Africa, this genetic relationship is also present.

When the first aboriginal people followed the great mammals into North America, the elk became an important source of food. Evidence of the significance of these animals in Native American culture is manifest in pictographs (rock paintings) and petroglyphs (rock engravings), left behind by these ancient peoples. These paintings and engravings depict scenes of elk and elk hunting activities. As well, elk hide, antlers, and bones were used by American Indians for clothing and tools. Elk were not only important as a resource, but like so many other mammals, they also played a significant role in the everyday and spiritual life of many North American aboriginal tribes.

Post European Contact: Prior to European contact, North American elk ranged from what is now New England to the far West, and from Canada to northern New Mexico and Arizona. However, by the early 1900s, their numbers had dwindled to less than 100,000. Of the six modern species of elk, the first to step into the sunset were Eastern elk and Merriam elk.

The Fossil Record: The elk alone is the quintessence of the family Cervidae. A deer among deer this animal has a rich heritage. During the geologic Pleistocene Epoch, which is characterized by appearance of modern man, there were at least 10 subspecies of elk in North America. The fossil remains of four elk subspecies were discovered in Wisconsin (C. Whitneyi Allen), New Mexico (C. lascrucensis Frick), California (C. aguangae Frick), and Alaska (Murie, 1951). Sadly, the Eastern elk (Cervis canadensis candensis) and the Merriam elk (C. Canadensis merriami) were decimated by settlers during the early settlement of this country. Only the Rocky Mountain elk (C. elaphus nelsoni), Roosevelt elk (C. e. roosevelti), Manitoba elk (C. a. manitobensis), and the diminutive Tule elk (C. a. nannodes) remain as a remnant of a herd that is estimated to have numbered 10 million elk ranging across the continent.

Weighing about 25-pounds at birth, elk calves grow fast and are able to join the herd quickly. Photo Credit: Rocky Mountain Elk Foundation

Both species were quickly eliminated by westward expansion and unregulated hunting. The Manitoba elk herds, who once mingled with the buffalo, were pushed to remote areas of Canada. Only a relic population can now be found in parts of Alberta and Manitoba. And by the early 1920s, the range of Rocky Mountain elk had collapsed into the Yellowstone-Jackson Hole area. Roosevelt elk survived only because their chosen habitat was the dark rain forest of the Pacific Northwest. The Tule elk that once numbered an estimated 500,000 animals were on the verge of total extinction by the mid-1800s. Fortunately, a California rancher provided a refuge for the remaining eight animals that were discovered living in a marsh in the San Joaquin Valley. This, the smallest elk subspecies, now numbers more than 3,000 animals, and can be found in several locations throughout California.

Benefiting from new conservation awareness, aggressive management, and efforts of hunters and conservation organizations, Rocky Mountain elk and Tule elk both have made an impressive comeback. At the dawn of the new millennium, the total North American elk population (Rocky Mountain elk, Roosevelt elk, and Tule elk combined) hovers at near one million animals, with continued herd expansion seen in most areas.

What is an Elk?: If you consider absolute size as the defining characteristic of the leading member of the deer family, then the clear champion in this arena would be the moose. Despite its imposing size, this weird-looking and phlegmatic behemoth seems to be a cartoon character. Similarly, both the caribou and the reindeer also don't rate very high in appearance or intelligence. While the whitetail and mule deer, and all of their various subspecies, can lay claim to both beauty and brains, neither group possesses the majesty of the regal elk.

Elk coloration ranges from the dark brown of their winter coat, to a light tan in the summer. This change of coloration is due to the growth of a darker, woolly undercoat in the fall, which is shed as the warmer weather of late spring and early summer approaches. This species also has a characteristic buff-colored rump patch and a deep-brown ridge of hair that hangs from beneath the chin to well between the front legs. At a distance, elk can appear reddish in color, with darker legs and head. Up close, however, the true tawny color is manifest.

Tiny Trophies: While elk antlers are impressive trophies, an elk's upper canine teeth are especially coveted. Called "ivories," "buglers," and "tusks," these thumb-size, slightly flattened, and rounded teeth are held in great esteem. The Plains Indians used them as clothing decorations, attaching dozens to their ceremonial dress. This alone is a strong statement as to the importance of elk in American Aboriginal culture. Even the American mountain men sought these tiny trophies and used them as trading stock. Today, several jewelry manufacturers produce personal adornments featuring elk ivories. Elk canine teeth are curious trophies and ones you'll want to save, even if for no other reason than creating your own unique collection.

Cow elk are only about one-half as big as a mature bull. Despite this size inequity, an older cow is usually the leader of the herd. Photo Credit: Bob Robb

are considerably lower than deer. For example, winter surveys of Rocky Mountain elk have establish that only 15 to 20 percent of any given herd consists of calves. Interestingly, calves have a series of creamy spots on their coats. No doubt, this serves as a protective camouflage. During the first few weeks of life, calves and their mothers remain on their own. When the calf has gained enough strength to keep up with adult elk, both cow and offspring will rejoin the herd structure. When less than a month old, most calves will feed on vegetation. Even though the calf will remain with its mother through the winter, by early fall it has become self-sufficient.

Elk are herd animals. This herd structure is based on a dominant cow. Only during the rut period do bulls have much influence. Even after a bull has formed a mating harem, a single cow still leads the herd. At the conclusion of the rut, herd bulls move off on their own. This leaves the cows and calves, with an occasional spike or raghorn bull mixed in, remaining together as a formal herd unit.

The breeding period, or the rut as it is known, can begin in midsummer and extend well into the fall. The farther south elk live, the earlier the rut will begin. I've watched Tule elk conduct breeding activity as early as late July. Correspondingly, bull elk in the northern Rocky Mountains have been known to respond to a rutting challenge into mid-October. The precise timing of the breeding period is dependent on many influences, including the physical condition of the animals, barometric pressure, and the length of the day. The height of the rut may only last a couple of weeks, with cows coming into and going out of estrus daily.

Like most male mammals, the bull elk stands taller than his female counterpart and possesses nearly twice the body mass. At either end of the elk spectrum you will find the Roosevelt and Tule elk. The Roosevelt elk is the largest member of this family, with bulls weighing from 850 to 1,300 pounds. Cows will tip the scales at 550 to 650 pounds. Conversely, a Tule elk bull will weigh about 400 to 450 pounds, while cows average 325 to 375 pounds. In between these two extremes, a Manitoba elk bull weighs in at around 800 pounds, with cows pushing the scales to about 600 pounds. Slightly smaller, a Rocky Mountain bull will go about 700 to 800 pounds, with cows weighing 525 to 575 pounds.

Life Cycle: An elk begins its life in early summer. Twins are rare, a single birth is the norm. By the end of the eight-month gestation period, the calf weighs about 25 pounds at birth. Reproductive rates in elk

On The Table: Aside from trophies on the wall and durable leather, elk venison is some of the best game meat available. A 3-ounce portion of cooked elk venison has less cholesterol, fat and calories than a similar cut of beef, lamb, or pork. Moreover, a mature Rocky Mountain bull elk will provide 300 to 400 pounds of boned meat. The taste of this savory flesh is similar to veal. Unlike beef, however there is little marbleized fat within the tissue structure. This eliminates the sometimes greasy under taste of beef. Cut into steaks, chops, and roasts, with the trimmings turned into ground meat, elk venison can be used in a variety of main dishes.

A bull's first set of antlers are prominent spikes.
Photo Credit: Jim Matthews

As a mark of sexual maturity, bulls will begin growing antlers sometime between eight months and one year. It will take somewhere between four and five months for the antlers to complete the growth cycle. During the months of August or early September, the animals will begin to strip the velvet covering off of their antlers. As they test their prowess, play battles will break out among the youngest bulls. When the rut comes to full bloom, however, the larger bulls will push the young spikes and raghorn bulls to the herd fringe. Since they are constantly revolving around the outskirts of the herd, these non-trophy animals are known as "satellite" bulls. After the rut, the immature bulls may rejoin the herd.

A bull elk is sexually mature shortly after his first birthday. And like all teenagers, a bull with a year or two under his belt is a sexual predator. Any young bull would like to get into the game, but these younger bulls are no match for larger animals—and they know it! The herd bull just won't tolerate competition for very long. Hoping to get into the action, any action, these youngsters drift from herd to herd in hopes of initiating a love affair. When they find a herd

bull that is busy defending his territory from a major competitor, one of these younger bulls will attempt to ease up to a cow. Most of these attempted liaisons are failures. Either the approach is rebuffed by the cow, or the herd bull gets wind of the affair. Occasionally, however, a spike or a raghorn bull will breed a cow in estrus. Most likely because they're young and stupid, there have been entire weeks when I saw nothing but spike bulls and raghorns on the move. I guess there's something to be said about youthful hormones.

As winter approaches, elk begin their annual migratory trek, often covering more than 50 miles in a single day's journey. A little snow doesn't seem to bother elk. While the first major fall storm can put deer to flight, elk may delay their departure until the snow is near belly-deep. Rocky Mountain elk generally have summer and wintering ranges that are miles apart and at differing altitudes. One of the best areas to watch Rocky Mountain elk migrate onto historic wintering grounds is the National Elk Refuge near Jackson Hole, Wyoming. Here, thousands upon thousands of elk congregate to feed and wait out the winter. The other elk species deal with winter differently. Since the Pacific Northwest receives little snow, Roosevelt elk may have only to move a short distance to escape the white stuff. Tule elk, like all California sun worshipers, enjoy a temperate climate. These miniature elk princes wouldn't understand the meaning of migration if it was explained to them. In the winter Tule elk might move from the foothills into low lying valleys and riparian areas.

During the winter, elk are most vulnerable to disease, starvation, and exposure. The loss of migration corridors and historic wintering grounds is most damaging to elk herd stability. Likewise, artificial feeding of elk during this period can also be detrimental. The best guarantee of elk herd health and survival is unmolested access through movement avenues, and protected wintering grounds with adequate food resources.

With the exception of the rut, a mature bull elk is a solitary creature. At most, he will tolerate the company of a few other bulls. These male patriarchs covet their peace and quiet and will be found in areas where disturbance is at a minimum. After weeks of chasing cows and challenging competitors, they need to rest and regain their strength.

Some bulls stay in the backcountry all winter long. With long hair, thick hide, and a substantial layer of fat, a bull elk can keep warm in temperatures that would kill a lesser animal. For feed, they find a high meadow where the wind keeps the grass free of snow. To obtain water, the elk can simply break the ice in a small creek with his hooves. Bedding out of the wind, the solitary bull is right at home. After dealing with the cows and the competition all through the breeding season, I am not sure that such a plan isn't the best course of action.

Feed, Water, and Shelter: Since elk are primarily grazers, the search for food demands a great deal of movement. These animals do move during daylight hours, but much of the time (especially during hunting season) movement is conducted at night. During the day, elk bed in heavy brush or dense timber and rumi-

As a bull matures, his antlers will manifest additional tines. Still in velvet, this 4-point bull is known as a raghorn.
Photo Credit: Jim Matthews

nate just like domestic cattle. As evening approaches, the movement toward open areas where they can feast on grasses will begin anew. While they are heavily dependent on grasses, elk will browse on Bitter Brush, Western Juniper, Mountain Mahogany, and other vegetation occasionally. And where acorns are available, they will gorge themselves on the fruit of the oak.

In the northern and western parts of their range, access to water generally isn't a problem. In the arid southwest, however, elk will travel miles to find water. In these regions, ponds, stock tanks, springs, and tiny seeps can be elk magnets. Moisture is also a source of mud, in which elk wallow to keep themselves cool. With thick hides and lots of hair, an elk can get overheated. A damp coat and a muddy covering are just like built-in air conditioning.

Besides the demand for food and water, elk also need shelter. Timber, with all of its enveloping closeness is home to an elk. The intervening tree trunks, limbs, branches, and leaves break the wind, repel rain and snow, and serve as insulation from all but the worst that nature has to offer. Within this protective verdant envelope, elk can even find isolated pockets of graze and browse. For an elk, spending the day in dark timber is like napping in a shady patio that adjoins a snack bar. In this environment, the hunter is at a disadvantage. The close proximity of several sets of eyes and noses make it almost impossible to get up close to a bull. Yet, this is where you must go if you can't catch up with that bull during daylight hours.

Because dark timber doesn't hold much in the way of graze or browse, elk move out into the fringes or open areas where more substantial food stocks can be found. However, here an elk is vulnerable to predators—especially hunters. For reasons of security, elk have developed nocturnal feeding patterns. This is why you seldom see elk out in the open during daylight hours. If you do find elk, it will be early in the morning and just before dark. If the moon is full, you might not even see elk at those times.

Antlers: Elk are defined by their incredible antlers. Bulls alone bear the antlers which may measure more than 5 feet in length, and exceed a foot in circumference at the base. The spread, or distance between the two antlers, may be nearly 4 feet. The first antlers that a bull produces are generally a pair of solitary beams, called "spikes." In the following year, the antlers will be multi-tined, most often three or four points to a side. In comparison to a more mature bull, these antlers will be slender with rather abbreviated tine length. These animals are called "raghorns," or "brush" bulls. Antlers produced in subsequent years will be heavier (greater in diameter) and manifest five, six, or even more points per side. Antlers are shed during the months of February and March. The massive beams loosen from their pedicles, or bases, and fall to the ground. In April, new velvet-covered antler nubs will appear which achieve their full growth potential by the beginning of the rut in September.

Beginning with the pearled ring around the base of the antler tine, ascending points are called the brow tine, the bez (or bay) tine, the trez (or trey) tine, and the royal (or dagger point or wolf tine) tine. Extending upward from this longest tine on the antler beam, additional sur-royal points give rise to distinct elk nomenclature. A six-point elk is called a "royal," the

While they're really not big enough to get into a serious battle with a mature herd bull, young elk will still spar with one another.
Photo Credit: Bob Robb

Sharing a common red deer ancestral heritage, both the Mongolian elk (this 7x7 bull was taken by outdoor writer Stuart Williams), and the Rocky Mountain elk look more alike than just distant cousins. Photo Credit: Bob Robb

addition of a seventh point establishes an elk as "imperial," and an eight-point bull is a "monarch." Interestingly, both Roosevelt and Tule elk tend to produce a number of extra tines in the uppermost part of the antler beam. These so-called, "crown points," are not unlike those seen on European "red deer."

Skin Game: A tanned hide from an elk, with or without the hair attached, is another treasure. American Indians used elk hide for clothing, blankets, sleeping robes, moccasin leather, and a myriad of other uses. Even today, a tanned elk skin with the hair left attached can make a great wall hanging, or couch cover. Furthermore, elk leather can be used for chaps, jackets, shoes, saddle scabbards, and many other useful personal and household items. I have a friend who covered all of the furniture in his den with elk leather. The look was magnificent and the leather has stood up to the wear and tear of more than 20 years.

A Family Success: The management of today's elk herds is nothing less than a wildlife success story. In both the United States and Canada, all species of elk have experienced phenomenal growth over the last two decades. In the 10 years from 1975 to 1985, elk numbers jumped almost 40 percent . And for the first time in this century—Arkansas, Kansas, Kentucky, North Dakota, Michigan, Pennsylvania, and Wisconsin—can list elk as indigenous animals.

Most of this growth has been seen in Rocky Mountain elk herds, but Tule elk also exhibited dramatic herd increases. Amazingly, in the 20-year period of 1975-1995, the North American elk population nearly doubled in size. Now, wildlife managers are seeking ways to slow, or reduce the herd increases in some areas. This has resulted in added hunting opportunities, lengthened seasons, and a rise in antlerless licenses.

Family Future: Interest in elk and elk hunting goes far beyond the North American continent. Hunts for elk in Asia and red deer in places as far-flung as northern and eastern Europe, the Iberian peninsula, South Africa, Argentina, and New Zealand are a reality. In North America, elk populations are enjoying continued expansion and there is a resurgence of interest in these majestic animals. While the elk segment of the deer family may have seen the loss of several members in North America, the future for that portion of the family tree is no longer bleak.

Chapter 2

Beat The Odds

Have an ace up your sleeve

Competition for elk hunting is becoming more intense every year on our public lands. And it is equally difficult for the unattached hunter to access private lands. More and more ranchers with elk on their properties are either posting "No Hunting" signs or leasing hunting rights to outfitters or small groups of well-heeled businessmen. As a result, many hunters are often squeezed together in what public land remains, during seasons that are too short and with lots of other folks who find themselves in the same boat. Consequently, trophy quality in many areas is declining, along with the hunter success rate. Quite frankly, the chances of experiencing a quality hunting experience—good numbers of bulls, pristine country, and low hunter pressure—is becoming harder and harder to come by.

Is December really too early to make elk hunting preparations? No, not if you want to hunt in Wyoming, Utah, or Montana. These states have big game license application deadlines in January, February, and March, respectively. Likewise, Colorado, Idaho, Nevada, and New Mexico follow closely behind with deadlines in March and April. Only Arizona, with their mid-June application deadline offers much in the way of lead time.

Most states use a drawing (computer selection) to allocate elk licenses. Statewide, most hunt areas are part of this system, so it's important to get started early. Also, don't put all of your license expectations in a single application, or even in a particular state. The current trend in game management puts license quotas well below demand in most prime locations. To insure drawing success, multiple application are an absolute necessity. You may draw more licenses than you can use, or you may not draw at all. Either way, the whole process is just part of the game. If you don't play, you can't win.

Make Up Your Mind: Decide where and when you want to hunt, then select a primary and one or more alternative hunt areas. If you've always hunted elk in a certain area, but over the years it has been increas-

If you want a crack at a bull like this, then you have to play the game Photo Credit: Jim Matthews

When To Apply For an Elk License: The process begins in winter. Granted, the holiday season is a tough time of the year for those who hunt the Rocky Mountains and the Southwest. Most of us are more concerned about our bank balances, than we are about next year's elk season. For many, next year's elk camp is nothing more than a fleeting dream wedged in between wrapping Christmas presents and recuperating from the annual New Year's eve bash.

Every state has a different system for allotting elk licenses. Regulatory booklets are the place to start. Photo Credit: Durwood Hollis

ingly more difficult to draw a license, then try applying for another region. Better yet, submit an additional application to a nearby state. This way, you increase your drawing odds by applying for another license. You might find yourself hunting in both areas (things could be worse), but that is better than having to forego the entire elk season.

Research is the Key: Like finding any good hunting spot, research is the key to success. Just because a state is offering a limited number of general elk licenses, or special-draw hunts for elk, doesn't mean that the area is overrun with trophy bulls. As mentioned earlier, many, but not all, special-draw areas are managed for herd structure, but that's not always the case. Also, a particular area in any given state may not have the right combination of genetics, feed, and soil mineral content required to grow eye-popping antlers, no matter how old the bulls live to be. For

Follow Instructions: While the license drawing is a great way to provide top-quality hunting opportunities, it can be messed up by careless applicants. How? Laziness is the number one way. Some don't take the time to read the application instructions. Be sure that all application forms are filled out exactly as specified. If you have questions, get them cleared up by telephone. While some read the instructions, they fill out the permit application haphazardly. Others fail to observe mandated submission deadlines, or forget to submit the required fee. An incorrectly filled out application will get you thrown out of the drawing every time. Furthermore, the application process, submission dates, and fee structure can (and often does) change from year to year. If you're really serious about elk hunting, then get serious about the application process.

In some states, bowhunters have better odds at drawing an elk license. Photo Credit: Bob Robb

example, the Roosevelt elk living on Alaska's Afognak and Raspberry Islands have huge bodies, but they simply do not produce trophy-quality antlers. If you're interested in a Roosevelt elk to put in the record book, then you'd better look somewhere other than Alaska. A trophy elk hunter would be better served by deciding that he wants to hunt only the biggest of bulls, then apply for special hunts in those areas throughout the region that have a proven track record for producing such animals. That's what I do. This type of research, in conjunction with a comprehensive study of the often complex application system of many states, is the best approach.

Ask Questions: Call the game department of the state(s) in which you're interested. Most agencies have a public relations or public information person that handles such inquires. In my experience, these folks are a wealth of information. Ask for their

Get Primitive: Most elk hunters are riflemen. However, there are a growing number of bowhunters and muzzleloaders who are also interested in pursuing elk. Most game departments recognize this interest and attempt to provide a primitive weapons hunting period outside of the normal rifle season. Since the number of elk hunters using a muzzleloader or archery tackle is extremely small, the odds on drawing a license/tag may be more favorable. Even better, the season may fall in the middle of rut, or during a winter migration period that can provide a better opportunity for success. If you really want to draw an elk license in a particular area, trying applying for an archery or muzzleloading tag.

upcoming year's hunting regulations, special-draw hunt application forms, and any pertinent information. Whatever you do, don't delay! Applications for elk licenses in some states can be due as early as the end of January.

While you're at it, ask about special hunts, land owners who allow access to their property, and newly opened hunting areas. Game biologists usually like to talk about their own areas of expertise. Use that knowledge to your advantage. Don't be afraid to ask questions—lots of questions. Ask about mountain ranges, drainages, landmarks, range conditions, old burns, elk migration patterns, and the all important—anticipated weather conditions. Surprisingly, I have easily obtained lots of cogent information right over the telephone.

Most states require that hunters send in the required hunting license and/or tag fee with the application form. The form of payment will be specified (cashier's check, money order, personal check, etc.), and those instructions must be followed to the letter. If the application instructions state that your check or money order is to be filled out to a specific governmental organization, use the exact wording that is provided—don't abbreviate. While it might not make any difference (money is money), there is also a possibility that your application may be rejected. Likewise, make sure that the envelope you use has the correct address (including post office box number and complete ZIP code), contains both the application and the appropriate fees, and has the necessary postage affixed. Don't forget to allow adequate time for mail transit and handling. When in doubt, send your application by express or overnight mail. Remember, the basic application rule: when all else fails—follow instructions!

License Fees: The cost of an elk license/tag often amounts to several hundred dollars (another reason many don't apply for these tags). Moreover, application submission deadlines can come up right after Christmas, right before or just after income tax time, or at some other inopportune financial moment. If you don't set aside the necessary funds early, you won't be able to get in the game. Some folks set up a special account just for their licensing needs. Funds are directed to that account on a regular basis and not withdrawn until the need arises. This way, the cost of an out-of-state license is spread out over a longer period of time. Some of my friends do side jobs, or "squirrel away" money that they would use for soft drinks, lunch, or other personal expenses.

If you do everything correctly, and the odds fall in your favor, then you'll receive the license (some states issue both a hunting license and a tag, each of which must be applied for separately) in the mail. If you don't draw, the licensing agency refunds all of the application fees, except for a small processing fee. How can you lose? However, make sure you get

started early. Out-of-state elk licenses are expensive. It's a sure bet that they will not be getting cheaper anytime soon.

Preference Points: In some cases, those who apply and do not draw a tag are given a "preference point" by the licensing agency. Preference point holders are given preferential treatment in the license drawings held in following years. Even with preference points, however, it may be several years before you're drawn. The reason for this is that there are more people with the maximum allowable number of preference points in the annual draw than there are licenses available. Let's face it, some applicants will get discouraged and fail to continue applying. Keep in mind that patience and persistence is the name of this game.

"Special" Licenses: Some states utilize more than one level of license/tag purchase price to provide enhanced drawing odds. Wyoming, for example, designated both a "regular" elk license at one price, and a "special" elk license at an increased cost. The basic difference is that fewer applicants are willing pay more money for the same tag that they may be able to obtain at a lower cost in the regular drawing. However, the smaller number of "special" license/tag applicants significantly increases the odds of drawing that particular license/tag.

Furthermore, a number of elk licenses/tags may be allotted to landowners, outfitters, political office holders, outfitter associations, sportsmen's organizations, and others for direct purchase or fund raising. Market demand governs the purchase, and coveted permits can carry a steep price tag. Many condemn such "check book" license/tag allocation systems, but the money usually goes directly to elk habitat enhancement or hunter access.

Some time ago, a group of my friends pooled their funds and submitted a party application for a particular elk hunting area. As luck would have it, they all drew the appropriate permits. At the last minute, another friend wanted to join the party. Unfortunately, the drawing had already taken place. Seeking an alternative approach, he contacted the game department and was informed that a small number of licenses/tags were allotted to an elected official (the Governor of the state). The cost was approximately three times that of a license/tag issued through the drawing process. That fact didn't seem to bother the hunter who was determined to join his friends. The check was written. The license was subsequently issued, and everyone was happy. You see, there is more than one (although expensive) way to beat the odds!

Special-Draw Hunts: What are they? In some western states, "special-draw" elk hunts are offered. Usually, this is a mechanism for game officials to manipulate bull-to-cow ratios, provide increased recreational opportunities, or meet a particular habitat management need. These licenses/tags are usually few in number, and may carry restrictions regarding the age (older, mature bulls) and sex (cows) of the elk. In most cases, these hunts are set up so that at least a few of the available permits can be obtained by non-residents. Competition for the hunts that are in the highest demand will be extremely fierce. The odds of drawing one of these licenses/tags can be somewhat improbable, but not necessarily impossible. The long odds discourage many hunters from applying, but someone has to draw those permits. If you draw, you're off on the elk hunting adventure of a lifetime. If you don't, you get your money back. Now, if that isn't a win-win situation, I don't know what is!

Another Way to Go: Staying abreast of all Western elk license and special-draw trophy hunting areas is a time-consuming process. States are constantly changing their programs, application deadlines, procedures, and fees. On top of all of this, the hot areas for elk seem to ebb and flow like the tide. The hot spot of five years

ago could have been impacted by development, fire, newly constructed road access, or even closure.

George Taulman's United State Outfitters (USO) is one of the largest outfitter concerns in the West. They got their start guiding on New Mexico private lands and have since expanded to several other Western states. Along the way, Taulman was constantly getting inquiries from clients regarding the best areas for elk hunting on public land hunts.

"I saw that many of the public land hunting areas around the West were offering the same kind of first-class trophy hunting I was providing on my private ranch hunt. Drawing a license or a special-draw tag for those areas was often a complicated process that tended to discourage applicants. However, it just made sense for a hunter to apply for these hunts, where he can enjoy quality hunting for the least expense," Taulman says.

"However, research is the key. If you draw a license in an area that holds only average animals, you may

If you've had difficulty drawing an elk tag, then try submitting for a primitive weapons license.
Photo Credit: Durwood Hollis

The cost of a fully outfitted elk hunt isn't cheap, but some states allocate licenses for just that purpose. Photo Credit: Durwood Hollis

get a great hunt, but take a mediocre trophy. By knowing the ins and outs of each state's licensing and special-draw programs, as well as where the best hunting for trophy-class animals can be found, I can match hunters with exactly what they're looking for. If someone calls me and says they're interest in a big bull elk, I can apply for them in the top one, two, or three hunts in the entire West," Taulman continues.

"If a hunter doesn't draw a tag, I place the tag draw money in an escrow account, then automatically reapply for the same hunt next year (hunters are required to put up the license and tag fees, plus application fees, just as they would if they were applying on their own). Because most of the good hunts are on the preference point system, if a guy stays with it, he's eventually going to draw a tag for the hunt of his dreams," he adds.

While the cost for world-class trophy elk hunts on private ranches in New Mexico where Taulman hunts is extremely high, comparable quality hunts can be afforded by special-draw tags in other areas. Permit winners can hunt on their own just as cheaply as they would if they went to their usual hunting area. Hunters pay USO an affordable one-time fee to enter the program. While USO would like to place hunters who draw tags with their guides, there is no requirement to do so. You are free to hire any outfitter or guide you want, or even hunt on your own.

"When people ask us about which hunts to apply for, we can tell them the areas best suited to backpack hunts, horseback hunts, using ATV's, going guided or going unguided. Our job is to match them up with the best hunt available, anywhere that meets their personal needs and preferences. Putting a hunter with one of our own guides is secondary to all of this,"

Taulman says. For more information about this licensing service, contact United States Outfitters, Professional Licensing Service, P. O. Box 4204, Taos, New Mexico 87571, or telephone 800/ 845-9929.

Another information and booking service that elk hunters should consider using is Garth Carter's Hunter Services, P. O. Box 45, Minersville, UT 84752, telephone 435/386-1020. Carter publishes a monthly newsletter with up-to-date information on Western hunting opportunities on all species of big game, including elk, on both public and private land. Membership in this service is $100 per year, and Carter provides assistance to members with non-resident tag and license applications. This is also a great source for locating fee-based private-land hunts.

The Best Chance of Drawing an Elk License: Based on total statewide elk population, the states of Arizona (25,000) Colorado (220,000), Idaho (118,000), Montana (100,000), New Mexico (58,000), Oregon (60,000), Washington (130,000) Wyoming (110,000), and Utah (63,000) have the largest number of animals and offer the greatest number of licenses. However, the states of Arizona and New Mexico are probably the best bets for a record book elk. If you want to hunt Roosevelt elk, then drawings held in Alaska, California, Oregon, and Washington are the only options. For a chance at a Tule elk, California is your solitary choice. Obviously, when it comes to the best license drawing odds, issues other than pure population numbers may play a part in your final decision.

Don't Waste Your Time: Despite the fact that Alaska, California, Michigan, Nevada, Oklahoma, Pennsylvania, and Virginia all have elk, the number of animals in each state is extremely small. Competition for allotted licenses is tough, hunting access can be difficult, and the cost of a hunt in some areas is beyond the budget of most working folks. Likewise, North and South Dakota also have elk, but only residents can apply for the limited number of licenses. Elk have been transplanted to Arkansas, Kansas, Kentucky, Minnesota, Nebraska, and Wisconsin, but the herds are not yet large enough to allow hunting. If you live in a state where elk license drawings are held, then try your luck. If not—forget it!

In Canada, the provinces of Alberta, British Columbia, Manitoba and Saskatchewan all have sizable elk populations. However, non-residents are only allowed to hunt elk in Alberta and British Columbia. Even there, you can't hunt without the services of a guide. Unless you can afford it, don't put either of these two Canadian provinces at the top of your elk hunting "places to go" list.

Tough Draw: The states of Arizona and New Mexico have some tremendous bulls, but drawing a permit is tough. While there's excellent elk hunting on public land in Arizona, that's not the situation in New Mexico. Much of New Mexico, like Texas, is held in private ownership. This means that access to elk hunting comes at a steep price (what else is new?). However, if you're serious about finding a record-book bull, then I would suggest that you start building preference points in the drawing process. The chances of drawing a license in Arizona are somewhat better than New Mexico. And the probability of success in the license lottery increases if you apply for either an archery or muzzloading permit.

Best odds in the West: Throughout the West there are areas in Colorado, Idaho, Montana, Utah, and Wyoming that deserve a closer look. Most areas have plenty of public land where the unattached elk hunter can pursue elk without the services of a guide. If I were planning an elk hunt in any of these states, here's where I would go.

Colorado has the largest number of elk in any localized geographic area of North America. In almost all areas, game managers report that elk herds are at, or above, expected population levels. In some game management units it is still possible for non-residents to purchase an over-the-counter bull license. While trophy hunters will be best served focusing on limited-draw units, there are lots of elk nearly everywhere in the state. Unlimited archery season begins in late August and runs through late September. Muzzleloader season runs for a week in mid-September, and there are three combined rifle hunt periods in October. The entire northwestern portion of Colorado probably has more elk per square mile than any other part of the state. Units 201, 2, 10, 3, 301, 4, 441, 5, and 14 all are good bets depending on weather.

For many years, the middle fork of the Salmon River in Idaho has been a favored elk hot spot. This is a tough hunt with straight up-and-down terrain, lots of timber, and limited entry points. This region can be accessed via the Camas Creek Road, northwest of Challis, Idaho, or by following the course of the Salmon River west of North Fork, Idaho. Another entry point is the road that leads to Big Creek, north of Yellow Pine, Idaho. Units 20A, 26, and 27 hold the best prospects, but be prepared for one of the most physically demanding elk hunts of your life. Idaho has a somewhat confusing license system, with hunters having to select either an A or B elk tag and confine their hunting activities to a defined Elk Management Zone. The A tag offers bowhunters and muzzleloaders an opportunity to take any elk (depending on unit and season), and provides rather generous seasons. The B tag is your basic rifle license with increased restrictions on seasons and type of elk.

The "Bee Hive" state of Utah has become an increasingly popular destination for elk hunters. While the southeastern portion of the state holds some tremendous bulls, hunting is restricted to limited-entry units and private land. But don't hold your breath when it comes to success in the license draw. The best bet will be the South Slope hunt in the north-

With more than 220,000 elk within its border, Colorado has a lot to offer. This fine Colorado bull, taken by Bob Robb in 1999 is evidence of this fact. Photo Credit: Bob Robb

eastern section of the state. This is tough country with limited access, lots of cover, no roads, and few established trails. Much of the region is designated federal wilderness, so access is by foot or horseback only. However, extended seasons, the opportunity to obtain both a bull and an anterless license under some circumstances, will make this an extremely attractive hunt. Archery elk season kicks off in late August and runs to early September. The general rifle season is held in mid-October. The general muzzle-loader season is held in early November.

The "big sky" state, Montana, has a burgeoning elk population. This is particularly true in southwest, south-central, and central Montana. The rifle season for elk in this state opens in late October and runs nearly to the end of November. Near the Idaho border, game units 321, 329, 328 and 302 have strong populations of older bulls. Because elk in these areas

tend to bail out over the state line into Idaho when the hunting pressure starts, I'd opt to hunt the first week of the season here. If you miss the opener, then shift your attention a little farther east to game units 423, 284, 293, 339, and 343. All of the units hunt well late and have enough hidden enclaves to hold some nice bulls. Drawing a general non-resident license can be tough, but if you use the services of an outfitter and pay for the higher price license you're guaranteed success in the license drawing.

The "Cowboy State," Wyoming, has always been one of my favorite elk spots. While there are excellent populations of elk in many parts of the state, the famed Thorofare area adjacent to the southeast corner of Yellowstone National Park is a consistent producer of good bulls. If you decide to hunt here, remember in a wilderness area all non-residents must, by law, have a guide. Outfitters hunt this area out of Moran on the

Game call manufacturer and video producer, Larry D. Jones, proves that Oregon can produce some great bulls.
Photo Credit: Bob Robb

west, and Cody on the east. Hunt units 59 and 60 are good early bets, with the archery season kicking off at the beginning of September. The general rifle season in these units also begins in early September and offers hunters a chance at bulls in the rut. A little father south, hunt unit 67 opens at the beginning of October and also provides top-notch hunting for big bulls. The elk license application submission period is January 1-31, so move quickly if you want to get in on the action.

In the Pacific Northwest, Oregon has some outsized Rocky Mountain elk bulls in the northeast, but it can be tough to draw a license. The real deal in this state is all of the wide-open opportunities for Roosevelt elk along the coast. True enough, you'll be hunting in dark timber, but the thriving population of elk makes up for all of your effort. Good hunting can be found on state and National Forest lands, from Reedsport in the south, to Astoria in the north. The elk population is saturated throughout this region and you can find them everywhere. Coastal hunters enjoy a near 15 percent success rate overall, and that's a lot to say for this state's elk hunting potential. Archery season begins in late August and runs nearly the whole month of September. Depending on the hunt unit, general rifle seasons are held in October and November.

When to Apply: All western states have specific big game license/tag application deadlines. The table below provides the latest application deadline information.

Western States Elk License Drawing Deadlines

Alaska	May 31
Arizona	June 15
California	June 2
Colorado	April 6
Idaho	May 31
Montana	June 1
Nevada	April 19
New Mexico	April 24
Oregon	May 15
Utah	February 1
Washington	June 11
Wyoming	January 31

Since these deadlines may change from year to year, hunters should write or call the respective game departments for current regulations, application procedures, and license and tag fees before making an application.

It may be a long shot, but you'll never draw an elk license if you don't get into the drawing process. Photo Credit: Durwood Hollis

It Can be You: Over the years, I hunted in almost all of the Rocky Mountain states, parts of the Pacific Northwest, the Southwest, and California. From Arizona to Montana, Utah to Colorado, and points between, pre-elk season planning has always made the difference between success and failure. However, it all begins with the timely submission of an elk license application. Odds are long on drawing some of the more coveted elk licenses, but someone has to draw and it might as well be you. But you can't draw if you don't play the game. If it can work for me, it can work for you—good luck!

Chapter 3

The Guided Hunt

How to pick the right guide, and the right hunt

The sound of horses and pack animals could be heard long before they burst from the trees. Uncharacteristically, the procession was moving at a fast trot. The guide, all dressed in black like a Johnny Cash wannabe, was in the lead. His horse was covered in a sweat. The string of mules he was leading was barely keeping it all together. And in the rear, his two hunters were doing their best just to stay aboard their horses.

We pulled off the trail and let the group pass. As the guide came abreast of us, he could be heard urging his hunters to "keep up." Quite frankly, I had never seen such a sight. The guide was yelling and cursing. The hunters were bouncing up and down in

the saddle. And the gear was flapping like sheets in a breeze. It was going to be a miracle if everyone and everything made it to camp in one piece.

When we pulled onto the trail again, my guide turned in his saddle and said, "That was quite a sight. It didn't look like anyone was having a good time— including the guide."

A couple of miles later, we ran into the same group again. This time, however, they weren't going anywhere in a hurry. Apparently, one of the mules had had enough high-speed trotting to suit its fancy. Like a broken sprinkler, the animal had spun out of control. The end result was gear thrown around every-

The right guide is often the difference between success and failure. Photo Credit: John Higley

where. Likewise, the entire pack string was disheveled, with ropes dragging on the ground and saddle panniers drooping like beltless trousers. The guide continued to curse everything, including his clients. By the look of things, this was one guided hunt that didn't get off to a good start.

On an elk hunt, there are many things that are simply beyond your control. The weather can turn ugly, or a horse can expire in the middle of trail (believe me, it has happened). Other than these rare situations (okay, problems with the weather aren't so rare), your guide should be able to get you and your gear to camp without too many problems. Obviously, that wasn't the case in the instance cited above.

There are guides, and then there are guides. Unfortunately, many so-called "guides" are really nothing more than horse wranglers (many aren't even good at that). Without any prior knowledge, the prospective hunter only knows what's in the advertising leaflet. Too often, that is about as close to an elk as you'll ever get. The guide may not be licensed, the camp from which clients hunt may be less than adequate, and the hunting area may be completely devoid of elk.

Elk Hunting Bargains: I have a friend who, while not wealthy, has enough means to book a hunt nearly anywhere. Despite his adequate personal income, he is always looking for a "deal" on a hunt. Once in a while, one of these hunts turns out all right. However, the rest of the time, something goes amiss. Now, I don't blame him for trying to save money, that just makes good sense. When you add up all of the trips that have been bummers, and compare them with those that have been successful, his elk hunting efforts have been less than satisfactory. The biggest reason why things haven't gone well is my friend's failure to book every hunt with a reputable guide, outfitter, or through a booking agency.

There is a nexus between the outlay of funds and the quality of most guided hunts. If you're always looking for a bargain, then maybe you're really not in the financial position to book a hunt after all. If that's the case, try saving up enough so you don't have to shop in the bargain basement for an elk hunt. You're better off paying for a licensed guide with a strong reputation for success, rather than wasting your money on what my father used to call "a lick, and a promise."

Ask The Right Questions: Once you've cut your selections down to one or two operations, then it's time to ask the really important questions. Here are some areas of discussion:

How long have you been in business? If the outfitter/guide has been in business a relatively short time (less than two years), I would suggest caution.

How many seasons have you been hunting your current area? My comfort with a particular hunting outfit increases with each year of operation in the same area.

What percentage of hunters book for more than one season? Repeat business is the best indicator of client satisfaction. If a client hunts with the same outfit more than once (even if they were unsuccessful), you can bet they got their money's worth.

What is trophy potential in your area? If most of the clients are shooting mediocre bulls, then you might want to move on to another operation.

What's the cost? Make sure you ask about the "total" cost, including such things as added charges for transportation (to and from the trail head, ranch, lodge, etc.), trophy preparation, meat care, extra charges for taking an exceptional animal, tips, gratuities, taxes, and anything not stated in the brochure or contract.

What about a written contract? Get everything in writing, including the outfitter/guide's license number, the name and address of the insurance carrier, and the name and address of the bonding company. If the operation is unable or reluctant to provide this information, it's time to move on to someone else.

How many days, including travel, can you expect to be in the field hunting? Most hunts include two days of travel (one day into camp, one day out of camp). If there are problems with the weather, guide illness, or guide absence, ask about compensation for days missed in the field.

What kind of accommodations and food will be provided? Most quality backcountry elk camps feature wall tents, heating stoves and lanterns, screened pit toilet, an outdoor shower, and plenty of hot water. Meals are generally a hot breakfast and dinner, with a sack lunch in the field.

How many hunters will be in camp? You're going on an elk hunt, not a family reunion. If camp is overcrowded, things can get out of hand. The number of hunters will be determined by the size of the hunt area.

What about support staff? Does your guide have to cook, clean, chop fire wood, take care of animals, or anything else besides hunting? An adequate elk camp has adequate staff. If the guide is the chief cook, dish washer, wrangler, blacksmith, wood chopper, tack and gear repair person, expect to spend less time in the field hunting.

Will you be sharing your guide with another hunter(s)? The best guided hunt is one-on-one. Any time you increase the number of hunters accompanied by an individual guide, the potential for hunter success drops markedly.

Outfitter, John R. Winter (standing) led the author (left) and another client to a pair of 6x6 Wyoming bulls.
Photo Credit: Durwood Hollis

Take Your Pick: Separating the "good, the bad, and the ugly" elk hunting service providers can be a real challenge for the uninitiated. The outfitter, whose camp was great two years ago, may be going through a divorce and his mind might not be on business. Even worse, is the operation that's in a financial crisis. I have seen cases where both the guide and the hunt deposit disappeared, leaving the client waiting at the trail head. If you talk to enough elk hunters, you'll run into someone that has a similar horror story.

The only way to keep up with things is personal knowledge. If you know the area you want to hunt, and are familiar with the outfitter or guide, then there's a good chance that things will go all right. If you're not familiar with either, then it's a gamble! The best substitute for personal knowledge is booking-agent knowledge. The booking business can't exist without hunter satisfaction. To stay ahead of the competition, a booking agent must maintain a solid reputation. This means putting hunters together with the best outfitters and guides. To understand the process better, let's explore the distinct role that "guides," "outfitters," and "booking agents," each play in the scheme of things.

The Guide: The dictionary defines a guide as someone "to point out the way; to direct on a course; to conduct strangers through a region." Simply put, an elk guide should have enough familiarity with the hunting area to insure your entry, safe passage, and return during the course of the hunt. Furthermore, the guide should be knowledgeable about elk and their traditional movements in the area. When the guide is an experienced elk hunter—all the better.

The Outfitter: An outfitter is a person who, by definition, "furnishes outfits." Specifically, the outfitter is the one who supplies the equipment for the hunt. Such equipment may include tents, cots, cooking and eating gear, game care equipment, riding and pack animals, and all other associated paraphernalia. In most instances, the outfitter is also a licensed guide. Other guides hunting out of the same camp may not be licensed, but work under the auspices of his outfitter/guide's license.

The Booking Agent: This person is the marketing representative of the hunting package. Acting as the agent of the outfitter/guide, the booking agent exposes the hunting opportunity to the potential consumer, handles the financial transactions, and follows-up on customer satisfaction. Usually, the booking agent has first-hand knowledge of the hunting package. The after-hunt follow-up serves as a continuing customer satisfaction indicator. Hunting operations that fail to meet contractual expectations are eliminated from the marketing presentation. In my experience, the booking agent can be the key to opening the door of elk hunting success. Booking agents make their profit the same way travel agents do, by a rebate from the outfitter or guide. So whether you use a booking agent, or purchase your hunt directly from an outfitter or guide, it all costs the same. The services of a booking agent are free of charge!

What About Costs?: Guided elk hunts are expensive. The base price for a seven-day backcountry hunt is about $4,000. Ranch hunts, or hunts on Indian tribal lands may be even more expensive—often a lot more. Paying $8,000 to $12,000 for an elk hunt isn't all that out of line in some areas. If you want to hunt Tule elk in California, for example, the limited number of available permits can put the cost right through the ceiling. When it comes to elk hunting, time and money are important considerations. Personally, I don't like flushing my money down the drain. The best way I know to tilt the odds in my favor is to use the services of a booking agent.

How to Get Started: There are many avenues to guided elk hunts. The back of most sporting maga-

Outfitter and guide, Tim Doud, has earned a reputation for success among serious elk hunters. Photo Credit: Durwood Hollis

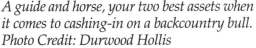

A guide and horse, your two best assets when it comes to cashing-in on a backcountry bull. Photo Credit: Durwood Hollis

zines has an extensive listing of hunting operations. Booking agents, outfitters, and guides can be encountered at local and national sports shows and hunting conventions (Safari Club convention, Rocky Mountain Elk Foundation convention, etc.). And you can talk to friends and associates who have used the services of such individuals.

Write, Call, and/or Visit: Corresponding directly with outfitters and guides that offer elk hunting opportunities will produce a colorful brochure, price list, and photos of the results of recent hunts. Speaking directly with these individuals can provide an even better sense of what their operation is all about. You can do this over the telephone, in person at a sports show or convention, or even visit their operation during the summer. If the booking agent/outfitter/guide offers summer fishing trips, you might consider booking a

trip to see how well things work. In some cases, fishing may be conducted out of the same camp as elk hunting. This will offer insight into the type of accommodations and food you can anticipate, as well as giving you a preview of the hunting area.

The Client List: Some oufitters/guides market their hunting operations directly to the public. As a potential hunt package customer, the best protection you have is a list of former clients. Any outfitter or guide that will not provide you with a list of previous clients should be avoided. When you request the list, make sure that you also ask for the names and telephone numbers of at least three unsuccessful clients. Once you receive the list, call three or four successful clients, and all of the unsuccessful ones.

Make Sure It's All Legitimate: During your discussion with the outfitter/guide, ask for a copy of his

In elk camp, it may be tents for shelter and wood rounds for seats, but the grub is great! Photo Credit: Bob Robb

business and guide's license, and if a membership is held in an outfitter/guide's association. Call each licensing agency and ask for any adverse reports on the operation. Then contact the outfitter/guide's association and request the same information. By the time you've boiled out the client list, and talked to licensing agencies and business associations, you will have a good idea of how business is conducted.

What's Expected of You?: Each hunter will be expected to arrive at a prearranged meeting point a day prior to the beginning of the hunt. Unless you've made transportation arrangement through the booking agent (some booking agents also handle travel), getting to that meeting point is your responsibility. You should arrive with a sighted-in rifle or bow, an adequate supply of ammunition or arrows, and all of your clothing, sleeping bag, and personal gear packed into two soft-sided bags. If you have any special needs (food allergies, special medications, health problems, physical limitations, etc.), discuss these matters candidly with your outfitter/guide. Finally, all financial arrangements should be settled prior to departure to elk camp. Failure to do this can result in hunt cancellation and deposit forfeiture.

What Can I Expect?: The initial meeting with your outfitter/guide may take place at a hotel, motel, cabin, ranch, or at the even at the trail head. Food and accommodations for that evening and the night have usually been previously arranged. If you've never been on a guided hunt before, some of my own experiences may shed light on just what you can expect

Two days before the opening of the 1995 elk season, I met outfitter/guide Tom Doud (Bliss Creek Outfitters, 326 Diamond Basin Rd., Cody, WY 82414, 307/527-6103), at a hotel in Cody, Wyoming. A room had already been reserved in my name, so it was easy to get settled quickly. Over dinner in the hotel dinning room, Tom, the other hunters in the party, and I got acquainted. In the morning, the entire group departed by vehicle to the trail head. At the trail head, our gear was packed on mules, we were put on saddle horses, and by midmorning things got under way. Along the trail, we stopped for a brief lunch, and shortly after nightfall arrival at camp became a reality. Once in camp, tent assignments were made and gear stowed. At dinner, camp rules were explained, hunt plans made, and each hunter was assigned a guide. In the field, the guide was my constant companion from

A warm fire and a hot cup of coffee, does it get any better than this? Photo Credit: Durwood Hollis

the time I stepped into the stirrups in the morning, until we returned to camp in the evening.

Likewise, during the three seasons that I hunted with John R. Winter (P. O. Box 182, Moran, WY 83012, 307/543-2309), of Moran, Wyoming, we initially meet up at his cabin. John put on a big dinner that evening and the hunters spent the night in the cabin. While we ate breakfast the next morning, our gear was taken to the trail head by members of the camp staff and packed on mules. By the time the hunting party arrived at the departure point, everything was ready to go. Each of us was provided with a sack lunch and a horse to ride. Six hours and 20 miles later, we arrived in elk camp. Upon arrival, tent assignments were made and we cleaned up for dinner. After dinner, the hunters returned to their tents and John and his guides made hunting plans. Long before the hunters awoke the next morning, the camp cook was already at work, and the guides were out catching horses. By the time breakfast was over, the only thing I had to do was get my rifle, binoculars, and a sack lunch. Once I was in the saddle, my guide and I were

inseparable. Each day it was the same drill until I scored on an elk. Then things shifted to meat recovery and trophy preparation.

In the early 1980s, I hunted with Arizonan Duwane Adams (204-Ave. "B," San Manuel, AZ 85631, 520/385-4995) and his elk camp was easily accessible by vehicle. We also met up the evening before the hunt began, ate dinner with the other hunters and guides, and slept in tents. Duwane usually doesn't hunt on horseback, so I anticipated lots of serious hiking. I wasn't disappointed! Just because you don't trek deep into the backcountry, doesn't mean that you can't score an elk. Some of the biggest bulls I've ever seen have been taken by Duwane Adam's clients, and they did it from start to finish on foot.

I've also hunted on private ranches where accommodations were a warm lodge with a hot shower and hunting transportation was provided by four-wheel drive vehicle. On one occasion, I traveled by jet boat up the Salmon River to a first-class hunting lodge that was about as remote as it gets. Conversely, I have met guides at trail heads when the transportation was

Hunting out of Tim Doud's Bliss Creek elk camp, the author took this 5x6 bull an hour into the hunt and less than a mile from camp. Photo Credit: Durwood Hollis

boot leather and we carried our own tent, food, and gear in backpacks. Plane, train, truck, boat, horse, or by foot, getting to elk camp is always an adventure.

If you're successful enough to score on an elk, primary field care will be provided by your guide. Your help is always appreciated, especially if you know what to do. If you don't know what to do, then do what you're asked. If you want to mount the head-skin, your guide will remove, salt, and roll the cape for transportation to the taxidermist of your choice. You can take the cape and antlers with you, or you can make arrangements with your guide to have the head mounted locally. I generally schedule a couple of extra days at the conclusion of the hunt to take care of meat and trophy matters.

Share, and Share Alike: The most expensive guided hunt is one-on-one (one hunter, one guide). You can save money by booking two-on-one (two hunters, one guide), but things might not work out as well as you would think. If the hunt is long enough (at least 10 days), and elk are relatively plentiful, then two-on-one will generally provide shooting opportunities for both hunters. However, in most instances one hunter gets a shooting opportunity, the other just tags along. If the second hunter gets a shot, it is usually very late in the hunt and at a mediocre bull. Of course, luck plays a part in all hunts. One hunter may score the first day out of camp, then the second hunter has the guide all to himself for the rest of the hunt. I've seen it happen both ways.

Longtime hunting companion, attorney Thad Young, and I once shared an elk guide. Thad's guide had to return prematurely to the trail head, and a replacement wasn't due into camp until the next day. Outfitter John R. Winter had been my guide for most of the hunt, so he asked if Thad could hunt with us. John knew that Thad and I have hunted together for so long that the decision about who shoots first, wasn't really a problem. Late in the afternoon, John located a bull bugling on a distance ridge. Together, the three of us made the long approach. I told John that if we got close enough, Thad could have the first shot. One thing led to another, and my friend managed to score. Later on that same evening, Lady Luck also smiled on me. When we rode into camp that night, Thad and I were both happy hunters.

The instance cited above was a case of two hunters and one guide getting lucky. However, it doesn't happen that way all the time. Two-on-one guiding can create a conflict of interest for the guide, as well as creating real problems between friends. When anger or hostility rears its ugly head, things can go downhill rapidly. If you've paid for the services of a guide, then you have every expectation of full value for those dollars. Tagging along isn't anyone's idea of a good time. Take my suggestion and spend the extra money for your own guide. Things just work better that way.

The Drop Camp: Other than hunting on your own, the most economical semi-guided hunt is a drop hunt. A guide can "drop off" several groups of hunters at various locations throughout his hunting area. He may already have camp set up, or you may use your own gear. The areas where elk frequent, and the best places to hunt will usually be pointed out on a map. And every few days, or on a prearranged day, the guide will check in on your camp and pack out meat if needed.

In a drop camp, the hunter(s) is(are) left on their own for the duration of the hunt. If you are an experienced elk hunter, know the area, and the elk population is good with a reasonable bull-to-cow ratio, you can be successful out of a drop camp. However, if the guide runs both guided hunts and drop camps, it doesn't take a rocket scientist to realize that you get what you pay for. It's as simple as that!

Guided Ranch Hunts: There are at least three kinds of ranch hunts that come to mind. First, there are ranch hunts that include deluxe accommodations in an upscale lodge, with vehicular transportation provided during the hunt. The elk on the ranch are free ranging, but due to an extensive network of roads, the hunt itself may not be very difficult. Usually, your guide will drive to a prominent location where elk can be spotted from a distance. Once

Arizona elk guides, Frank Morales (left), and Duwane Adams (right), teamed up to put their client on this spectacular bull. Photo Credit: Duwane Adams

While many booking agents, outfitters, and guides offer two-on-one (two hunters, one guide) hunts, one-on-one (one hunter, one guide) eliminates a lot of potential problems.
Photo Credit: Bob Robb

you've located the bull you want, it's a simple matter to stalk close enough for a shot. These hunts have limited hunting pressure, high elk populations, and cost lots of money.

The next kind of ranch hunt requires the payment of trespass fees, and if you're successful—a trophy fee. This type of hunt may be unguided and hunters must provide their own accommodations and food. However, if a guide is included in the package, it is generally a ranch hand or a local resident who has some knowledge of the area. Success on such a hunt can be high, but the costs can also be staggering.

Finally, there are ranch hunts that feature a captive (fenced-in) elk population. Depending on the size of the ranch, the elk may be as wild as free-ranging elk, but this is not always the case. Accommodations are generally first class and hunter success is 100 percent. And since the elk are owned by the ranch owner and not the state, hunting license requirements may not apply. If this, or any type of ranch hunt interests you, then by all means check it out. However, for many elk hunters it isn't elk hunting if it isn't a tent camp in the wilderness.

Tips: There is really no obligation to tip your outfitter, guide, or members of the camp staff. However, a gratuity of any form is always appreciated. If you decide to tip, your guide should receive the largest sum, with members of the camp staff receiving lesser amounts. Tipping can also be accomplished by giving your guide a pair of binoculars, a custom knife, or even a rifle. Gratuities are a sensitive subject and must be approached tactfully. Whatever you do, make sure that good manners and courtesy prevail.

The Bottom line: Guided hunts are expensive, sometimes—really expensive. If you don't live in an elk area, or don't have the time to scout things out, engaging the services of a guide is the way to go. The use of a booking agent can help sort out the good guys from all the rest, but nothing is an absolute guarantee. A guided elk hunt is like going on an ocean cruise. You pay the price and hope that it's a good experience. Depending on a multitude of variables (including bad weather, poor food, and less than optimal accommodations), you may, or may not have a good time. And that, my friends, is why it's called hunting!

Chapter 4

New Frontiers

Successful public land elk hunters learn to break the barriers

The winding dirt road ended abruptly and we swung the truck in a full circle to park. Illuminated momentarily by the vehicle's headlights, a black and eerie ocean of junipers seemed to stretch endlessly on all sides.

"We're here," said my hunting companion, Thad Young, as the truck slid to a stop in a billowing cloud of dust.

With only the soft glow from Thad's flashlight illuminating the way, we left the truck and stepped off into the enveloping darkness. When we stopped to catch our breath, I asked where we were going. He explained that when the area was homesteaded,

ranchers quickly snapped up the prime farming and grazing areas. What remained were thousands of acres of rugged juniper-covered terrain. Most of this land ended up in the jurisdiction of the Bureau of Land Management. Even though much of this acreage may be landlocked by private holdings, often a narrow entrance corridor can be found when one corner of a Bureau of Land Management holding intersects a public road. Through some careful map work, Thad had found just such an entrance.

Struggling through the tangle of junipers made us feel as though we were being swallowed whole. The

Unlocking public land elk hunting secrets will take its toll in sweat, sore muscles, and boot leather—lots of it!
Photo Credit: Bob Robb

thick trees and rugged terrain served as a barrier to all but the most tenacious hunters. At first glance, the area seemed impenetrable, but looks are deceiving. After the better part of an hour, we finally topped out of the enveloping vegetation into some very huntable mixed cover.

"Just like having your own private hunting preserve," said Thad.

Unlocking the secret of that juniper barrier first took a lot of exertion. But through the years, that particular piece of government ground has given up enough good bull elk to make it all worthwhile. Secreted well away from the mainstream hunting crowds, heavy cover can open up into some promising elk hunting hot spots. But, getting to the good stuff can take a toll in sweat, sore muscles, and boot leather.

Terrain Barriers: I can recall one particularly rugged canyon in south-eastern Arizona that the locals don't even hunt. Spurred on by the knowledge that most hunters wouldn't even think of hunting the gorge, I plunged deep in the folds of that hellhole on foot. Once below the rim, I had my own personal hunting paradise. It was steep, dry, and foreboding, but the canyon gave up a fine bull about two hours

into the hunt. Several tough hauls out of that cut in the earth put the meat in the freezer (next time, I'll bring a frying pan and eat the elk on the spot) and a set of impressive antlers on my wall.

The dry hills and rugged canyons of the West and Southwest can be silent barriers to all but the most dedicated hunter. While herds may be few and far between, if you can find a source of moisture, shade, and food, you might just find elk. Since there is little hunting pressure in these areas, bulls often live long enough to grow impressive racks.

I know of a particularly ugly range of hills right in the middle of Wyoming's high desert country. Most hunters wouldn't think a respectable elk could be found in the region. I say so, because that's just what I thought. However, while hunting deer in the area, I found the opposite to be true. One morning, just after daylight, I worked my way along a twisting ridge that seemed to run for miles. Below me and spreading in both directions, junipers covered the slope. Farther down the ridge, a splash of alders and sage ran well out into the flatlands. If there was ever a place that looked like mule deer country, this was it. About an hour after dawn, I sat down to glass a couple of nar-

Finding the right spot can take every tool in your bag, including serious map work. Photo Credit: Bob Robb

row draws that tailed off the ridge. To my surprise, a very nice 6x6 bull elk broke out of the junipers. The bull wasn't in a particular hurry, he was just traveling from one place to another. Off to the side, I could see a handful of cows moving through the junipers. Who would have thought this to be elk country? However, it most certainly was all of that, and then some. The next season, I returned and found myself the only elk hunter for miles.

Since many barriers prevent vehicle access, you'll often have to find your own way into—and out of the best hunting country. Most of the time, your method of transport will be a good pair of boots. If you're successful, field dressing, skinning, and possibly even butchering an animal at the kill site will be necessary. Some type of backpack, large enough to carry your lunch, a jacket, elk quarter bags, a canteen (sometimes two), and other needs for the day, will be an essential part of your plans. And, don't forget a map, compass or GPS instrument, and the ever-important flashlight. Tough terrain makes for tough access, but once beyond the barrier, it really is "like having your own private hunting preserve."

Water Barriers: In many areas, rivers, swamps, and lakes are your barriers. Several years ago, when my Montana hunting guide picked me up at the airport, there was a canoe lashed on top of his truck. The next day, we drove along a river where there were no bridges, stock crossings, or access to the other side for miles. The watercourse was too deep to wade and too treacherous for horses, but that didn't prevent us from crossing in the canoe. Once on the other side, we found ourselves in untouched elk country. During the next few days, I saw lots of elk and not one hunter. When I finally tagged the bull I wanted, it was a simple matter to field dress it, quarter the carcass, and haul the quarters down to the river. Once there, we loaded the meat into the canoe for the return river crossing.

During a summer fishing trip, I noticed that there was access only on one side of the lake we were fishing. While shore fishermen could work their way up and down part of the lake shore, an overland journey to the opposite side was virtually impossible. During an afternoon lull in the fishing action, my companion and I cruised along the far side of the lake in our boat. It was there that I noticed several canyons that looked like good elk country. Later on in the fall, I stopped by my fishing partner's home to see if he'd finally caught the trout of his dreams. When I pulled into his driveway, there was a huge set of elk antlers leaning up against the side of his garage. Subsequent conversation

revealed that he had also made note of the canyons on the opposite side of the same lake. Realizing that there wasn't any way around the shoreline, he figured that his boat could open up some new hunting country. Obviously, my friend made the right choice.

Once, while slogging across a narrow strip of boggy ground between two mountain ridges, I jumped a nice bull and three cow elk right out of a wallow. Evidently, the soggy tangle of vegetation served the elk as a protective envelope and the mud eased the heat of the unseasonably warm September weather. It seemed that the elk didn't give a second thought about a little mud and water. Boggy areas that escape hunting pressure can serve as home for many reclusive, heavily pressured elk. More than one trophy bull has come out of such a spot, especially after opening day when the smart elk retreat to these areas.

Adjacent to many lakes, rivers and similar regions, potential elk hot spots can be found. But, before you crank up the outboard motor, or throw a canoe on top of your suburban utility vehicle, check local regulations about ownership, access, and any other special regulations. There may be provisions against hunting within a certain distance from the riverbank or lake shore. Other laws can also apply. Even if there are some regulatory constraints, many of these types of areas still deserve investigation. Aquatic barriers can often mask the avenue into an untapped elk hunting resource.

Highway Barriers: There a thousands of miles of interstate highways throughout the country. In some areas, posted signs prevent anything other than emergency parking along these thoroughfares. Even when there's access, it may only lead to one side of the highway. Since law enforcement frowns on crossing a busy interstate on foot, one side of the highway may be completely free of hunting pressure.

A few years back, I discovered just such a highway barrier. Along a stretch of this thoroughfare, a solitary off-ramp led to a frontage road that provided access to only one side of the freeway. On the opposite side of the highway there was no access at all for miles. I reasoned that if a way could be found across the interstate, it might just open up some new elk country. So, I pulled off of the freeway and began to explore the frontage road. Behind a screen of tumbleweeds, a large steel culvert presented a possible avenue under the interstate. After walking several hundred yards through the culvert's dark interior, I emerged on the opposite side of the freeway. By finding a way under the highway barrier, I had discovered a pathway into a new hunting area.

Get Physical: Pre-hunt physical conditioning can help ease the strain of an extended stay in the woods. If you arrive at the trailhead out of shape, you're definitely not going to have a good time. Likewise, if you can't leave work stress, marriage stress, and child-rearing problems at home, then everyone in elk camp will have to suffer—all because of you. Elk hunting ought to be stress relief.

With hundreds of square miles of public land elk habitat, you'll have to give it more than a just a casual once over.
Photo Credit: Bob Robb

Between freeway off-ramps, the possibility of untouched hunting areas always exists. If you want to explore, find a place to completely exit the roadway, park your vehicle legally, and make sure you're aware of local hunting regulations. Lands adjacent to a major highway may be a mix of both public and private holdings, so make sure you're always on the right side of any property line. When in doubt about the legality of access, seek permission first.

Perception Barriers: Season after season, many hunters drive right past some great hunting areas. To the casual observer, these regions often seem inaccessible or simply too tough to hunt. That's just how Al Kavalauskus and I felt when we pulled off the road along side of a steep, dry, juniper-covered set of hills on the flank of a sizable mountain near Thermopolis, Wyoming. Neither of us had ever hunted the area before and from the looks of it, I could understand why. The only apparent water source for miles was a foul-smelling creek, a foreboding sign at best. About the only thing those rugged hills had to offer were lots of juniper, rocks, dry grass, and a smattering of sage. It simply didn't look like elk country. A mutual friend had recommended the area. However, both of us wondered whether or not we were the butt of a joke.

Stepping off into the half-light of a new day, we held little hope of seeing any elk. At the lower elevations there was plenty of antelope sign and a few deer tracks, but evidence of elk activity was non-existent. Once we got into the high country, a scattering of elk

In the West, there are thousands of square miles of publicly-owned elk habitat. These areas are open to you. All you have to do is get there and be willing to hunt hard. Most of the bulls I've taken have come off government ground. You can be successful. I know, because I've been there, and done that! Start out being prepared for the worst, and graciously accept success when it comes to you. If you keep in the game, you're bound to be a winner somewhere along the way. If that success turns out to be a heavy-antlered 6x6 bull elk—all the better!

On public land, recent fires can open up acres of prime elk habitat. Photo Credit: Bob Robb

tracks could be seen. Finally, we caught sight of a couple cow elk. A good omen, but still I wasn't impressed. While I watched the cows with my binoculars, a few yards away Al had a very different vantage point. Unseen from my position, a bull elk was feeding a short distance straight below us. Al caught my attention and I turned to see the bull hightailing down though the trees.

Things and places are not always what they seem. If I hadn't had confidence in our information source, no doubt we would have chosen to hunt somewhere else. The place just didn't look right, and it was that perception that formed a barrier to our hunting interest. No doubt, other hunters shared the same opinion and had driven right on by in search of a better looking area. No, it wasn't access or a terrain barrier that discouraged hunting, it was simply the perception that no elk in its right mind would ever live there. Obviously, we were wrong!

Crowd Barriers: If you're like me, you hate crowds—especially when they're other hunters. However, there once was an occasion when an orange-vested throng worked to my advantage. An

acquaintance had given me a tip on a secret elk spot that he had hunted during his college years. Of course, it had been more than 15 years since the bearer of the tale had hunted there. Not to be discouraged, I decided to participate in the out-of-state license drawing. In the due course of time, an envelope containing an elk license for the area arrived in my mail box. A few weeks later, and more dirt roads than you can imagine, I discovered the exact location.

It was two days before the season opener, so I had enough time to scout things out. By the end of the first day, I managed to locate lots of fresh sign, a couple of major game trails, and two small herds of elk. Things were definitely looking good. The next day, I made all of the necessary preparations for opening morning. By late afternoon, however, other hunters began showing up. Obviously, the once secret elk spot wasn't a secret anymore.

It just so happened that during my scouting foray, I had located a narrow pass from one drainage to another. The game trail in the bottom contained enough telltale tracks to give away the true secret of this location. However, getting there in darkness would mean rolling out of my sleeping bag three hours before dawn, hiking by flashlight in tough country and getting into position well before the rest of the crowd even finished breakfast. Under normal conditions, I wouldn't even think of hunting anywhere near such a large group of hunters. Without any other options available, the only thing left to do was to use the crowd to my best advantage. Hopefully, they would push some elk in my direction.

At 3:00 a.m., my tiny alarm clock did its best to wake me from a fitful slumber. Looking outside of my camper, I couldn't see another light anywhere. Hopefully, the freezing temperature would keep everyone else in their sleeping bags for another hour or two. Dressing quickly, I slipped out of the truck, and took off into the darkness. By the time the pass came into view, the first rays of light were just beginning to

color the eastern horizon. I picked a stand well up on the ridge, overlooking a major game trail. No matter what happened, I was in a position to ambush any bull that took that route.

The area was too steep and stony for horses, so I knew the other hunters would be limited by the distance they could cover on foot. I have found that if hunting is conducted on foot, most hunters will only go about one mile from their vehicle. A tenacious few will cover an additional mile. And only a handful of hardy souls will push on a third mile. The narrow pass and the game trail were a tad father than three miles from camp.

Just before dawn, I could hear faint sounds of truck doors slamming and hunters yelling back and forth. The smell of camp fires and bacon even drifted to my nose. Obviously, hunters don't realize how far sound

A hidden elk wallow has real potential, but you may have to hike through miles of blow-down timber to find it. Photo Credit: Bob Robb

Beyond the barriers—highways, crowd, and your own perception—you just might find a fresh elk rub. Photo Credit: Bob Robb

and smells can carry in the woods. Shortly after daybreak, some scattered shooting broke out. And by the time the first rays of the sun began to warm my face, I could see orange vests all over the lower flank of the mountain. It was beginning to look more like a military exercise than the opening day of elk season!

The first group of elk boiled out of some trees about a mile and a half down the mountain. Weaving their way in and out of the timber, the animals eventually passed right below me at less than 150 yards. A few minutes later, a raghorn bull and a spike came down the same trail in a big hurry. "So far, so good," I thought to myself.

An hour or so passed and only a couple of other groups of elk had traversed the game trail. And a bull of any significance was conspicuous by his absence. While the mob of hunters below had thinned out con-

siderably, several could still be seen trudging up the mountain. In another hour or so, at least a couple of hunters might overrun my position. Quite frankly, I was running out of time.

Something moving in the trees caught my eye. Finally, the dusky shape of elk could be seen. Using the binoculars, I managed to pick up a flash of ivory. Further glassing revealed even more optical information. This animal was a bull—a very good bull—with at least five-points on one side of his rack. Now, things were beginning to get interesting! However, this particular bull wasn't a dummy. After watching him for a few minutes, it became obvious that he wanted to stay out of sight. With all the hunters on the mountain, I didn't blame him one bit. If he stayed in the trees, getting a clear shot a this big boy was going to be a challenge.

Just because it doesn't look like elk country, doesn't mean it isn't. Photo Credit: Bob Robb

As I watched, the bull drifted through the heavy cover towards my position, minutes turned into the better part of an hour. He was still too far away, and there were too many intervening trees to be sure of a shot. For a moment, I considered moving closer. But that plan was quickly discarded as an exercise in futility. No, I would have to wait the bull out.

Just then, a hunter appeared about a quarter of a mile below me. Since there was a slight uphill breeze, it only took a minute or so before the bull picked up his scent. Watching through my binoculars, the animal could be seen testing air. Then he began moving away from the unfamiliar odor and right towards the pass. This was what I had waited for all morning. The bull dropped out of the timber, hit the game trail, and started to trot towards my position. At 200 yards distant, I picked him up in my scope. And when he came broadside, I squeezed the trigger.

At the shot, the elk bunched up in the middle and took off at a run. With bullet-compromised lungs and a failing blood supply, he didn't go far. By the time the nearest hunter realized what happened, I was already elbow-deep into field dressing chores.

Rather than being obstructed by the crowd, I had overcome the barrier it presented. No it wasn't easy, but I had been willing to pay the price. If you want to beat the other guy at his own game, then you too will have to pay the price. And that cost may entail rolling out of bed in freezing weather, hiking long miles by flashlight beam, and then patiently waiting for your chance. It's tiring, frustrating, and demanding, but that's what it's all about.

Mental Barriers: Elk hunting on public land is never easy. To be successful, you may have to hike miles into bad country. At some point in time, the weather will probably be cold and wet, and it might even snow. After a day or two on the trail, you could develop blisters, experience high altitude headaches, and otherwise feel simply miserable. Worst of all, the elk can be tough to find.

When contemplating a public land elk hunt, it's easy to get discouraged. The hunter success rate, even in the best elk states, is less than 25 percent and drawing a license isn't a sure thing. Then there's the cost, the special clothing and equipment, and the deplorable weather. Elk hunting isn't a casual sport. You have to be serious, to be successful. Serious about finding a place to hunt. Serious about the license drawing game. And even more serious about getting an elk.

When public land hunting pays off, it often does so with big dividends. This bull came from Idaho's Selway/Bitterroot Wilderness. Photo Credit: Bob Robb

Elk camp is no place to complain, whine, or wimp out. You have to leave everything behind in a relentless pursuit of success. On one elk hunt, I watched a hunter ask daily to be taken to the top of a distant ridge so he could use his cell phone. All day long this guy subjected anyone who would listen to a rant about how much money he was losing. After two days of this claptrap, the outfitter hid the telephone. After that, the hunter had a good time and got his elk. My best advice, stay focused. If you can't, don't go elk hunting.

Some folks can't seem to keep their mouths shut. Every little thing sets them off. They can't sleep right because their tent mate snores (ever heard of ear plugs?). Their butt gets sore after a day in the saddle (try walking). And everyone else has gotten an elk, why can't they score? (if you'd quit complaining, your luck might change). Successful elk hunters don't complain, and complainers aren't usually successful.

I've been on elk hunts that never panned out until the last hour of the last day. Sometimes you just have to gut it out. Complaining doesn't make things better, it just serves to discourage you and everyone else. If you have a specific problem, discuss the matter with your guide. You're the paying client. Most outfitters and guides will go out of their way to make your hunt a success.

When you're seeing lots of elk, anyone can have a good time. When things get tough, however, that's when the worst in all of us can bubble to the surface. An upbeat, positive attitude will go a long way towards making a tough elk hunt bearable, even enjoyable. I've been on hunts when nothing seemed to go right, but I still had a good time. Don't let the situation, your physical condition, or your mental attitude be a barrier to a successful hunt. Remember, any day in the field (even a bad day), is better than a day at the office. And that, my friend, may be a cliché, but it is also a fact!

If you've had trouble finding a place to go, then learn how to break through the obstacles to find new hunting ground. Each individual region is different, but search out the areas that have barriers to hunter access, find a way across, into, or through those hindrances, and you'll discover hunting opportunities you never knew existed. Likewise, don't let anything, or anyone get in the way of your success. Use the tools at hand to overcome license access barriers, physical limitations, and people (even yourself) with sour attitudes. Public land hunting isn't easy, but it isn't all that bad either.

Chapter 5

Elk Hunting Strategies

It's not what you do. It's how you do it.

One fruitless September afternoon, deep in the wilds of Wyoming's Thorofare country, I posed what was no doubt one of the most muddle-brained questions of my elk hunting career. "Where are the elk?", I asked John R. Winter, renowned outfitter and guide.

"Elk are where elk are, and they aren't anywhere else," John replied.

My first thoughts were, ask a dumb question, get a dumb answer. Giving the matter serious consideration, I realized that John's reply was really a tidbit of sage elk hunting wisdom. Elk are herbivores and they consume vast quantities of food. While these animals will browse, they prefer to graze. To find enough food, elk often have to cover many miles. Consequently, these animals seldom stay in one place very long. The key, then, to finding elk is discovering evidence of recent activity.

Despite manageable weather, the right gear, and lots of fresh elk sign, there are times when you can come up empty-handed day after day. A modern idiom, "been there, done that"—expresses my feelings on the subject. If elk hunting was easy, then it wouldn't be called "hunting." To be consistently successful there are times you must abandon proven techniques and just get radical!

Get High: Big game animals are more aware of danger approaching from below, than from above. Gaining the high ground well before first light gives the hunter a distinct advantage. This places you in a position that allows for rapid response. When you're on top of the landscape, you can cover more ground with less energy. And covering ground is what finding elk is all about.

Arizona big game guide, Duwane Adams is a firm believer in getting high. Duwane always gets his elk hunters into position before the eastern horizon even has a glimmer of light. "The only way to catch a bull out in the open is to get high early. If you're still trying to make it to the top, and daylight comes, you're too late.

It takes preparation, hard work and lots of strategy to put a bull like this on the wall. Photo Credit: Jim Matthews

Hunt the Pockets: Traditionally, elk move from cover to feed, and back again. However, there are times when they don't move at all. Whatever movement occurs usually does so in a relatively small area in a much larger habitat. If you can't find elk in all of the usual places, then you're going to have to look in the unusual spots. In these protected environmental "pockets," elk can find all they need. Here they will remain until lack of food, human intrusion, or the weather stimulates a move.

Four elements of successful elk hunting strategy: map, compass, binoculars—and a sensible scheme. Photo Credit: Durwood Hollis

Leave early and get into position while it's still dark. When you find a bull, move quickly to where you can get a shot. It's better to wait on the sun, then have the sun wait on you," Dwane told me during a recent hunt.

Tim Doud, is a "pocket" hunter—pocket meadows, pocket wallows, even pocket timber. I know, because this Wyoming outfitter and guide led me into just such a spot a few seasons ago. Hunting out of Tim's Bliss Creek camp, we tried all the usual elk haunts without any success. Sure, we found plenty of elk sign, but no animals were present.

"This is strange. I saw several small groups of elk in this area just last week," Tim said.

Well, Tim Doud isn't a man that gets discouraged easily. When the usual didn't work, it was definitely time to try something different. Pointing to a distant rocky bluff, Tim said, "There are a couple of pocket meadows that run up toward that rim. Let's see if we can't find some elk there."

Sure enough, there were two narrow openings in the timber that offered excellent elk forage. We hunted across the first stretch of grass without success, then as we approached the next opening, the sound of an elk bugle came to our ears. That bugle was just like giving Tim a kick in the posterior. He took off like a shot, motioning for me to follow along. A hundred yards later, the bottom edge of the second pocket meadow came into view.

"The elk are here, I can smell them," Tim whispered.

The musky scent of elk, reminding me of the smell of cows in a barn, drifted through the trees. Momentarily we caught sight of the first elk—a cow. A few minutes later, another cow joined her, and then another, and another. Before long, the whole herd was feeding out in front of us.

"Here comes the bull," Tim said anxiously.

The next few seconds were blurs. However, I do remember placing the crosshairs of my scope just behind the bull's shoulder. At the shot, the herd patriarch leapt, high into the air and hightailed it for the timber. After giving things a few minutes to settle down, we found the bull just inside the trees. There

*Hunting "pockets" of feed and cover can pro-
duce bulls. Photo Credit: Jim Matthews*

was no need for a follow-up shot. Obviously, Tim Doud's pocket meadow strategy worked. And it's worked for him more than once.

In a Pinch: Elk don't waste energy. When they move, elk do so along defined trails that take advantage of natural terrain features (passes, plateaus, cuts, and benches). Trying to locate a herd of elk at any point along one of these routes can be as difficult as finding "a needle in a haystack." However, you can take the guesswork out of finding elk by planning an ambush at a pinch point.

Careful interpretation of a topographical map can assist you in finding places where elk move through a narrow corridor, or along a particular constricted trail. Search the map for potential passages from one drainage to another, from food to water or from feed to cover. It may be a narrow pass, a winding bench, or even a line of timber across a rocky slide. When you find such a place, search it out and look for sign—tracks, rubs, scat, anything. If you discover evidence of recent elk activity, then you're in business.

Hunting in a pinch point requires patience and an iron will. This is especially true when a lack of elk is combined with discomfort in the lower posterior. If you can remember how hard those wooden church pews were when you were a kid, then know that patience is directly related to comfort. To stay alert, your stand must be comfortable. A non-absorbent foam pad can cushion your posterior, as well as keep cold and dampness away from the seat of your pants. Select a location that offers good visibility, puts the wind in your favor, and provides adequate protection from the elements.

Whatever you do, watch the wind.
Photo Credit: Bob Robb

I've spent many an hour waiting on elk at a pinch point. Most of the time, it's boring beyond comprehension. I remember sitting on a narrow pass from one drainage to another for three entire days. There was no doubt that elk were using this avenue, but all of their movements seemed to be after dark. Nonetheless, one bull decided to take that passage while there was still enough light to see him clearly in my rifle scope. When a pinch point produces a bull, it couldn't be easier.

Cross Over on The Other Side: The number of times I've followed herds of elk through the timber have been legion, especially during bow season. No matter what I did, getting close to the herd bull, just didn't seem to be in the cards. Either the wind would change unexpectedly, my presence became known by one of the cows in the herd, or I just got frustrated and abandoned the project. No matter the reason, trailing a herd of elk hasn't always been my most productive hunting strategy.

Waiting for elk at a "pinch point" demands patience, but it can pay-off with big dividends. Photo Credit: Bob Robb

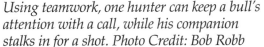
Using teamwork, one hunter can keep a bull's attention with a call, while his companion stalks in for a shot. Photo Credit: Bob Robb

Once during the Colorado bow season, I encountered a small herd elk feeding along through an enormous stand of aspens. After two hours of following this group of animals at a discreet distance, I decided to circle around and get ahead of them. Taking careful note of the wind, I moved to a position about 300 yards ahead of the elk. Just about the time I thought the elk had taken a different course of travel, the first cows started showing up. It didn't take long before the bull passed right in front of me at less than 25 yards.

An elk's olfactory sense is highly developed and operates like early warning radar. If you decide to circle around a herd, or even a solitary bull, remember that your scent can spoil the best of plans. Subtle changes in air current should influence where and when you move. Likewise, the position of the sun should play a role in the direction of your approach and where you make your stand. With the sun at your back, the elk will have more difficulty seeing you.

Sometimes you just have to give up one approach and try another. If you can't get up on a bull through one avenue, then switch paths and try another method. I'd always rather have an elk come to me, than the other way around. The next time you can't seem to get close enough for a shot, try circling around and waiting for the bull to come to you.

Double Up: Two hunters working in a tandem can sometimes be successful in situations where a solitary hunter would only meet defeat. In the early 1990s, I hunted with outfitter and guide, John R. Winter, in Wyoming's Two-Ocean Pass country. The weather was unseasonably warm, even for mid-September.

Every decent bull in the country was buried deep in the dark timber and they weren't about to come out. After a week of trying every trick in the book, I was ready to give up.

On the last evening, of the last day of the hunt, we spotted a couple of bulls feeding in some mixed cover. You could only see the tops of their antlers; nevertheless, it was our only opportunity. The problem that presented itself was making an approach. Once we dropped down into the cover, it would be impossible to see either of the bulls until you were right on top of them.

John pulled out his elk call and bugled. That's all it took. Both bulls sounded off loudly and looked in our direction to see what the fuss was all about. After about 10 minutes of verbal sparring, it was obvious that neither elk was going to move.

"I'll stay put and use the call to keep their interest. You try for one of the bulls," John instructed.

I didn't need any further encouragement. Keeping my eyes on the tips of the closest bull's antlers, I plunged into the head-high cover. In the meantime, John kept up a steady stream of bugles and grunts. Surprisingly, the bull had no idea that I was anywhere around. The cover was so thick that I had to get within 20 yards just to make a shot. A few square inches aren't much of a target presentation, but at close range that didn't make any difference. When the echo of the shot died away, the bull was mine.

Using one person to keep a bull's interest going with a call, while the hunter moves in for a shot, has worked for me several times. This strategy is effective during the rut, after the rut, and in every hunt period, including the general rifle season. If a bull won't

Get ahead of the bull and wait him out.
Photo Credit: Jim Matthews

come to you, then focus his attention on something else, and you go to him. Like I said, sometimes you have to get radical.

Dark Timber: I don't know anyone who really likes to hunt dark timber. You can spend days in the timber and never even catch a glimpse of an elk. Just because you're in the worst hellhole on the mountain, it doesn't guarantee a bull behind every tree. My suggestion is to cover as much ground as possible until you encounter fresh sign. When you do, then it's time to move like a snail. You'll be looking for a piece of elk—a flash of ivory, the flick of an ear, or a splash of buff and creme in an otherwise verdant tangle.

While not as phlegmatic as the moose, nor as over-wrought as the deer, elk depend heavily on the herd community to serve as an early warning system. The presence of many eyes and noses within the group provides a sense of security. What is perceived as a threat to one, is a threat to all. Even so, when feeding or bedded, elk seem more relaxed than most members of the family Cervidae. And this point of vulnerability offers an edge to the hunter when hunting dark timber.

Elk are never quiet when they are feeding, especially a whole herd of animals. Even when they're resting, they still mew and chirp, and even stand up and move around. Don't worry too much about making some noise when you're hunting in the timber. Of course, talking out loud can be as disturbing to an elk as a fingernail on a chalkboard. If you must converse with your hunting companion(s), develop a series of hand signs as a method of silent communication.

When you move through timber, watch where you step. Try to roll each footstep from initial heel strike to toe push. This way, you distribute your weight evenly over the length of each step. Also, vary your stride so that the pattern of movement is random (like an elk feeding), rather than predictable (like approaching danger). If you happen to spook an elk, get on your cow call immediately. If the animal(s) hasn't (haven't) caught your scent, then there's a good chance that the call alone will settle things down.

If you decide to hunt the dark timber, lace your boots up tight, stuff a sandwich in your pack, and prepare to do battle. This is elk hunting at its very worst. Roosevelt elk lives in this kind of habitat in

Sometimes, you've just got to make like a worm and crawl to get to the good spots. Photo Credit: Durwood Hollis

coastal Oregon and Washington. The tenacious hunters who go after them enjoy a reasonable level of success, so hunting dark timber can't be all that bad. Timber work can, however, be frustrating, even hellish to the point of discouragement. Unfortunately, at times it's the only game in the woods.

Throw Caution to the Wind: While I advocate stealth in hunting strategy, sometimes you just have to get aggressive. Here's a good example of what I mean. Once, while riding with my guide up a steep incline, we rounded a corner in the trail and ran smack into a whole herd of elk. The animals were right in the open and spread across a broad area. Traditional hunting strategy suggests that we ride into the nearest timber, dismount, and try to approach on foot. However, that wasn't what my guide suggested.

"Keep on riding, they don't know what we are," the guide hissed through his teeth.

Even in the backcountry, elk see horses and men on horseback all the time. Without catching a whiff of man scent, I am not sure an elk knows the difference. Banking on this piece of animal psychology, the guide felt that we had a chance for one of the bulls in the herd.

"Get ready to dismount on the offside of your horse without stopping. Pull your rifle out of the scabbard, and set down. I'll keep on going. Your horse will follow mine. When we're clear, shoot that bull right in front of us," the guide whispered.

The plan worked like magic. I slipped off the horse without missing a beat. In one fluid movement, the rifle came free from the scabbard. While I was still hidden behind my horse, I sat down and draped the rifle across my knees. Once the guide and the horses were clear, I found the bull in my scope. That old boy didn't know what hit him. In fact, the other elk didn't even realize anything was amiss until I stood up and spooked the whole herd. Sometimes you have to consign traditional strategy to history and throw caution to the wind.

Go Late: On my first elk adventure, a veteran who had hunted more years than I had lived gave me a solid piece of elk hunting advice. "Opening morning is worth the rest of the season," he stated with authority. After more than three decades of elk pursuit, I must admit that there is value in that statement. However, the converse can be equally as true. What do I mean? If you get some weather (read that as serious snow), a late-season hunt can produce spectacular results.

Wet and sloppy, or dry and powdery, it's not easy trudging through a couple of feet of snow. It can take all day before you locate a bull, so start early (even earlier than that) and plan on staying late. When you find a bull, sometimes there's more than one in the

"Elk are where elk are, and they aren't anywhere else," John replied.

same area. With the rut over, these guys are interested in one thing—food and lots of it!

When it snows, the very first elk to move will be cows, calves, and the smaller bulls. Mature bulls will wait it out until the snow is a couple of feet deep. In the meantime, they often elect to spend their time feeding on south-facing slopes where the sun melts the snow quickly. Here, they can rebuild the fat layer that was lost during the rut period. I've even seen bulls laying right out in the open catching some midday sun.

Many of the traditional late season migratory trails are well known, especially by those who hunt places like the boundaries of Yellowstone National Park. Like fans waiting for a chance at tickets to a football game, hunters line up at a "firing line" and wait for the elk to come out of these protected areas. Most of the mature bulls have learned to avoid this gantlet of hunters by moving under the cover of darkness. By first light, these animals are well past the danger.

If you're lucky enough to draw a late-season elk license in one of these areas, try setting up away from the crowd. I like to find a ridge overlooking the intersection of several major migratory trails. If there's evidence of elk activity, then it is just a matter of waiting until a bull comes your way.

Hunting buddy, Zieb Stetler, used this approach on several occasions to score. Hunting near Grand Teton National Park, Zieb has a favorite narrow slot, between two drainages, that has produced more than one migratory bull. The area he hunts is several miles away from the local "firing line," and that doesn't seem to inhibit its big-bull potential. "I just set up before daylight, and then wait and see what shows up," Zieb told me recently. A few seasons ago, Zieb put his wife on a bull using this strategy. When you enter the Stetler home that same bull is displayed prominently in their front room.

Even though the area you hunt may not have a late season, watch the weather anyway. More than one unseasonable snow storm has put elk in motion. Even if the weather only moves some elk, it can still make things easier. If you only find spikes and raghorns with the herd, then you'll know to look for a big bull where snow-free forage still remains in the backcountry.

When hunting snow, my suggestion is to get high and use your binoculars. Dress warmly and be prepared to glass all day. After a major storm, all the usual rules won't apply. Elk can, and do, move throughout the day. Against the snow-draped background, they are easy to spot. Once you find the bull you want, then get into position for a shot.

Another late season possibility is following tracks. In snow, elk leave tracks that a blind man can follow.

Early or late, there are times that the only place to find a bull is in heavy timber. Photo Credit: Jim Matthews

However, just following any elk tracks is usually a waste of time. Well-shaded tracks can look extremely fresh, even though they are hours old. Tracks of mixed sizes are often made by groups of cows and calves. If the tracks have been made recently, they will manifest sharp, well-defined edges. Sometimes, small pieces of loose snow will be scattered out between tracks.

Don't get in the tracks and follow blindly. Tracking in snow can make a lot of noise. If you try to pursue a bull in a straight line, the sound of your approach can give you away. Likewise, air currents may not be favorable and can carry your scent well ahead of you. If the bull hears you, or winds you, the game is over. The best strategy is to loop ahead of the tracks and catch the bull unaware. Keep the tracks in sight, but climb well above them. Then as you move, use binoculars to scan ahead of your line of progress. If the tracks are fresh and made by a bull, you might stumble on him right in front of you. The rest of the time—luck is a player in the game.

Pump It Up: When it's warm, elk like to cool off. That's when they head for the nearest wallow. The location of every one of these mud holes in a particular area, no matter how well hidden, is common knowledge to an elk. Finding a wallow isn't all that easy, but when you do it's time to get busy.

Not all wallows are in use all the time. This being the case, I try to tip the odds in my favor. If a wallow shows recent use, I try to make it more attractive to a bull. Since a bull elk can detect a cow in estrus for a considerable distance, I try to give him what he wants. The discreet application of a little cow-in-heat scent can really turn just any old wallow into the best spot on the mountain. The odor of the concentrated mating scent is carried through the entire drainage and any interested bull will find the source of that scent.

Squirting cow-in-heat scent on the ground doesn't seem to work as well as applying it to a strip of cloth and suspending it from a tree branch. I keep several strips of pre-soaked scent cloth in a plastic bag. Using a length of monofilament line, the strips are attached to points along each wallow entry trail. Depending on the proximity of the wallow to elk in the area, you can expect some action within a day or two. It's a waiting game, so exercise patience. When the bull comes, he'll be right where you want him.

Scent trails can work almost anywhere. On one occasion, I watched a bull feed into a patch of open grass two evenings in a row. This opening was quite large and any attempt at predicting where the bull would come out of the timber was impossible. Since I was hunting with a bow, the need for a close shot was paramount. After watching his entry into the area twice, I had a general idea of the direction he would take. The next afternoon, I attached a scent strip to a tree branch at the edge of the grassy area and settled in to wait.

Right on time, the bull came out of the timber about 150 yards away. Then suddenly, he turned and disappeared right back into the cover. I couldn't figure out what happened until he reappeared nearly on top of me. I was so unhinged that my arrow flew right over his back. While the bull spooked at the noise, he didn't see or scent me. Even before I could get on my cow call, he was back again. Overwhelmed by the scent in the air, nothing could dissuade him from his love quest. This time, I didn't miss.

Shut Up: Most elk hunters have tried their hand at bugling elk. Bugling elk can be an effective hunting method at the right time (peak of the rut). The rest of the time, it's a waste of time. Any bull elk that's lived more than one hunting season has been fooled by a call once. If that bull has survived, he's gained a valuable education. Since every hunter in the woods has an elk bugle, any bull with good instincts knows that the elk he hears may not be the real thing. Too many hunters waste time bugling. Keep at it long enough, and you're sure to blow a sour note. All it takes is one mistake to let the bull know you're not the real thing. If the elk figures that out, he's gone.

Rather than attempting to call the bull to you, try an opposite course of action. When you hear an elk bugle, get on the move. Look at it this way—the bull is calling you, rather than the other way around. When you move, move fast—run if you have to. Do whatever it takes to get close while the bull is vocal. If

Elk wallows often need the addition of a little scent to "pump" them up. Photo Credit: Jim Matthews

he falls silent, then you won't be able to pinpoint his position. If his bugling falls off, try using a stick to rake a couple trees. Make a lot of noise. Get an attitude. Pound the ground like a bull stomping out his dominance. Sometimes this is all it takes to get the bull fired up again.

Look at it this way, what have you got to lose? If you bugle, the bull could gather his cows and take off for parts unknown (the usual response). If you're silent, you might just be able to get close enough for a shot. Based on my experience, you'll be surprised how easy it is to stalk right in on a bull by keeping quiet and listening.

Something Old, Something New: Sometimes you get lucky on the first day of a hunt. The rest of the time, it can be tough to find a bull. When things get tough, you need to get tougher. Break all of the rules and see what happens. That old gas pipe elk bugle your uncle used in the 1940s might just do the trick in the new millennium. You never know what will work. Rest assured, however, that nothing works all of the time. I like to mix up my hunting strategies. Traditional with a twist of unconventional is probably the description of my own special hunting cocktail.

Chapter 6

Let's Get Physical

If you're going to be an elk hunter, then it's time to shape up!

If you're like me, you've noticed that the mountains get a little steeper with each passing season. The 20 miles on horseback that used to be enjoyable now becomes an annual form of punishment. It's more difficult to slip out of that warm sleeping bag and get dressed in a cold tent. Your muscles ache after a long day's hunt and the words "Let's take it easy" have a whole new appeal.

It takes a stout heart and tough legs to pack out an elk one quarter at a time. Even the antlers and a fresh cape can weigh more than 50-pounds. Photo Credit: Bob Robb

As much as I like to hunt elk, there have been times when a hiatus has put me on the "injured-reserve" list. A torn ligament, spousal pregnancy, the birth of a child, work, school, all at one time or another have kept me at home. I remember one time when almost five years went by without an elk hunt on the horizon. When I finally hit elk camp again, I wasn't prepared for the long hours in the saddle. At first, my knees ached, my posterior was sore, and the inside of my thighs were chaffed to the point of tears. Even worse, my lungs and legs weren't in shape for all the hiking we had to do. Simply put, I was a mess.

Since that experience, I've tried to begin elk camp preparation at the beginning of the summer, not just a few days before elk season opens. Sure, it's not easy to find the time. I am as busy as the next person, but finding time for exercise isn't impossible. Playing with the dog, taking a walk with my wife, or even shooting hoops with my teenage son can make a difference.

It's a fact of modern living that most of us are carrying around more weight on our bodies than we need. If this wasn't true, then we wouldn't be so fixated on diet and weight-loss programs. However, diets can only do so much. Once you reach your weight loss goal, you'll eventually put the weight back on. So, if you want to keep weight off, you need to change both the way you eat and your overall lifestyle.

When it comes to exercise, about the only time most folks heart rate goes up is when they have to look for the television remote. Long ago I realized that there are more calories on the dinner table than opportunities to burn them. This prompted me to balance my food intake with my daily level of physical exertion. While I don't claim to be a diet and exercise guru, calorie management and exercise has been a continuing concern with me.

You don't have to join a health club to drop a couple of pounds, just institute some subtle changes in the way you handle your daily activities. Rather than using a vehicle for transportation, try walking. If your office has both an elevator and stairs, the choice is obvious. And

You don't shoot elk out of the front seat of a pickup truck. Preparation for the hunt takes a lot of hard work. Photo Credit: Rocky Mountain Elk Foundation

consider getting involved in some form of exercise that strengthens your legs and increases stamina. But before you take up jogging, aerobics, or some other form of exercise, check with your physician.

Walk: It's a fact that Americans don't walk anymore than we have to. We use moving walk-ways at the airport, escalators at the mall, elevators in our office building, and our automobiles as much as possible. I am as guilty as anyone else when it comes to not walking. A supermarket is located about two long city blocks away from my home. If my wife asks me to go to the store for something, I seldom walk. It seems that we are always in a hurry, so walking somewhere, anywhere, is out of the question.

One of the best exercises you can do is to walk. Now, I am not talking about strolling to the end of the block and back again. If you want to gain any benefits from walking, you're going to have to walk for extended distances. At a reasonable pace, most humans cover about 3 miles per hour on foot. If you're fairly sedentary, start out with 30 minutes of walking at least five days a week. After a couple of weeks, you can extend your walk to 45 minutes, and then a full hour. Walk at a brisk clip and put some uphill grades into your route when possible. Walking doesn't pound the feet, ankles, hips, and

knees like jogging, so even older folks can benefit from this type of exercise.

In my area, a narrow greenbelt runs from one housing development to another. There's a paved walkway, a winding grassy lane, and lots of trees. It's actually quite a peaceful setting right in the middle of the concrete, asphalt and steel so typical of most urban areas. My wife and I often enjoy a good walk down the greenbelt after dinner. It provides us with some serious quality time together and it can be quite romantic (love in the park?).

However, the benefits of this exercise go far beyond personal interaction. I've noticed that we seem to walk longer and longer distances. Our leg muscles have become more limber, and both of us seem to have developed enhanced stamina—just from walking.

Another suggestion is to become a mall walker. Sure, you'd rather watch the game on television. Who wouldn't? However, doing a little power walking through one of the mega-malls is definitely stimulating (okay guys, get your minds on a higher plain). First of all, you can always stop into one of the sporting goods stores and look over the selection of outdoor gear. Next on your mall agenda could be several trips up and down the stairs to subsequent levels (big malls usually have

The benefits of exercise—even if it's nothing more than a brisk walk on a regular basis—cannont be overemphasized. If shooting practice is helpful and packing the proper gear important, then physical conditioning is *vital*.

Backcountry elk hunting takes stamina, and lots of it! Every shooting opportunity will demand that you control your breathing and heart beat. Photo Credit: Bob Robb

more than one level of stores). Of course, you could even walk from one end of the parking lot to the other (what better way to look over the selection of new sport utility vehicles folks are driving these days). In short, malls are never boring.

Jog: In local neighborhoods, college campuses, even outside of hotels during conventions, the jogging phenomena is all too apparent. An excellent exercise to build lower leg muscle mass and lung capacity, jogging is the exercise of choice for millions. You don't have to be a long-distance runner to benefit. Start by jogging short distances and then work up to your own personal goal. Proper footwear, along with some initial leg muscle stretching, are necessary to prevent injury.

Like any exercise, jogging gets boring after a while. Try running up and down the bleachers at your local high school, or along a backwoods path to ward off boredom and enhance your workout. Another good suggestion is trade your jogging shoes for the boots you intend on wearing this coming fall. Then slip on a backpack with enough weight in it to simulate actual field conditions. You might even talk

one of your elk hunting buddies into joining you. In time, you will begin to realize that jogging can be stimulating, even enjoyable.

Hike: If you live in close proximity to the outdoors, spend some time hiking on a regular basis. In the late spring, summer, and early fall, days are long enough to get in a little hiking after work. In the winter, when it gets dark early, try to spend a hour or two hiking on the weekends. Even if the closest you can get to the outdoors is your local park, put on your hunting gear and take off. Pack a sandwich, something cool to drink, and make sure you take your binoculars along.

As soon as you get serious about hiking, the whole experience will begin to dramatically change. You'll see wildlife (even in the park) you've never even noticed before. Everything in your hiking environment becomes significant, even important to your newly honed visual and olfactory senses. You may find that watching birds takes on a new meaning. Reading animal tracks in the dust can cry out for understanding. Even the smell of wild flowers will begin to demand your attention. Hiking not only

Traversing elk country on horseback can be tough on your legs and knees. A little pre-hunt bicycling will help you get used to the saddle a lot quicker.
Photo Credit:
Durwood Hollis

builds muscles and endurance, it can also help you gain heightened knowledge of the outdoor world. And If you choose to hike near your hunting area, this can even provide an opportunity to scout for elk before the season opens.

Bicycling: Whether you're hunting on foot, or on horseback, in elk country your legs will take a beating. I've spend many nights dealing with legs cramps and muscle soreness after a hard day on the trail or in the saddle. Bicycling is the answer to a prospective elk hunter's physical conditioning needs. Jogging, even jogging stairs or bleachers, is boring. Likewise, even walking gets old after awhile. Riding a bike, even a stationary bike, never seems to get old.

In recent years, adults have begun to reacquaint themselves with the bicycle. Providing a physical workout that's superior to walking, bicycling takes much of the boredom and strain out of exercise. Of course, a protective helmet is recommended (I am sure you remember those bike crashes of your youth), and you should avoid riding during rush-hour traffic. Other than these simple safety suggestions, bikes are great fun and a fantastic workout for your legs and lungs.

If you're up to it, mountain biking will really put you in shape. You'll need a beefed up bike to handle all of the rocks, ruts, and other dirt trail obstacles. And I wouldn't even think about trail biking without the necessary protective equipment, so make sure you wear knee, elbow, and wrist guards. I have a friend who got so into mountain biking that he now hunts off his bike. Wheeled vehicular transport isn't legal in wilderness areas, but lots of elk live in areas well suited for the use of a bicycle. The last time I spoke with him, he had just returned from an elk hunt in Washington. Interestingly, the bike was his key to a 5x5 Roosevelt bull. Many of the roads in his hunting area were closed to vehicular traffic, so using the bike he was able to cover far greater distant than those hunting on foot. What a way to combine exercise and elk hunting!

Even stationary bicycle riding can work wonders. Rather than collapsing on the couch and watching the evening news, try climbing aboard a stationary bike while you watch television. When someone tells me they don't have time to work out, or that the weather prevents them from going outdoors, I am quick to suggest a stationary bike as an alternative to riding on city streets. Bicycling works all of the same muscle groups that horseback riding does, so you'll be better prepared for extended hours in the saddle, if you've spent some time aboard a bicycle.

Swimming: When it comes to a total body workout, there's nothing better than swimming. This exercise utilizes lungs, heart, and all of the major muscles groups. However, not everybody knows how to swim and access to water can be limited. You should seek out an indoor or outdoor aquatic environment where you can swim safely. Health clubs,

the YMCA/YWCA and college pools are other good places to swim. My wife even suggested that the warmer water in Hawaii would allow me to swim more often. Think of it, Hawaii as the preparation grounds for next year's elk hunt. I told you swimming was a good thing. Of course, like any type of exercise, the benefits from swimming come with time and commitment (does that mean a trip to Hawaii every year?).

Aerobics: Unless you live in elk country, you're going to find yourself short-of-breath in elk camp—at least for the first few days. Mountain altitude doesn't contain the same amount of oxygen as that found at sea level. The higher up you go, the thinner the air. Without adequate oxygen in your blood stream, your lungs will scream for more. This becomes readily apparent when your guide hasn't even begun to break a sweat, and you can't seem to get your breath. The worst case scenario is altitude sickness, which can land you in the hospital.

Aerobic is simply defined at "with oxygen." Aerobic training, or aerobic exercise focuses on conditioning your lungs and circulatory system. Pushing your heart rate up a few notches on a regular basis can do you a lot good. Aerobics combine calisthen-

Elk hunting isn't a casual sport. If you want to be successful, then get into shape before you hit camp. Photo Credit: Bob Robb

On an elk hunt, the day-after-day demands of the hunt can extract a toll on your body. Photo Credit: Bob Robb

ics, dance, and music in a workout that can stretch and tone your muscles as well as improve your breathing. Many companies, schools, churches, and gyms offer regular aerobic workout classes before and after working hours. If you're short on time, you might try tuning into a televised aerobic workout program and follow along in the privacy of your own home. Also, there are plenty of workout videos and classes available at your local spa or gym. Even if you only participate once a week, aerobics can make a huge difference in how well you manage the physical demands of elk hunting.

Weight Training: Most of your pre-hunt training should focus on building leg muscles, enhancing lung capacity, and building endurance. Even so, some work on the upper body using free weights isn't a bad idea. Hopefully, part of the hunt will involve lifting and carrying elk quarters. Even carrying a set of elk antlers can put a hurt on you after a few miles.

Try combining weight training with walking or jogging. Simply work out with a free weight in each hand. Start out flexing with light weights, 5 pounds or so, in each hand. As your strength builds, increase the weight. Mix in some push-ups, chin-ups, and

even a pass on the monkey bars in the local park. In time you can put together a real work out with minimal investment in equipment. This doesn't have to be an everyday thing (you'll burn out quickly at that rate), but a couple of times a week can work wonders.

Exercising can be boring, no doubt about it. Try jogging alone in the predawn and you'll be quick to agree. I haven't found any way to totally escape the boredom, but there are some things you can do to make it more bearable. Avoid repetitive exercise patterns. If you walk or jog, use several different routes and mix them up occasionally. When possible, exercise with a friend and include some hiking, bicycling, and swimming in your weekly program.

A few seasons back, I joined some other hunters for a week-long horseback elk hunt in Wyoming's Bridger-Teton Wilderness. In the group, there was one middle-age guy, somewhat overweight and out of condition. To be sure, he was an enthusiastic hunter with a bubbly personality and all the right gear. But about an hour into the six-hour horseback ride to base camp, I knew he wasn't going to have a good time. By the time we hit camp he could hardly stand up. Three days later he threw in the towel and returned to the

It takes upper body strength to draw a heavy bow. Pre-hunt training with free weights can help condition those muscles. Photo Credit: Bob Robb

trailhead with less than one full day of hunting under his belt. It was a sad ending to a hunt he'd planned on for several years.

The benefits of exercise—even if it's nothing more than a brisk walk on a regular basis— cannot be over-emphasized. If shooting practice is helpful and packing the proper gear important, then physical conditioning is vital.

Just plumb worn out! An elk hunt will do that to you. Photo Credit: Durwood Hollis

Chapter 7

Make The Grade

Don't let a breakdown foul-up your elk camp plans

Not far from my home, a major interstate highway runs north to the heart of the inner-mountain West. Millions of travelers, including countless hunters bound for elk camp, use this blacktop ribbon. Unfortunately for some, this roadway takes its toll in vehicular failure. And one stretch of it is particularly gruelling.

You see, over a distance of about 10 miles, the roadway rises some 3,500 feet in elevation. Worse yet, weather conditions over the top can range from excruciating daytime heat in September, to snow and ice in October and November. There's never been a time that I've traveled over that pass that there hasn't been at least one vehicle broken down along the highway.

Fellow hunter David Long knows all about the grade. For as long as he's lived in the area, that highway has always loomed larger than life as elk season approached. "I can't tell you how many times that

The worst trip to elk camp scenario—winch and shovel time! Photo Credit: Durwood Hollis

first 10 or 15 miles of the interstate has ruined opening day of elk season," David admits. "The first time I broke down it was probably a radiator hose, the next season the trailer popped loose from the hitch, and there've been more flat tires and broken shocks than I care to remember," he adds.

Now, David takes good care of his vehicles. But when you combine a fully-loaded camper, three or four hunting companions and all of their gear, and mix in a steep, winding grade, you have a prelude to disaster. Making the trip to elk camp becomes dependent on one question: Will your vehicle make the grade?

No matter where you hunt, vehicle failure can wreck your plans. While there are no absolute safeguards, there are preventative measures to increase your odds of making it to camp on time and within your budget.

Engine Tune-up: Currently-manufactured vehicles can run trouble-free for a long time. Tune-up intervals of 30,000, 40,000, and even 50,000 miles are not uncommon. The downside of low engine maintenance requirements is that it's easy to push the performance envelope a little too far. So, if it's been a while (more than six months or 20,000 miles) since your vehicle has been tuned, then have the work done prior to elk season. The tune-up should include the replacement of spark plugs, adjustment of points and timing, carburetor adjustments, fuel filter replacement, and an oil change, as well as the inspection, adjustment, and repair of any other systems related to engine performance.

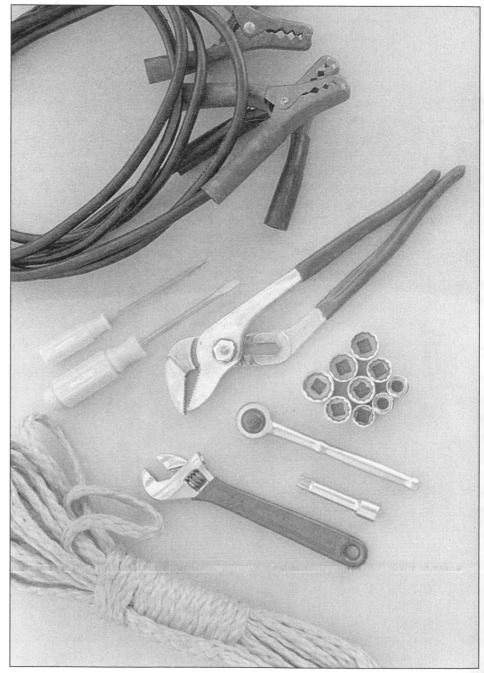

Essential vehicle travel extras include: jumper cables, pliers, screwdrivers, socket set, adjustable wrench, and most importantly—a tow rope. Photo Credit: Durwood Hollis

Belts and Hoses: Probably the single most common cause of breakdown is cooling system failure. A simple inspection, adjustment and replacement (if necessary) of all belts and hoses connected to the radiator, fan, air conditioner, brakes, or power steering system can prevent most problems. If any hose is cracked, replace it. If any belt is loose or worn, either make the necessary adjustments or get new ones.

Fluids: Check the fluid levels in your radiator, battery, power steering unit, and brakes. Add fluid where necessary and make sure that the fluid seal is adequate. Pay particular attention to your radiator. If the radiator fluid is discolored with rust, then it's time to have your cooling system flushed and the coolant/antifreeze replaced. It's a good idea to carry an extra gallon of coolant/antifreeze along with you on the trip.

Brakes and Tires: Rain, sleet, snow, and ice all place added demands on brakes and tires. Make it a priority to have your tires and brakes serviced, well in advance of departure. Worn tires or faulty brakes can result in an accident. If your tires exhibit significant signs of wear, do yourself a favor and replace them.

Other Measures: Put together a vehicle survival package that includes tire chains (make sure they're the right size), road flares or reflectors, a tow strap, a length of rope (at least 100 feet), a small tarp (so you can work under your vehicle without getting your clothes dirty), a flashlight, electrical tape, duct tape, hand cleaner, a roll of paper towels, a small shovel, and an assortment

> ## If it's been a while since your vehicle has been tuned, than have the work done prior to deer season.

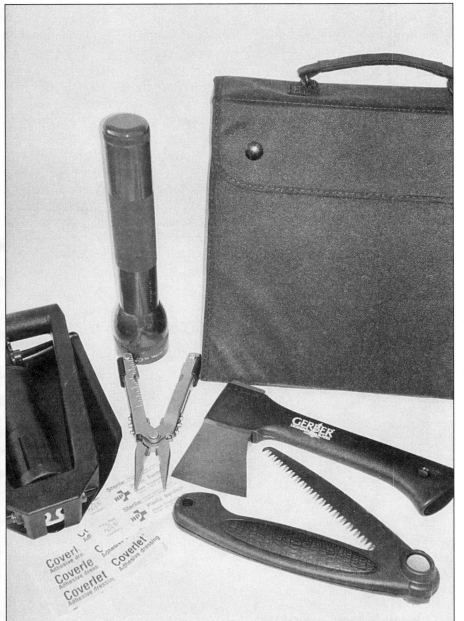

This Gerber SUV emergency tool assortment—shovel, axe, saw, multi-tool, flashlight, and first aid supplies—all in a convenient case, can be handy in an off-the-road emergency. Photo Credit: Durwood Hollis

of hand tools (adjustable wrench, reversible screwdriver, socket set with handle and an extension). If you have a problem on the road, there are times when even a professional mechanic and all of his tools can't fix the mess. However, the minimal tools and equipment I've outlined above have been an answer to my prayers for more than 40 years behind the wheel.

Off-Road Considerations: Don't even think about pulling onto a dirt road without carrying a shovel and an ax. Of course, a High-Lift jack and some type of pulley-hoist are other off-the-road essentials. Also, I've found that extra rope, a wide tree strap, radiator Stop-Leak, canned flat-tire foam, and a gallon of gas can be vital when you're deep in the backcountry without a service station in sight.

Recreational Vehicles: Those who use a trailer, tent trailer, or motor home should carefully check the electrical, braking, and other systems (cooking, heating, and water supply). Special care should be taken to make sure that the propane/butane flow to any cooking or heating appliance is turned off at the tank during transport. I'd hate to tell you the number of times I've seen a motor home or trailer along side of the road completely engulfed in flames. The primary cause of such infernos is usually a faulty propane/butane system and/or failure to terminate the flow of gas at the storage tank.

Don't Leave Home Without It: It takes more than guns, gear, and hunting strategy to pull off a trip to elk camp. Before you ever back out of your driveway, make sure that your vehicle is in shape for the trip. Even when you've thought of every conceivable contingency, something can go wrong. In that case, make sure you have enough pieces of green paper with pictures of dead presidents imprinted thereon—or plastic in your wallet—to handle the situation.

Chapter 8

Dress And Pack For The Occasion

Clothing, gear, and gear containment makes the elk hunter

It had been a tough day. Earlier in the afternoon, I'd taken one of the biggest bulls of my hunting career, but the celebration had been tempered by deteriorating weather conditions. Returning to camp through miles of blowdown and ankle-deep mud, my gnawing sense of fatigue had grown to a crescendo. My rain suit, water-repellent boots, and knit gloves had offered only initial protection against the downpour. Now, after four hours of nonstop rain, I was drenched to the skin.

In a normal squall, my lightweight nylon rain suit would have worked as well as anything. But in this deluge of Biblical proportions, the coated fabric failed miserably. Even though I'd changed my socks a couple of times, my feet were still wet. When it comes to the gloves—well, let's just say that knit gloves weren't the best choice! So, I cursed the manufacturers of the rain gear and boots, blamed myself for the poor choice in gloves, and continued on my journey. As tiring and uncomfortable as that experience was, it taught me a lesson that I'll never forget. Pack the right gear for the occasion.

Selecting the right clothing should be as important as sighting in your rifle. Start by inventorying what you already have on hand. As a rule, most week-long fall hunting trips require long underwear, two pairs of trousers, two shirts, a sweater or sweatshirt, a jacket or coat, gloves, hat, boots, and rain gear.

Layering: In the mountains, the ambient temperature can change from below freezing to uncomfortably hot in the space of a few hours. Add to this temperature roller-coaster dripping-wet fog, rain, sleet, hail, and snow and you'll quickly realize just how important it is to dress for the occasion. Wearing several tiers of clothing, rather than just a single insulated garment, allows the option for garment manipulation as the need arises. If you're like me, this can be an ongoing process.

You won't have the option of carrying an entire wardrobe with you in the field, but you can select

clothing that keeps your internal body temperature evenly regulated. You'll want to dress warmly when it's cold, yet have the option of cooling down when

Nothing beats wool on an elk hunt. This red/black Woolrich coat and pant set is the ultimate in cold weather outdoor wear. Photo Credit: Woolrich/Images Group

Take the bite out of cold weather with a pair of long underwear. Photo Credit: Durwood Hollis

things heat up. In the coldest weather, you can work up a sweat. Conversely, in moderate daytime temperatures, you can get cold.

Unless it's unusually hot (a rare occurrence in elk country), I generally wear long underwear, a medium-weight shirt and pants, sweater, insulated vest, jacket, gloves, and a hat (with ear flaps). The multi layering of outerwear provides the option of clothing removal as my body temperature demands. One thing you never want to do is to start sweating. At the first sign of body heat build up, I start removing garments. Likewise, if I begin to feel cold, it's time to put something back on.

A day pack comes in handy as a mobile closet of sorts. Instead of tying a jacket and sweater around my waist, I simply stuff them in the pack. And there they remain ready for use if conditions change. Of course, I never leave camp without some kind of wet weather protection in my day pack.

A review of what to wear, layer-by-layer, can assist in making the right selection of both inner and outerwear as you prepare for elk camp.

Underwear: While in elk camp, most hunters don't take the time to wash anything more than their hands (some don't even do that!). So, keeping clean can be difficult. Combine the dirt and grime of hunting camp with white undergarments, and in a couple of days even your best unmentionables will look a bit scary.

My suggestion is to select dark-colored undergarments (shorts, tee shirts, and long underwear), so that the fabric hue conceals much of the wear and tear of hunting camp.

Cotton long johns provide only marginal insulation, absorb and hold moisture, are slow to dry, and, when wet can chafe the skin. The only thing that can be said for cotton underwear is that it's inexpensive and machine-washable. A better choice is one of the new synthetic fabrics (polypropylene, Thermax, Coolmax, Caprilene, etc.) that dries quickly when wet and provides enhanced insulation. Silk long underwear is also a good choice with similar properties. Although you'll pay a premium for this kind of underwear, it's worth the expense in the long run. If you plan to be in camp any longer than a few days, pack an extra set in case you get wet.

Trousers: Like most hunters, I'm fond of jeans. Despite the fact that they're made out of cotton-denim—which soaks up moisture like a sponge—jeans are just damn comfortable. In days gone by, jeans were all the same. Now, you can select from a wide range of colors, patterns (look for "relaxed," or "loose" fit), and fabrics. For cold-weather wear, lined denim jeans are also available. Besides being comfortable, jeans are affordable, machine washable, and durable. These are features that have made them a time-honored tradition in hunting camps.

Warm, even when wet, woolen clothing (shirt and pants by Woolrich) is the best choice for cold weather wear.
Photo Credit: Durwood Hollis

I'll be the first to agree that jeans aren't always the best choice. This is especially true when it comes to cold-weather hunting. Here, fleece, or wool is the fabric of choice because it performs well in the cold. While wool absorbs moisture, unlike cotton, it provides warmth even when wet. However, wool can shrink. Buy your trousers with room to spare. The firms of Codet (Derby Rd., Newport, VT 05855, 800/992-6338), Filson (P. O. Box 34020, Seattle, WA 98124, 800/624-0201), Johnson Woolens (51 Lower Main East, P. O. Box 612, Johnson, VT 05656, 877/635-WOOL) and Woolrich (1 Mill St., Woolrich, PA 717/769-6464), all manufacture top-quality wool hunting pants. Wool clothing is expensive, but the fabric provides services like no other. I've worn a pair of Woolrich wool Malone cloth trousers for more than 30 years and they are still in great shape. The initial cost of a new pair of wool trousers can be staggering. If you're on a budget, shop for bargains in used wool trousers at your local surplus store. Don't forget, most wool clothing must be dry-cleaned, not machine-washed. However, the folks at Woolrich Woolens now offer a line of Nippenose Washable Wool clothing that deserves a closer look. A durable blend of 85 percent wool/15 percent nylon, this wool fabric is specially designed to be machine washable and line dried.

Fleece is lighter and less costly than wool. This material offers body heat retention similar to wool, but it must have an inner laminate to be waterproof or wind-resistant. While fleece can get wet, it dries quickly. Available in several different camo patterns, and absolutely quiet in heavy cover, fleece outerwear is often the choice of bowhunters.

Cotton long johns provide only marginal insulation, absorb and hold moisture, are slow to dry and, when wet, can chafe the skin.

Belts and Suspenders: On most hunting trips, I generally lose a little weight. Sometimes it's a lot of weight. So much so, I have a hard time keeping my pants up. Furthermore, I generally carry extra cartridges, a canteen, a knife, and a flashlight all on my belt. The combined weight of this gear, even with my belt at the last hole, seems to assist in the relentless southward movement of my trousers. Faced with the prospect of being arrested for indecent exposure, I

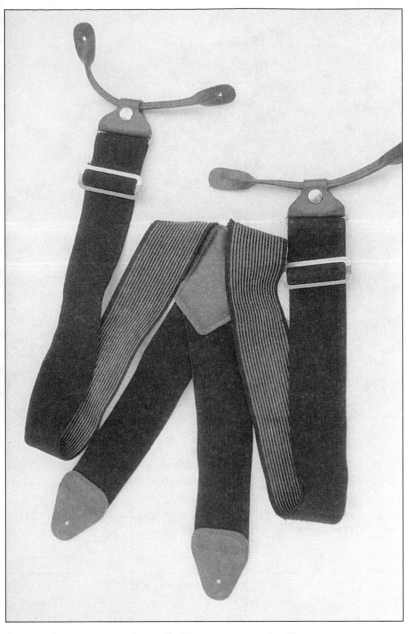

Suspenders are more than a fashion statement in elk camp.
Photo Credit: Durwood Hollis

thing when you bend over. Since shirts take the brunt of wear, you'll want to pack at least two so there's always a clean spare available. Personally, I lean toward heavyweight cotton-flannel or lightweight wool.

Sweater, Sweatshirt, or Vest: A sweater, sweatshirt, or insulated vest provides added warmth without extra bulk. As the hunting day progresses, you can peel off this extra layer when the temperature dictates. A vest is probably a little more versatile (you can open it up without taking it completely off) than a sweater or sweatshirt, but I am hard pressed to advocate one over the other. A single article of clothing in this category should be sufficient to meet your needs.

Jacket or Coat: Whether I wear a jacket or a heavy coat afield depends on the expected daytime temperature, my level of physical exertion, and method of hunting. If still hunting is the primary game plan, then I'll opt for a jacket. On the other hand, if I'm on horseback or expect to be stationary for an extended period of time, then the heavy coat gets the nod. Since it is quiet in heavy cover, warm when wet, and tough as nails, wool is always a great choice in the outdoors. The only drawback to a wool jacket or coat is that if it gets soaked, it takes a long time to dry. Other fabrics, including synthetic blends, fleece, and saddle cloth, may offer distinct advantages over wool. I particularly like designs that feature a zippered liner which allows the wearer to adapt the coat/liner combination to a wide range of temperatures.

Gloves: If you're traversing rocky terrain, hauling game, or making a stalk on your hands and knees, a pair of gloves offers invaluable protection. And in adverse temperatures, gloves protect your hands from the cold. Knit gloves work well in dry weather and as glove liners. Heavy fleece, leather, or insulated fabric gloves (both with and without liners) are the best choice for cold weather. But when it comes to wet weather wear, there's no substitute for neoprene. In extreme temperatures, mittens keep your fingers together and provide better body heat retention than gloves. Pack at least two pairs of gloves, so even if one pair gets wet or lost, you'll have a backup.

Headgear: A wide variety of caps—with or without ear flaps, some with insulation, some without — are common in elk camps. Hot-weather hunting caps usually feature a breathable mesh crown and an absorbent inner sweat band. Cold weather caps offer an insulated

decided to acquire a set of suspenders. What a difference they made. Even if you're not used to wearing them, in elk camp suspenders are the height of fashion and functionality.

Shirts: All kinds of shirt fabrics—cotton, flannel, chamois, fleece, and wool—are available to the elk hunter. You might consider packing both lightweight and heavyweight shirts to cover a wide range of temperatures. When you select a hunting shirt, avoid the tailored look. You'll need lots of room under your shirt for long underwear. Make sure the shirttail is long enough to stay tucked into your pants. Breast pockets should have button-flap closures so you won't loose any-

Whatever you do, expect the worst and hope it never comes to pass.

Worn on top of long underwear and a shirt, this Woolrich Polartec fleece pull-over and wool vest add warmth to the body core. Photo Credit: Durwood Hollis

crown, tuck-away ear flaps and, possibly, a laminated moisture barrier. Easier to wear, and pack (when you travel) than a full brim hat, the cap is often my choice.

Knit caps are the ultimate in cold weather wear and can be rolled down to cover your ears. While you might offend the traditional sensibilities of hunters in the West, in really bitter weather, you'll see knit caps on more than one hardcore cowboy. Best of all, you can carry a knit cap in your pocket and pull it out if the weather turns bad.

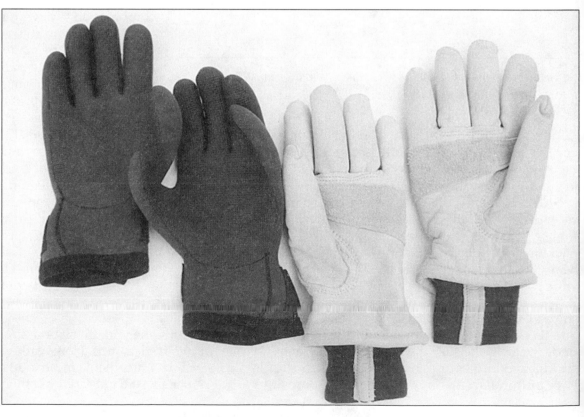

Either neoprene gloves with silk liners (left), or insulated leather gloves (right), can protect your hands from the rigors of the hunt. Photo Credit: Durwood Hollis

The traditional wide brim western hat will keep the sun out of your eyes and serves as an excellent rain buffer and windbreak. Off your head, the domed crown can even serve as a makeshift rifle rest. Western-style hats are made of straw (real cowboys don't wear straw), or wool felt. If you like this type of headgear, make sure you purchase your hat slightly larger than normal. This way, when the wind kicks up, you can pull the brim down low on your head and weather the worst blow. Also, make sure you obtain a slip-on blaze orange cover. The cover allows compliance with local hunting regulations without interfering with the fit of the hat. Available in a wide range of sizes, brim widths, crown heights, and colors, this style of headgear has a lot going for it.

For most purposes, a pair of quality leather boots will provide excellent service. In warm weather, anke-high leather/fabric/ synthetic composite boots are light and offer enhanced comfort.

Socks: Once a cotton sock loses its cushioning ability, any seam, fold, or a ridge can wreak havoc on your foot. Some of the recently developed cotton/synthetic blends, or other similar sock materials will provide superior cushioning and wick moisture away from your foot where it can evaporate. Like any piece of quality gear, good socks are expensive. Don't try to pinch pennies when it comes to socks, buy the best you can afford. Pack one pair for every day you expect to be in camp, and carry an extra pair afield for a change when necessary.

Boots: Last season, there were several guys in elk camp from the Northeast. To a man, all of them wore rubber-bottom pacs with leather uppers. After the first rainstorm and subsequent snowfall, my leather boots were soaked through. However, I noticed that all of the New Englanders had dry feet. Now, I pack two pairs of boots. One pair of leather boots intended for general use, and a pair of pacs for wet weather wear. Even an old dog can learn new tricks.

If you hunt rough terrain, you'll bless the day you opted for lug soles. However, in wet weather or snow, lug soles will load up with muck and you can say goodbye to traction. If you expect to encounter wet weather, consider one of the alternative tread patterns

When it comes to keeping dry and warm on the trail or in the saddle, elk hunters will appreciate pac-boots with replaceable felt liners, like this pair from Sorel.
Photo Credit: Durwood Hollis

Cold feet will put you out of the game faster than anything else. Pack two pair of socks for every day you're in camp. Photo Credit: Durwood Hollis

(air bobs, ripple soles, etc.) that are self-cleaning.

Another consideration when it comes to boots and horseback riding is the fact that lug-soled boots don't slide into and out of saddle stirrups easily. If you have to dismount quickly, you might find yourself in a world of hurt. So, if horse travel figures into your hunting plans, either have the regular stirrups replaced with oversize versions, or purchase boots with a less-aggressive sole pattern.

There are so many boot choices that the subject is worthy of an entire chapter all by itself. For most purposes, a pair of quality leather boots will provide excellent service. In warm weather, ankle-high leather/fabric/synthetic composite boots are light and offer enhanced comfort. At the other temperature extreme, there are times when uninsulated or insulated pacs are the best choice. Expect to pay at least twice as much for boots as you'd pay for dress shoes. You can never pay too much for boots. You can pay too little and that will cost you much more.

Rain Gear: There's nothing more miserable than being wet and cold. If you don't believe me, then ask those tenacious hunters who stalk the damp forests of the Pacific Northwest (or anyone who's hunted Alaska). The key to dealing with wet weather is to have the right clothing.

Some wet-weather fabrics are advertised as water-resistant, water-repellent, or waterproof. Don't accept any of these claims at face value. Put on your rain gear at home and have someone douse you with the hose. After a few minutes of soaking, you'll know whether or not it works as advertised.

If you hunt on foot, then some type of lightweight poncho, or two-piece rain suit can usually handle your wet-weather needs. Coated nylon is the lightest waterproof material, but it doesn't breathe and you'll get clammy after you wear it for a while. Waxed cotton works well, but it's heavy to walk around in and noisy in the brush. Moisture-barrier laminate materials (Gore-Tex) offer outstanding protection while allowing your skin surface to breathe. However, there's probably no single best choice in rain gear for every situation. Personally, I use a lightweight rain suit for still hunting (fleece with a moisture-barrier laminate), and a full-length waxed cotton Australian storm coat on horseback. Both kinds of rain gear are designed for particular conditions and I

Personally, I've never been on an elk hunt when it didn't rain.

would suggest you consider both. Like I said, there's nothing more miserable than being wet and cold.

Sleeping Bags: In elk camp it can get cold at night—really cold! Selecting the right sleeping bag should be one of your primary considerations. A down-insulated bag offers the best relationship of weight to warmth. However, moisture is a nemesis to down. If it gets wet, down loses its heat-retention properties. Personally, I've never been on an elk hunt when it didn't rain. And sometimes it rained a lot! Even with the best of care, your sleeping bag gets dripped on, splashed on, or downright soaked. Unlike down, synthetic sleeping bag insulation (Qualofill, Holofill, etc. won't retain moisture. Even if a synthetically-insulated bag gets wet, it dries quickly. Best of all, such bags weigh little more than their down counterparts. For my money, a synthetically-insulated sleeping bag is the right choice for elk hunters.

Other Considerations: Hunting trips generate lots of dirty clothes. Pack a mesh laundry bag for soiled garments rather than tossing them on the floor of your tent or on top of clean clothing. To prevent mildew, make sure all wet articles are thoroughly dry before packing them away.

> ## My best advice, plan for the worst case scenario—take an extra box of shells.

A small bag or kit to hold toiletries (toothbrush, toothpaste, hair brush, a comb, soap, shampoo, medicines, insect repellent, etc.) will help keep all of these related articles together. If you don't have a toiletry kit, you can use quart-size Zip-Loc bags. The clear plastic allows you to see the contents, and protects the rest of your gear from an accidental spill. Don't forget, your hands can really suffer under the ravages of cold, dry weather. A small tube of hand cream (unscented) or skin softener will keep your skin from cracking and should be a part of your essentials kit.

Don't forget to pack some first-aid supplies. Include several different sizes of adhesive bandages (fingertip, knuckle, strips, and extra large sizes), a pair of tweezers, folding scissors, one-time use foil packets of antibiotic ointment and burn cream, a patch of self-adhesive mole skin for blister prevention, and lip balm.

For personal hygiene and cleaning up, pack some unscented baby wipes to give yourself a once-over on a daily basis. I found that a few paper towels folded up and placed in a sealed plastic bag can come in handy for lots of cleaning purposes. And don't forget to pack some regular toilet paper.

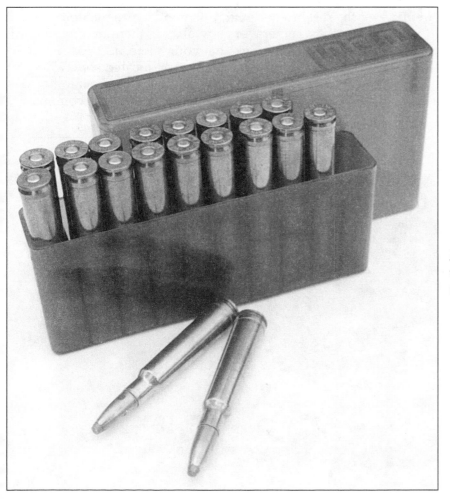

Factory cartridge boxes don't hold up very well. A molded alternative offers better protection. Photo Credit: Durwood Hollis

Other items that you might want to include in your gear are a portable gun cleaning kit (it's impossible to clear mud or snow out of your rifle barrel without it), a small screwdriver/allen wrench set to fit your firearm (including the scope and mounts), some type of lubricant, oil-impregnated gun wipes, and an optical lens cleaning kit for your binoculars, scope and camera lenses. And don't forget to include a small flashlight, supplemental batteries, and an extra bulb in your gear.

When it comes to camera, forgo packing your single-lens-reflex (SLR) model, and purchase a pocket-size "point-and-shoot" camera. These handy cameras are generally small enough to slip into a shirt pocket, easy-to-use, reliable in adverse weather, and affordable. Since some of your activities may take place under less than optimal light conditions, make sure whatever you select has a flash option. While you're at it, slip several rolls of color print film into your gear. Film is cheap, elk hunts are expensive, so shoot a lot of film. This way you can enjoy your adventure for years to come.

Finally, pack two full boxes of shells. Remove the shells from their original boxes, repack them in plastic shell containers, and tape them closed. Under normal conditions it may take you years to work through the first box. However, if you knock your scope out of alignment, or a screw comes loose (it does happen), you can use up an entire box re-sighting your rifle. It can be a long ride back to civilization. Even when you get there, the local gun store may not carry shells for your particular rifle. And if you find the right caliber,

Separate your gear into distinct groupings—personal clothing and hunting gear.

the bullet weights available may not be what you've sighted-in with. My best advice, plan for the worst-case scenario — take an extra box of shells.

Gear Containment: I've packed my gear in everything from hard luggage to a government-issue duffle bag. Hard luggage might be nice in an automobile or on an airplane, but it doesn't pack too well in a boat or on a horse. From my years in the military, I can tell you that a duffle bag can hold a lot of gear. But when you're trying to find something, what you're looking for always seems to be at the bottom of the bag.

Heavy denier Cordura nylon, Ballistic cloth, and canvas are all solid choices in duffle bag fabrics. Look for waterproof bottoms, close stitching, heavy-duty zippers, and reinforcements at points of strain. Two medium-size duffle bags are better than one large one, and lots of zippered outside pockets allow better access to smaller items.

How to Pack: Separate your gear into distinct groupings—personal clothing (underwear, trousers, shirts, socks, boots, and toiletries), and hunting gear (jacket, coat, a hat, gloves, extra shells, a backpack, saddle bags, binoculars, field dressing gear, etc.). Then pack each gear group into its own separate duffel. If you pack in this manner, you'll be able to find individual items without making a mess out of all of the rest of your gear. Cushion any fragile items (binoculars, camera, etc.) by placing them in the center of the bag. Make sure that your name, address, and a daytime telephone number are located somewhere inside and outside of both bags (a plastic laminated business card works great). Finally, a tiny combina-

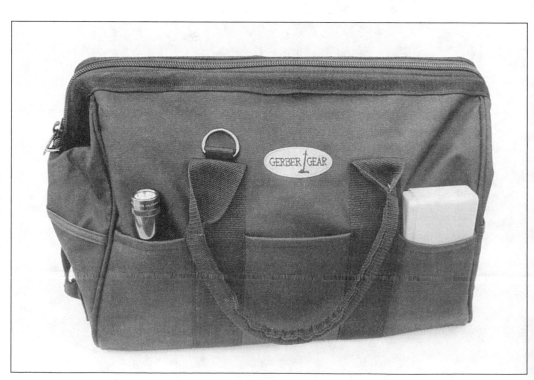

A couple of heavy-duty gear bags will allow you to separate your clothing from necessary hunting equipment.
Photo Credit: Durwood Hollis

tion padlock (lock combinations are easily remembered, keys can accidentally be left at home), or other type of security fastener (plastic electric wire ties) will help keep luggage handlers honest.

The Last Word: Several years ago, one of my hunting buddies obtained a coveted out-of-state big game license in a highly competitive drawing. Not wanting to lose the license, he gave it to his wife for safekeeping. When it came time for him to leave, he asked his spouse for the license. So much time had passed, his significant other couldn't remember where she put it. Well, he rectified the situation with a couple of last minute long-distance calls to the game department and an additional payment for a replacement license. However, it could have turned out differently. There are game officials who would have simply said, "Too bad!"

Hunting licenses, airline tickets, passports, etc., should be kept secure and close at hand. I usually lock such documents in my gun safe. During trip preparations, these papers are removed and packed directly into my gear or on my person. I put my license and tags into a plastic holder (the kind many hunters attach to the back of a jacket or vest), and then use the safety pin to attach the whole mess to the inside of my gun or bow case. While I could overlook my license when packing for elk camp, I am unlikely to forget my rifle or bow. Before I pull out of the driveway, or step onto an airplane, I double check to make sure that my hunting license(s) and any other significant documents are in my possession.

I haven't ever forgotten my hunting license, but I have left my gloves at home—and more than once. I don't know what it is about gloves and me. You'd think after dozens of elk hunts I'd get the message. I have resorted to writing myself a hunting gear packing list. The list is checked twice (sometimes three times) before I leave home. However, I still occasionally fail to pack something important.

Even with the best planning, it's possible to overlook something, take the wrong gear, or even lose a bag en route to camp. On one flight to an out-of-state hunting camp, my rifle was stolen during baggage handling. Fortunately, a credit card provided a hasty replacement. It took a little time to adjust the trigger, mount a scope, and sight-in, but I had planned an extra day at the beginning of my trip for just such an eventuality.

Finally, if you drive to elk camp, an extra set of vehicle ignition keys can come in handy. Give the extra set to your hunting buddy and hope you never have to use them. Keys have a way of getting lost in the field. I would hate to tell you the number of times my keys have fallen out a pocket. One time they even landed in the body cavity of an elk during field dressing!

Every hunting trip is an education and you'll learn from your mistakes. While my suggestions are based on years of experience, there are no hard and fast rules when it comes to packing for elk camp. But, whatever you do, expect the worst and hope it never comes to pass.

Chapter 9

In The Saddle

The do's and don'ts of backcountry equine transport

If you're a serious elk hunter, then at some point a horseback hunt may figure into your plans. However, just because you grew up watching Western movies doesn't mean that you're automatically an accomplished horseman.

Many years ago, I became involved in a ranch partnership that offered instant ownership of four horses. As the years went by, my understanding of horses and riding experience increased. While I am certainly not an expert, I've learned a thing or two that might just make your horseback hunting experience a little easier.

Leave It To the Professionals: My advice to any first-time horse rider—or even someone who rides occasionally—is to leave all of the stock wrangling to the professionals. Each horse or mule has its own individual personality. Just like you understand the personalities of your children or friends, outfitters and guides know and understand their own horses. You wouldn't like someone else handling your kids, so don't try to manage someone else's horses. Even if you're an accomplished horseman, ask first before you do anything with the pack or saddle stock. Most guides welcome some assistance, but your safety always comes first.

It all begins at the trailhead, where your gear will be packed for the trail. Then it's time to "saddle up" and head for elk camp.
Photo Credit: Bob Robb

With his stirrups adjusted properly, this hunter is sitting comfortably in the saddle. Photo Credit: Durwood Hollis

Riding Hints: Most likely, the guide will try to pick a saddle and horse combination that fits your frame and suits your riding abilities. The saddle should be comfortable; if it seems to rub you the wrong way, ask for an adjustment or change. Make sure that the stirrups fit. You should be able to stand in them and have about 4 inches of clearance between the saddle and your backside.

To mount, approach the horse on its left side. Take hold of the reins and drape them over the animal's head so that one rein is on each side of the neck. Do not release the reins from your grasp. Stand next to the left stirrup, facing the rear of the horse. Grasp the saddle horn with your left hand. Use your right hand to twist the left stirrup around 180 degrees so that you can place the toe of your left boot into it (when you

Safety First: If you hunt on horseback very much, you'll eventually see everything—including hare-brained stunts and outright stupidity. Nothing is more stupid than placing a loaded rifle in a saddle scabbard. You'd be surprised at just how many times hunters forget to remove the live shell from the chamber of their rifle. A fully-loaded magazine doesn't present a safety problem, but a live shell in the chamber does. Placed in a saddle scabbard, the rifle safety can accidentally move to an "off" position. A good jar (the horse jumping over a downed piece of timber) can trip the hammer, causing the rifle to fire. If this should happen, serious injury (read that as a gun-shot wound) to you, the horse, or both, can result. Even if nothing serious occurs, your guide will most likely inflict considerable verbal pain to your ears. While completely unloading a muzzle loader isn't necessary, you must remove the cap and release the hammer. Even with the projectile and the powder charge in place, without the priming cap and with the hammer covering the nipple, there is no possibility of ignition. Make it a habit to check your rifle each and every time it is returned to the scabbard. Likewise, if you're a bowhunter, make sure all of the arrows in your bow quiver are secured. Whatever you do, think safety: first, last, and always!

begin to mount, should the horse move forward, you'll automatically swing around into the saddle). Step up into the stirrup, swing your right leg across the top of the saddle and engage the right stirrup with the toe of your right boot. If things go right, you'll find yourself in the saddle. When things go wrong—just hold on!

Under no circumstances should a right-side mount be attempted without first checking with the guide. If you try to mount from that side, you'll probably be in for a learning experience. If you find yourself on the low side of the trail, just turn the horse around so that its left-hand side is facing uphill—or the high side of the trail—then mount as you would normally. Once in the saddle, you can turn the horse around.

When you ride, sit up straight and loosely hold the reins in your left hand. Those new to the saddle will probably find comfort in holding on to the saddle horn for stability, but more accomplished riders will

Each horse or mule has its own individual personality. Just like you understand the personalities of your children or friends, outfitters and guides know and understand their own horses.

use their legs to grip the horse. If you want the animal to turn left or right, simply lay the reins on the opposite side of its neck (left side if you want to make a right turn—right side if you want to make a left turn), to produce a response. If you want to go forward, then let the reins fall slack in your hand and verbally encourage (click your tongue) the animal. If the horse is slow to respond, give it a gentle nudge in the ribs. To stop forward movement, pull back gently on the reins. Finally, when you're riding uphill, lean forward in the saddle, downhill, lean back.

Long hours in the saddle will give you a new appreciation for the term saddle sore. Since the discomfort will be most noticeable in the seat of your pants, your knees, and inner thighs, I've found that wearing long underwear under your trousers provides some cushioning. Likewise, a pair of pantyhose (just don't let your hunting buddies see you putting them on in the morning) will also ease the pain of

Leave horse and pack stock problems to the guide, he's the expert. Photo Credit: Bob Robb

long-distance riding. The slick surface of the panty-hose will prevent your trousers from rubbing you the wrong way, in all the right places. For those who experience knee pain, try lengthening the stirrups a bit or wear elastic knee supports. If the miles in the saddle really get to you, there's no shame in slipping a small piece of foam padding under your bottom. Let's face facts. When it comes to horseback riding, most of us are, in the vernacular of the West— "dudes." Don't be surprised if it takes several days of riding for you to get used to the saddle. After that, there shouldn't be a problem.

Most horseback travel will be at a gentle walk. If you lag behind, then you may want to move the pace up to a trot. To initiate a trot, lean forward in the saddle and nudge the horse with your heels. Don't worry. The animal knows what to do. When you trot, stand in the stirrups to prevent the saddle from hammering your rear end. Once you catch up, resume your original pace. Running the horse isn't necessary. Unless there's a grizzly bearing down on you, keep things at a slow pace.

Close Contact: When you move around a horse, make sure the animal knows what to expect. This is especially true when you move from one side of the horse to the other. When you walk around the rear of the animal, lightly lay the palm of your hand on its hindquarters to maintain direct physical contact. This way, the horse is aware of your movements and less likely to kick out. If you don't feel comfortable that close to the rear end of the animal, then step completely away and walk around to the opposite side.

Likewise, if you cross under the horse's neck, keep the flat of your hand on the animal at all times. The physical contact not only reassures the horse, but it also maintains a measure of control. Whatever you do, don't shout or wave your arms around in an excited manner. This will only serve to scare the animal and can result in a dangerous situation. If there's a need for strong discipline, leave those actions up to your guide. Remember, you're the client, not the wrangler.

Stay Alert: Horseback riding is great therapy. After a mile or so in the saddle, you'll settle into the rhythm

> **If the miles in the saddle really get to you, there's no shame in slipping a small piece of foam padding under your bottom. Let's face facts. When it comes to horseback riding, in the vernacular of the West— most of us are "dudes."**

of the trail. However, the horse's ability to remove you from the saddle in an instant must never be underestimated. The moment you become complacent, the balance of control can shift to the animal's favor. Without immediate restraint, an unfavorable outcome can result. Most of the time there is no soft spot on which to land if you suddenly find yourself out of the saddle.

While returning from elk camp deep in Montana's Bob Marshall Wilderness, my inattention resulted in an unplanned departure from the saddle. About 5 or 6 miles into the trip, the pack string following me started to act up. It wasn't anything serious, just one mule harassing the other. I didn't give it much thought, but my horse didn't take to the mess behind him. Without warning, he bolted up the trail. Unfortunately, my left foot slipped out of the stirrup. In an attempt to regain my balance, my other foot also came free. In an instant, the horse and I parted company. Landing upside-down in the middle of the muddy trail was a painful and rude awakening. While my ego was bruised, it wasn't damaged nearly as badly as my severely dislocated shoulder. Eight hours later, six of those on horseback (read that as unrelenting agony), an emergency room physician finally put me back together again. Even now, the dull ache in my right shoulder is a somber reminder of the episode.

Horses and humans are a companionship of elk hunting necessity in the backcountry. It is an association that I am never quite sure is well appreciated by either horse or rider. Just when you think you have things under control—you find out that you don't! Take it from me, never let the trail or your riding experience lull you into a false sense of confidence. If you do—some horse, at a point in time—will probably remind you of your failure!

The Daily Drill: In elk camp, by the time you roll out of the sleeping bag, attend to morning personal hygiene matters and eat breakfast, your guide will usually have a horse saddled and ready for you. Your only responsibility is to stuff a sack lunch into the saddle-bags, secure your rifle in the scabbard, and step into the stirrups. However, the emphasis here is on the word "usually," because sometimes things go awry.

The End of the Trail: When it comes to hunting with horses, it's all about attitude and patience. You have to take things as they come. A horse can bite, kick, buck, and even roll over on you, but in the mountains, equine transport is often the only way to get where you want to go. So, despite all of their inherent negative qualities, horses are often necessary—even tolerable at times.

Horses and pack mules may not be a pickup truck and a string of cargo trailers, but in the backcountry it's the next best thing.
Photo Credit: Durwood Hollis

Even hobbled, horses can wander off during the night. If I were faced with the daily prospect of carrying some overweight dude all over creation, I would go missing during the night as a standard operating procedure! While saddle animals are often referred to as "dumb," there are times when a modicum of rationality manifests itself in their actions. So don't blame the outfitter or your guide for this rather common event. After all, horses are still just horses.

Should your trusty steed decide to leave for parts unknown, the camp wrangler or your guide must locate, catch, and return the animal (usually there are several equine escapees) to the camp corral. All of this takes time and can delay your morning departure. If it happens, don't get steamed up. Find your way back to the cook tent and have another cup of coffee. Remember, things could be worse—but we won't go there!

During the day, the horse is your basic vehicle of transportation. You can expect to ride from one location to another, tie up, and then glass for elk. You may even hunt through an area, returning to the horses an hour or so later. Always follow the guide's lead—ride when he rides, and when he dismounts, you follow suit. The guide knows his horses, so don't question his judgment in this arena.

At the end of the day, the responsibility for care and feeding of the saddle stock falls to the outfitter or guide. If you're competent in such matters, some assistance unsaddling the animals, brushing them down, and putting out feed is always appreciated. However, if you do nothing more than collect your gear, and disappear into a waiting tent, no one will think ill of you.

Tie Up: When you head off to hunt on foot, make sure you tie your horse securely. There's nothing quite so embarrassing as returning to find the animal gone! If you're in doubt about how or where to tie up, follow your guide's lead. When I was new to the horseback hunting scene, I used a simple overhand knot to secure my animal to a convenient tree. There wasn't any problem until the horse got bored and started pulling the loose end of the rope. It was only a matter of minutes before my trusty knot came untied.

While the horse didn't wander off, the guide gave me a dirty look when we returned to the horses. Don't depend on the security of your tie knot, ask the guide to check it for you.

When you tie-up, make sure that articles of clothing and other items are kept well away from the animal. Even if you only dismount for a short break, don't leave your hat, jacket, or rifle where the horse can get at it. Horses are curious animals and they may decide to see if what you've left nearby is something to eat, or play with. If you don't think this is a serious matter, then you haven't seen what horse teeth can do when you're not watching. Personally, I like my hat in one piece!

Lead Out: A saddle horse wears both a bridle and a halter—one on top of the other. The reins are attached to the bridle and serve as a two-piece equine steering wheel. The lead rope, however, is attached to the halter. This rope is much longer than the reins and is used to tie-up and lead-out. A horse can be lead by the reins. However, the reins are rather short and it's easy for the animal to accidentally step on you. When leading a horse over uneven ground, the longer lead rope gives you greater latitude of movement. If you don't think this is important, then you haven't had a horse hoof placed squarely on top of your foot, or had a 1,000-pound animal roll over on top of you. Believe me, it's not fun! You'll find the lead rope secured around the saddle horn, or attached to the front of the saddle. When it comes time to walk your horse through tough terrain, eschew the reins and use the lead rope.

To avoid getting stepped on, use the lead rope to guide a horse or pack animal over rough terrain. Photo Credit: Hubert Hollis

When you lead your horse, try to avoid walking directly in front of the animal. Also, put as much distance between the horse and yourself as possible. This allows the animal to negotiate difficult ground without running over you. When leading your horse, always keep an eye on the animal in case it starts to loose its footing. If something happens, then you'll be able to get out of the way quickly. Getting into a wrestling match with a horse isn't my idea of a good time!

Working With Pack Stock: If you get an elk, then pack animals will come into play. While some outfitters use pack horses, most depend on mules to haul out harvested game. Mules can carry significantly larger pack loads than a horse—even a pack horse. Furthermore, mules are more "sure-footed" than a horse when carrying a heavy load. This ability allows these animals to negotiate terrain that would intimidate most horses. In tough country you can usually (there's that word again) depend on a couple of mules to pack elk quarters, the headskin cape, and antlers back to camp without having a problem.

Getting your elk back to camp or to the trail head may take place the same day you make the kill, the following day, or over a period of several days. The weather, time of the kill, and distance to camp can all play a role in this decision. When you return to the kill site with pack animals, the carcass will be split into four quarters (usually with the hide left on for meat protection). Then the quarters are divided equally between the mules and placed in panniers. Finally, the panniers will be attached to the pack saddle and the cape and antlers tied on top. My advice during this procedure is to stand back and let the outfitter or guide deal with this chore. If your help is needed, you'll be asked. However, don't be overly helpful. Just do what you're asked, and do it when you're asked to do it.

Animals, like humans, have bad days. When they go off, it usually only results in some gear getting strewn about. However, these outbursts can spread to other saddle and pack animals. Should a horse or a mule have a problem on the trail, quickly move away from the animal. A hoof strike can break bones and have the potential for fatal implications. Should things fall apart on the trail, try to avoid being part of the problem. Since the guide is the equine expert, leave the resolution of such problems up to him.

How well I recall Wyoming elk guide, Bob Smiley, getting kicked full in the chest by a mule. We had just finished loading some elk quarters. I was check-

Wyoming elk guide, John Winter (foreground) is getting some client assistance tying off the load. Photo Credit: Durwood Hollis

ing to see if we had left anything behind, when suddenly, the sound of a distinct thud came to my ears. Turning around, I watched as one Wyoming elk guide flew through the air. When he hit the ground, the large hoof imprint on the front of his coat told the story. Apparently, Bob was pulling a rope tight and had his foot on the rear of the mule to gain leverage (not a good plan). It was at that point that the mule decided to teach him a lesson. Bob escaped with only bruises, but things could have been worse. Getting kicked, bitten, or stomped by a mule (or a horse) is no laughing matter.

Horse Gear: While many guides can provide a saddle scabbard for your rifle, you can bet it won't be an exact fit. A better approach is to arrive at the trail head with your own saddle scabbard. Most leather scabbards are usually made to fit a particular type of rifle and barrel length, so make sure you get the right size. If the saddle scabbard comes with an optional hood, pay the extra money and get it! Enclosed in scabbard and hood, your rifle has the ultimate in protection from the elements.

There are alternatives to costly leather scabbards. The Allen Company (525 Burbank St., P. O. Box 445, Broomfield , CO 80020, telephone 800/876-8600) markets a zippered, pile-linned, blaze orange, Cordura nylon gun case (Model 990) with "D" ring tie-downs for saddle attachment. If you are a bowhunter, then you'll also need some type of saddle scabbard for your bow. Whatever you select, remember that a saddle scabbard isn't a QuickDraw holster. Protection from the weather, security, and safety are what you should consider when selecting a scabbard.

A set of saddle bags is another piece of horse gear hunters consider an absolute necessity. Leather saddle bags are often the choice of many, but those of fabric construction (water-resistant canvas, padded Cordura nylon, etc.) are less expensive and equally serviceable. Saddle bags should be large enough to pack your lunch, a camera, and other minimal essentials—however, don't overdo it. A cantle bag, which fits just behind the saddle (at the cantle) is another possibility. This type of bag is large enough to hold your lunch, extra shells, even a light jacket and other

There's a storm brewing and these two elk hunters are wearing full-length waxed cotton dusters for rain protection. Photo Credit: Durwood Hollis

Home from the hills! If success is judged by the size of the antlers, it looks like this guide's hunters did alright. Photo Credit: Bob Robb

essentials. Also, there are smaller individual and paired bags that slip over the saddle horn to carry a canteen, small camera, sunglasses, or other items you want to have at hand.

Rain Protection: If you spend much time hunting in the mountains, you can count on rain. When you're on horseback, there's little chance to get under cover. Seated some 5 feet off of the ground, you'll face the full force of the weather as your horse continues along the trail. Whatever you do, never forget to carry some type of rain gear every time you leave camp on horseback. Usually, there are two lengths of leather, right behind or just in front of the saddle, which can be used to tie the rain gear to the saddle. Secured in this manner, it will be out of the way, yet readily available.

When a horse moves through brush, blow-down timber, and other cover, it doesn't go out of its way to make it easy for the rider. In such situations, you'll find yourself constantly riding through more clothes-shredding cover than you'd imagine. After an hour or so in heavy cover, lightweight rain gear can come out in tatters. A full-length, waxed-cotton Australian riding coat is the only type of rain protection I know of that can handle the rigors of bad weather and horse travel with equal aplomb. A waxed-cotton jacket, in conjunction with overpants made of the same fabric, also offers solid protection. Waxed-cotton garments are expensive, so expect to lay out some hard-earned bucks for the best quality. If there's an optional jacket or coat liner, get it! When the weather turns wet and cold, you'll be glad you made the investment.

Trail Gear: Three other pieces of trail gear—chaps, neck scarf, and a pair of gloves—are considered as riding essentials. During the first few hours of the day, riding through dew-laden vegetation can soak your pants. Then when the moisture starts to evaporate, your trousers will feel like a refrigeration unit. I solved this problem by including a pair of waterproof Cordura nylon chaps in my gear. The chaps are lightweight and easy to put on and take off, and cost a fraction of the price of leather chaps.

The constant movement of a shirt collar across my neck while riding is a nuisance. After a day or so in the saddle, a shirt collar can rub me raw. To prevent irritation, I usually tie a silk bandanna around my neck. Not only does the silk prevent collar burns, it also provides an added measure of warmth on those frosty mornings.

I never step into the stirrups without a pair of gloves. Should the horse get headstrong, gloves will prevent the reins from tearing my hands open. Furthermore, gloves keep my hands warm and prevent them from drying out in the mountain air. Deerskin gloves are the most comfortable and they will stay pliable even after repeated exposure to moisture.

Preparation: Just because you grew up watching John Wayne reruns on television, horsemanship isn't transferred by optical osmosis. Long before you depart for elk camp, put some time in at a local stable. Not only will the experience toughen up your rear end and knees, it will provide an excellent refresher course in basic riding techniques. Riding a bicycle can help build leg muscles and is an excellent form of exercise that can make long hours in the saddle bearable. Likewise, deep knee bends, leg stretching, and jogging can also help limber up muscles and tendons. However, if you have an old injury that might be aggravated, go easy with the training. Make sure you consult your physician first, then begin physical preparation long before hunting season comes around.

> ## Horses and humans are a companionship of elk hunting necessity in the backcountry.

Chapter 10

Kit And Caboodle

Gear and gadgets to make your elk hunt successful and survival possible

Recently, my wife, youngest son, and I made a trip to the drive-through window at our local fast-food establishment. When our order arrived it was neatly contained in a paper bag, complete with individually wrapped entrees, eating utensils, napkins, condiments, salt and pepper. In the car, we were easily able to distribute the food among ourselves, season it to taste, and then, after eating, clean up.

I am sure that most of you have had similar experiences. However, when you don't get everything you ordered (French fries) or intended to get before you left the restaurant (extra condiments, a few napkins), it can be troublesome. Either you turn around and go back to the fast-food establishment, or you try to make do with what you have. Elk hunters also need all the right stuff. Once you are in camp, usually miles away from anything resembling a store, the opportunity to acquire a missing item is not in the offering. Sometimes, it's not easy to make do in elk camp. Worse yet, if you get caught out overnight, your life may depend on that particular piece of gear.

Throughout this book, various accessories (game calls, scents, special sights, binoculars, scopes, clothing, game care products, etc.) are mentioned that can make your hunt more successful. Commentary in this chapter will focus on all of the rest of the gear and gadgets that an elk hunter will find useful. While you can't bring all of the luxuries of urban existence to camp, there are a few necessities that can make getting around, living, hunting, and surviving in the backcountry just a little easier.

Find Your Way: If you don't know where you're going, it's a good bet that you won't get there. This is where a map can come in handy. You'll need lots of maps—road maps, topographical maps, Bureau of Land Management maps, National Forest maps, and most importantly a state Atlas and Gazetteer.

Individual state road maps can be obtained through the Automobile Club (if you're a member), at state transport weigh stations, some vehicle service stations, and in the form of a bound guide at many book and magazine sellers. This type of map is useful in getting you from one point to another, but generally lacks enough specific detail to be used for anything other than vehicular travel.

The DeLorme Atlas and Gazetteer (DeLorme, Two DeLorme Dr., P. O. Box 298, Yarmouth, ME 04069, 207/846-7000) is a unique set of topographical maps

Preparing for elk camp takes more than just packing an extra pair of trousers, a rifle, and a handful of shells.

Elk hunters need maps—road maps, topographical maps, and sportsmen's maps—to find their way around. Photo Credit: Durwood Hollis

covering individual states in book format. These handy books provide excellent detail, delineating private from public land, topographical features, roads (even dirt roads), lakes, swamps, ponds, water courses, and other important topographical information. The current series covers 34 states and is available at major book sellers. Large, full-color, and easy to read, elk hunters will find these state map books a valuable resource.

For computer users, DeLorme also markets Topo USA 2.0 on CD-ROM. This mapping software provides up-to-date seamless topographic coverage for the entire United States. Now, it's easy to locate any place in the country quickly and effortlessly. You can conduct your search by place name, geographic feature, or latitude/longitude designation. The topo-

graphical maps show contour at 30-foot intervals, and the program includes over 300,000 miles of backcountry trails. Using this software, you can print high-quality, detailed topographic maps of anywhere in the United States. Best of all, you are able to customize your maps with symbols, text, and Global Positioning Satellite (GPS) coordinates—and a lot more.

Another great computer map source is Maptech (655 Portsmouth Ave., Greenland, NH 03840, 603/433-8500). Their CD-ROM Toposcout software provides up to 250 high quality USGS state topo maps per compact disc. The maps can be printed out in four-colors or black and white, in a variety of scales, as needed. The map software is equipped with a GPS interface for direct electronic download/upload of coordinates. If you're ready to become a computer-age elk hunter, this firm's products are what you need.

U. S. Geological Survey (USGS) topographical maps are even more specific in detail and cover smaller units (quadrangles) of land than an atlas or gazetteer. The best known of these maps are the 7.5-minute, 1:24,000-scale quadrangle series. By way of explanation, a 7.5-minute map shows an area that spans 7.5 minutes of latitude and longitude, and it bears the name of the most prominent feature in that quadrangle. Topographical, or "topo" maps, use brown lines to show the terrain contours, and areas of vegetation are shaded in green. Water courses, lakes, ponds, swamps, etc., are colored blue. Elevations are generally shown in feet. Topographical maps are available at backpack shops, sporting goods stores, gun shops, and directly by mail. You can write to USGS Map Sales (Box 25286, Denver, CO 80225), or call 1-800-USA-MAPS, for further information on how to order maps for specific area(s).

The Bureau of Land Management (BLM) controls huge blocks of public land throughout the western United States. This agency also makes maps of its holdings available to the public at a nominal charge. Write or call the following agencies for map information: Arizona State BLM Office, 3707 North 7th St., P. O. Box 16563, Phoenix, AZ 85011, 602/640-5547; California State BLM Office, Federal Bldg., 2800 Cottage Wy., E-2841, Sacramento, CA 95825, 916/978-4754; Colorado State BLM Office, 2850 Youngfield St., Lakewood, CO 80215, 303/239-3600; Idaho State BLM

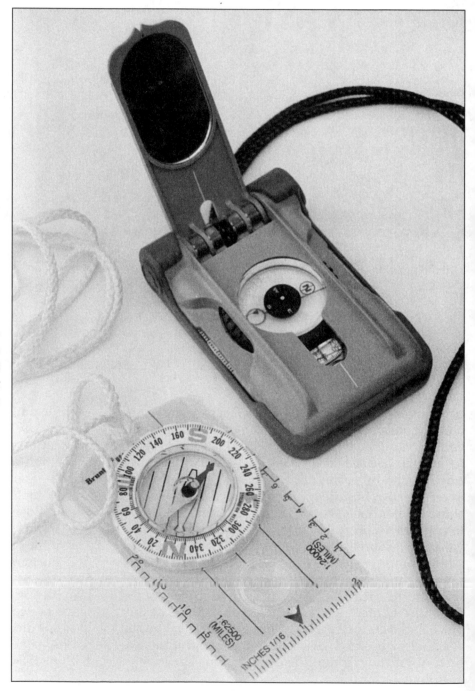

A orienteering instrument—basic or sophisticated—should be in every elk hunter's pack. Either of these two Brunton compasses can get you where you want to go, and back again. Photo Credit: Durwood Hollis

Office, 3380 American Terrace, Boise, ID 83706, 208/384-3000; Montana State BLM Office, 222 North 32nd St., P. O. Box 36800, Billings, MT 59107, 406/255-2808; Nevada State BLM Office, 850 Harvard Way, P. O. Box 12000, Reno, NV 89520, 702/785-6586; New Mexico State BLM Office, 1474 Rodeo Road, P. O. Box 27115, Santa Fe, NM 87502, 505/438-7400; Oregon/Washington State BLM Office, 1300 Northeast 44th Ave., P. O. Box 2965, Portland, OR 97208, 503/280-7001; Utah State BLM Office, 324 S. State St., Suite 301, Coordinated Financial Service Bldg., Salt Lake City, UT 84111, 801/524-3146; Wyoming State BLM Office, 2515 Warren Ave., P. O. Box 1828, Cheyenne, WY 82003, 307/755-6BLM. Computer access to each state's BLM Web site can be found at www.wy.blm.gov ("wy" is the designation for Wyoming; substitute the appropriate two-letter abbreviation for the state BLM Web site you want to view).

National Forest Maps can be obtained from these regional offices: Region 1, Montana, northern Idaho, 406/329-3089; Region 2, Colorado, part of Wyoming, 303/275-5350; Region 3, Arizona, New Mexico, 505/842-3076; Region 4, Nevada, southern Idaho, western Wyoming, 801/625-5262; Region 5, Califor-

Why Carry A Survival Kit: The impetus for the creation of my own survival kit, as well as the items selected for inclusion, came from an experience related to me by one of my hunting buddies. That individual, Craig Kitts, had a real-life survival ordeal as a teenager. By sharing this incident I hope to demonstrate how easily a day afield can turn into a survival crucible.

Although more than 30 years have past, Craig Kitts still retains a vivid memory of how he spent two frightening days alone during the 1968 Utah big game opener. "Even though I was just a teenager, my dad had a certain level of confidence in my level of maturity. I'd been a Boy Scout and learned many outdoor skills. I guess my independence just came naturally. Besides, we'd hunted in that particular part of Utah for several years and I knew it as well as my own backyard," Craig said.

Little did young Craig Kitts know that all of his knowledge of the area wouldn't help him survive the unexpected snowstorm that struck midday. Caught out alone, the boy tried to return to camp. "It wasn't all that far back to camp. I knew which way to go and what trails to follow, but the snow was coming down so fast and hard that it was impossible to see. When I stumbled into a little cluster of trees that I recognized, I decided to stay put and wait the storm out," Craig said.

When the light began to fail, young Craig grew even more anxious. "I tried to leave the trees, but each time the snow stopped me cold in my tracks," Craig went on to say.

In his jacket pocket, Craig carried a butane lighter. The lighter provided a steady flame which made fire making a lot easier. "I'd had trouble lighting a fire with matches before, so the choice of the butane lighter was something that came out of my days as a Boy Scout," Craig explained.

The boy also carried a space blanket, lock-blade knife, a canteen full of water, and some extra high-energy food. With shelter from the storm, the young boy felt a little more secure. "I thought the storm might last through the night. My choice of accommodations wasn't upscale, but then it wasn't all that bad. I had enough clothes in my pack to keep warm—even in freezing weather. I used the space blanket as a wind break. The fire kept me warm, and the food in my pack kept my stomach from growling. While the prospect of spending the night in the woods wasn't my idea of a good time, I knew it was better than wandering around and getting lost in the storm," Craig stated.

Well, the storm didn't clear by morning, and snow fell throughout the following day. When the evening of the second day approached, the lad knew he would have to spend another night out alone. Meanwhile, stranded in camp by the blinding snowfall, Craig Kitts's father knew just how perilous the situation had become. By the time the boy had been missing 48 hours, his dad began to fear the worst.

By the dawn of the third day, the snowfall let up. However, the constant wind whipped the fallen snow around in a blinding flurry. Even with self-imposed rationing, Craig's meager food supply was exhausted. Available fire materials had been reduced to almost nothing and when the boy thought he might have to spend another night out, he was "plenty scared."

Sometime during the third night, the wind stopped blowing. Craig's father assembled a search party, and at the first hint of light the group left camp. By this time they weren't looking for a lost teenage boy. They were searching for a body. But that wasn't the case. Upon awakening, young Kitts could see clearly. "You can't imagine my relief. I grabbed my pack and headed off towards camp as fast as I could go. About halfway down the mountain, I ran smack into dad!"

nia, 415/705-1837; Region 6, Oregon, Washington, 503/808-2971). Computer access to the U. S. Forest Service Web site can be found at www.fs.fed.us.

Other locally-produced maps can be found in retail stores where hunting gear is sold. Often, these maps can provide the best up-to-date information on local land owners, and recent transfers of private-to-public land conversion. Obtain all of the maps you can and use them!

Orienteering Instruments: The use of a compass and a Global Positioning Satellite (GPS) instrument is the best insurance you can buy to prevent getting turned-around (read that as lost!) in the woods. The compass is the most basic orienteering tool and should be in everyone's pocket or pack. I've used a Brunton (620 E. Monroe Ave., Riverton, WY 82501, 800/443-4871) compass for years and have found it to be completely reliable. When you're in camp take a

compass reading on several prominent terrain features. Then you'll know how elk camp relates to each one. If you become unsure of your position, use the compass to determine where you are in relation to one of those terrain points. Since all orienteering instrument manufacturers have easy-to-read product guides, I won't spend time with a lengthy discussion of compass use. If you don't have a compass — get one and use it!

Likewise, a GPS instrument is another solid piece of "lost-proof" insurance. If you have the opportunity to do some pre-season scouting, the locations of water holes, wallows, rubs, and major game trails can be saved in your GPS unit. Back at camp, you can electronically retrieve each location and plot them all on a topographical map. This allows you to plan your hunt strategy with an enhanced level of confidence. Furthermore, the GPS unit can help you negotiate in total darkness, in fog, or rain when terrain features may not be visible. This mean you can get to your hunting area and back to camp, even in the dark, with little fear of getting lost. The firms of Magellan (960 Overland Ct., San Dimas, CA 91773, 909/394-5000), and Garmin (1200 East 152st St., Olathe, KS 66062, 913/397-8200), both make top-quality GPS instruments. You don't have to get the most expensive unit, even the lower priced models provide all the orienteering information you'll need. Until you become GPS literate, simple is better than sophisticated.

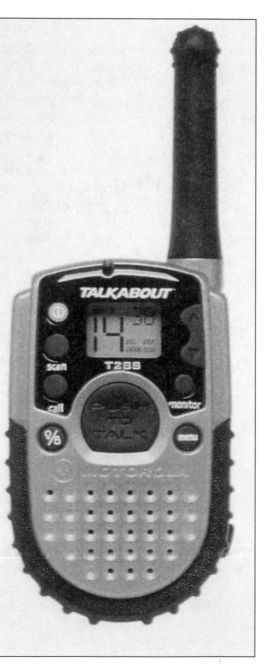

Keep in touch! A pair of two-way radios, like this Motorola Talkabout, can keep companions close at hand. Photo Credit: Motorola Corporation

Keep in Touch: While hunting alone in remote Alaska, fellow outdoor writer, Bob Robb, got in the way of a loose bolder the size of a small car. Needless to say, he came out second best in the fray. His injuries were so serious, there was no way he could have gotten back to civilization on his own. Fortunately, Bob carried an emergency radio and was able to contact the pilot of a Federal Express transport jet flying overhead. The pilot informed authorities in Anchorage, and help was on its way. Without the radio the end result of this incident could have been entirely different. Even a couple of small one-channel walkie-talkies can keep you in touch with your guide, a hunting buddy or camp. I don't know

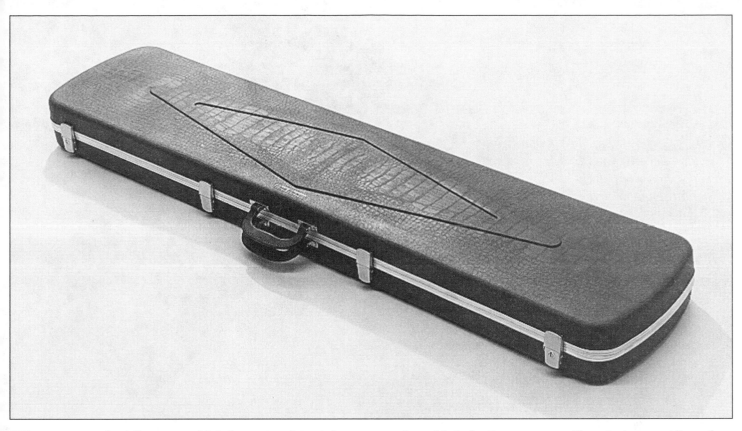

When you travel to elk camp, a high-impact resistant, luggage grade molded plastic gun case will protect your rifle and scope from possible damage. Photo Credit: Doskocil

about you, but I want to make it back from elk camp in one piece. The small size and light weight of a hand-held radio, or a pair of walkie-talkies, makes them a sensible addition to any elk hunters gear.

Let There Be Light: If you've ever tried to field dress a bull elk in the dark, then you'll appreciate the light-giving advantage of a reliable flashlight. There are a number of good flashlights on the market, and a whole bunch of bad ones! Personally, I carry a slender, 2-cell, AA battery-powered MAG-LITE, Mag Instrument (1635 S. Sacramento, Ontario, CA 91761, 909/947-1006). The flashlight weighs almost nothing and is easily carried in a factory-supplied nylon webbing belt sheath. These lights are available in a number of different sizes and colors, in AA, AAA, C, and D battery configurations, feature a machined aluminum housing, and have an adjustable light beam-on/off switch. Best of all, an extra light bulb is carried inside of the battery case for ease of replacement in the field. There are other good flashlights, but my MAG-LITE has proven its worth on more elk hunts than I can recall.

Rifle and Bow Transport: Safe and secure transport of your rifle, or bow from home to elk camp can present problems. If you're traveling by vehicle, a soft gun case or bow case may be all that's necessary.

However, if you go by air, special containment is called for. Each airline has specific requirements for the transport of firearms, and these requirements may also cover bows. All carriers demand that firearms are contained in a hard-sided, lockable case. Even though it might not be spelled out by airlines, bows demand the same level of transport protection. Baggage handlers can be tough on luggage. I would suggest that you purchase the most rugged rifle or bow travel case possible. While you're at it, slip your rifle into a soft case or scabbard before you place it inside of the hard case. This way, your firearm will be have double the protection. Use small combination (keys are easy to lose) padlocks to secure the case.

Obtain all of the maps you can and use them!

Sling It: Carrying a rifle any distance can be burdensome. A shoulder sling takes all the pain and strain out of this task. Made from leather, nylon webbing, neoprene rubber, and segmented plastic, the modern rifle sling is heaven-sent to the backcountry elk hunter. Most rifle slings are attached by means of stock-inserted swivel points. However, traditional blackpowder riflemen often use leather loops to attach a sling to the wrist and barrel of their smoke poles. The best slings distribute the weight of the rifle evenly and are wide enough to not cut into your shoulder. The sling can also be used as a shooting aid.

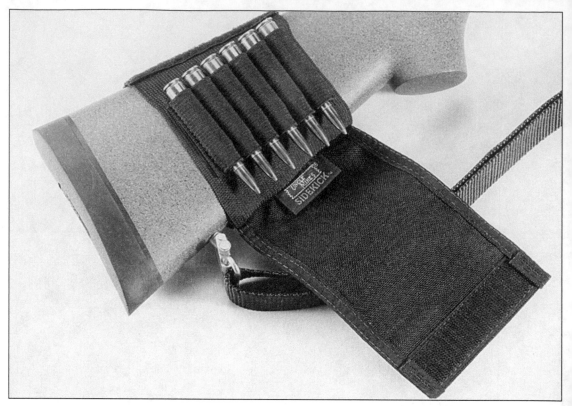

In addition to a sling, another great rifle accessory is a buttstock-mounted ammo carrier. This model, made by Michael's of Oregon, features elastic shell loops and a cover-flap. Photo Credit: Michael's of Oregon

Simply insert your left arm (right-handers) through the sling, reach around the sling and grasp the rifle forend, and apply outward pressure on the sling with your forearm. This provides added stability when shooting in any position. Obviously, a rifle sling does more than dangle!

Firearms Cleaning Gear: If you accidentally plug your rifle barrel with mud or snow, and don't happen to have a cleaning rod, you'll be in a world of hurt. Blackpowder shooters have an easy time of it. They can simply use the ramrod attached to their rifle. However, centerfire rifle users have no such luxury. Several manufacturers produce gun cleaning kits, complete with wire brush, patch jag, patches, cleaning solvent, and oil, in break-down configurations. Find a kit that meets your needs and then slip it into your duffel bag. Just let it rain or snow, and everyone in camp will want to use your cleaning gear. In short time, you will understand how easily a gun cleaning kit can solve more than one firearms predicament.

Optical Cleaning Gear: Most of us don't pay much attention to optics care until the viewing image in our binoculars or rifle scope is blurry, cracked or spotted. Water spots, dust, tiny pieces of debris or finger print oil can make a mess out of the best lenses. If you're in the habit of simply blowing away the big particles, spitting on the lenses, and using your handkerchief to wipe them clean—stop it, right now! Unless you want to permanently scratch the optics beyond redemption, then start using a cleaning solution and lens paper. Shop for these inexpensive products in your local camera shop. While you're there, pick up a

retractable lens brush. You'll find the brush the easiest and safest way to remove dust, grit, and debris from the surface of lenses.

The Elk Hunter's Pack: Gone are the days when I thought all I needed to hunt elk was a good rifle, a handful of shells, and a pocket knife. After more than three decades of elk hunting, I've learned a few things. If you're going to pursue elk on your feet, you'll need a quality backpack. Elk hunters need to carry certain items with them every day. This gear includes a rain suit, a warm jacket or heavy coat, gloves, extra pair of socks, extra shells, map, compass or GPS unit, flashlight, first aid gear, skinning knife, a small ax or a saw, lunch, and a some water. This may sound like a lot of stuff, but believe me you need every item.

There are several backpack options, including external-frame packs, internal-frame packs, and frameless day packs. For extended backcountry hunting and serious meat hauling, there is no substitute for an external-rame pack. A popular external-frame pack for elk hunters is the Freighter Frame available from Camp Trails (625 Conklin Rd., Binghamton, NY 13903). This frame is made from lightweight aluminum with a non-reflective powder-coat finish. A removable fold-away support shelf and frame extender bar prevents load shift when hauling. And the nylon mesh back support, contoured shoulder straps, breast strap, and padded hip belt offer comfortable frame suspension. A pack bag can extend the use of the frame beyond that solely as a meat, hide, and antler hauler. There are a couple of different bags,

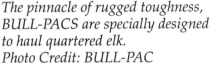

The pinnacle of rugged toughness, BULL-PACS are specially designed to haul quartered elk.
Photo Credit: BULL-PAC

each with lots of straps and zippered pockets, that fit this frame.

One of the most durable external pack frames designed especially for elk hunters is the BULL-PAC (825 Juniper Ct., Lewiston, ID 83501, 208/798-3299). Made from aircraft-grade square aluminum tubing, this frame has been tested to hold more than 200-pounds. Featuring welded construction, stainless steel fittings, and one of the most comfortable suspension system available, this is a serious heavy-hauler. A couple of different pack bags made from Saddle Cloth with a storm-proof liner, are also available to fit

this frame. If tough and rugged elk hunting is your game, then this is definitely the pack for you.

Another external-frame pack choice is the Quik-Packer from Cross Creek Trading Company (800/488-5075). This is a unique take-down pack frame that eliminates all the hassle associated with wearing a frame pack all day long. This frame can be carried in a day pack, or a fanny pack, and assembled in minutes—without tools. When put together, the frame and its padded hip belt and load harness are ready to carry meat, cape skin, or elk antlers. Unconditionally guaranteed to handle loads to 100 pounds, this is one

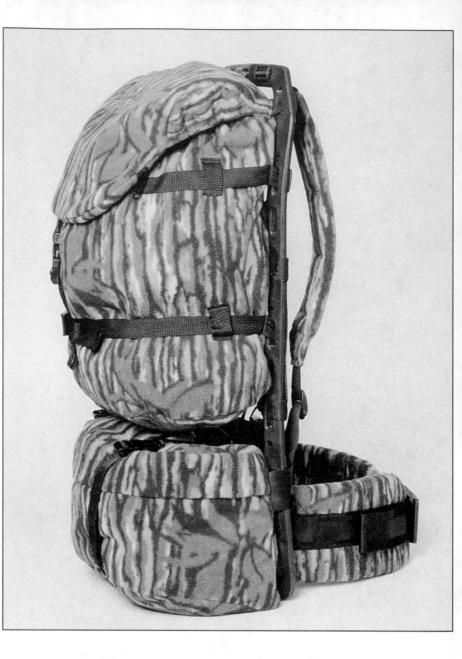

The Dwight Schuh hunting pack by Fieldline combines a molded external frame with a detachable two-piece fleece pack.
Photo Credit: Fieldline

frame pack that deserves serious consideration.

A new addition to the Fieldline (1919 Vineburn Ave., Los Angeles, CA 90032, 323/226-0820) pack line is the Dwight Schuh Hunting Pack. Dwight Schuh is a well-known outdoor writer and dedicated big game hunter, specializing in bow hunting. This Fieldline adaptation of Dwight's basic conceptual design pairs an injection molded frame with a two-part camo fleece pack. The upper pack offers generous capacity and has compression straps for load adjustment. The bottom pack is detachable and can be used separately with the waist belt as a fanny pack. The ergonomically-designed suspension system is engineered to provide the best in load-carrying comfort. A great pack for elk hunters who count boot leather as one of their most valuable assets.

An internal-frame pack won't carry the volume of meat or gear that an external-frame will, however, this pack configuration fits your body a like a glove.

This makes it easier to negotiate heavy cover and uneven ground without getting off balance or making a lot of noise. Made with ergonomically-designed shoulder straps, waist belts and bag support systems, an internal-frame pack offers the ultimate in carrying comfort. Lots of zippered pockets and tied-down attachments means that you can keep all of your gear organized. Bad Lands (1414 South, 700 West, Salt Lake City, UT 84104, 801/978-2207), Bianchi (100 Calle Cortez, Temecula, CA 92590, 909/676-5621), and Crooked Horn Outfitters (26315 Trotter Dr., Tehachapi, CA 93561, 805/822-3635), all make fine internal-frame hunting packs.

A hunter's frameless daypack is just the ticket for most all-day elk adventures. A daypack will carry all the gear you need, and then some. Better quality daypacks feature leather, molded or reinforced bottoms for enhanced wear, contoured shoulder straps, a breast strap, and a padded waistbelt. Select from

Wheels afield! With a folding game cart on his back, this elk hunter is prepared for success. Photo Credit: Durwood Hollis

models crafted from Cordura nylon, ballistic nylon, fleece, or saddle cloth. Look for a single main compartment and several outside pockets. Nearly every backpack manufacturer makes one or more daypack models. I particularly like the daypack models manufactured by Badlands and Crooked Horn Outfitters. Designed especially for hunters, these packs are available in your choice of camouflage or blaze orange.

It's a Long Haul: If you don't have access to pack stock, then there are only a couple of other meat retrieval choices. You can use a backpack and make several trips, or you can use a wheeled game cart and make fewer trips. Hauling elk meat out of the woods on a packframe isn't my idea of a good time. In some situations (designated Wilderness Areas), pack stock or back packs are the only hauling options available

to the hunter. Where they are legal to use, however, a wheeled cart is an effective gear and game transport mechanism. While you probably can't roll a whole elk out of the woods, it is possible to wheel a couple of quarters at a time. Mail order hunting equipment suppliers usually list several game cart models in their catalogs. Safe and simple to use, a game cart can definitely lighten the load.

Leave a Mark: In the children's tale, "Hansel and Gretel," the kids, after being captured by the evil witch, dropped bread crumbs along the way so they could find their path home again. Early frontiersmen used an ax to blaze their own trails through the forest. Today, I am sure the environmental crowd would frown on such a practice. However, leaving a trail behind is still a good idea. Instead of bread crumbs or toilet paper (both of which dissolve in a good downpour), use plastic engineer's tape. The tape comes in several different fluorescent colors (red, pink, orange, green, and yellow), in handy rolls that contain enough length to last all season long. If you need to mark a trail, pull off a length of tape, tie it to a convenient bush or tree at appropriate intervals, and continue on your way. When you return, you can remove the tape. Sporting good stores and gun shops sell rolls of blaze orange plastic tape, and other colors can be found at your local hardware store. Inexpensive, easy to carry, and highly visible at a distance, marking tape can save you a lot time looking for the right trail, a hidden wallow, or a downed elk.

First Aid: Scrapes, blisters, burns, cuts, chapped lips and an occasional headache are just part of hunting. Being careful and using common sense (something in short supply at times) can keep most medical problems at bay. However, there are times when things go awry. When one of those times manifests itself on an elk hunt, a first aid kit is your first line of defense. Most elk camps are required by law to have a rather well-supplied first aid kit, but you may be a long way from camp when a problem arises. My advice is to pack your own first aid supplies. You don't have to purchase a commercial kit (not a bad idea), just gather together a few basics and seal them up in a heavy-duty ZipLoc plastic bag. The basis of any first aid kit is a good selection of self-adhering bandages (make sure you include some finger, knuckle, and extra large sizes). A small tube of antibiotic cream, some headache tablets, anti-diarrheal medicine, sun screen, tweezers, individually-packaged alcohol wipes, and some type of lip protection should all be a part of your kit. You can add other items as needed, but keep it simple.

Survival Kit: Every elk hunter should make up their own survival kit. I usually slip a space blanket and an extra sweatshirt in a plastic bag. Tucked in my pack or saddle bags, both items take up little space and weigh virtually nothing. My canteen is always with me, and a couple of high-energy food bars complete the hydration/nourishment package. Finally, I keep a lighter buttoned into one of my shirt pockets. This helps to keep the butane warm enough so that the fuel source can ignite in freezing temperatures.

Craig Kitts's story (see sidebar, page 103) isn't

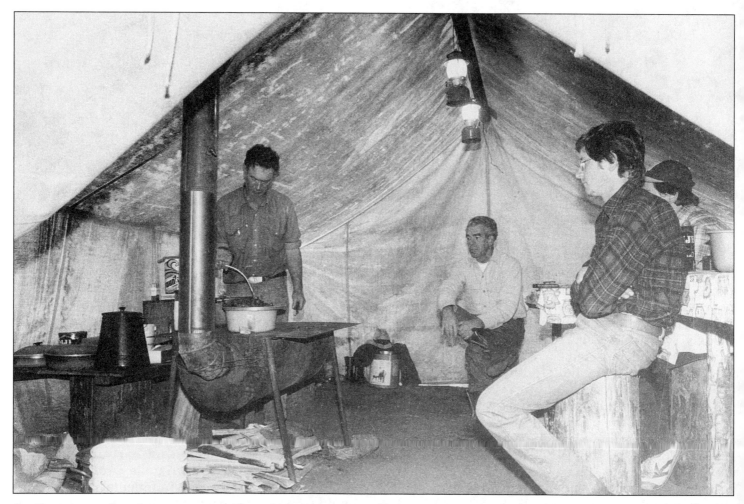

In elk camp, you're a long ways away from the conveniences of home. Choose your gear wisely and pack all the right stuff. Photo Credit: Bob Robb

unique. Every year similar survival situation arise in the outdoors. These challenges come without warning and often carry with them the most severe consequences. Some may feel that Craig's survival was the result of his early Scout training, or his level of maturity or some other variable. No doubt all of those factors made a difference. When asked, however, Craig told me that his "preparation for survival" made the difference.

In some emergencies, a shard of bottle glass might cut you out of a pinch. However, there are times when a chain saw, flame thrower, down comforter, five gallons of water, and a whole pile of hamburgers couldn't keep you safe, warm, hydrated, and nourished. Somewhere in between these extremes, the right gear and a level head can tilt the survival odds in your favor.

Get Started: Elk hunting can be tough on hunters. The weather is often unfavorable and the terrain brutal — just to mention a couple of negative facets of the hunt. Preparation is the key to your enjoyment and survival. Start assembling your gear long before hunting season rolls around. Pack everything you need. Your success and survival may depend on it!

Chapter 11

Bores And Bullets

When it comes to elk hunting, use enough gun

Few elk hunting topics will start a lively debate as quickly as will that of rifles and calibers. Everyone has their biases, and I'm not the exception. Based on three decades of successful elk hunting with a wide range of calibers and bullet weights, it is my belief that a 7mm, 175-grain bullet, is the minimum caliber and bullet weight that should be used on elk. Many may take issue with this, but I feel that there is sound practical evidence to confirm my position.

Nothing clings to life with the tenacity of a wounded elk. Even with a fatal wound, an elk will cover a surprising distance on adrenaline alone. In 1995, I shot a bull with a .338 Winchester Magnum, using a 220-grain Winchester Power Point bullet, at a distance of approximately 160 yards. The bullet

The moment has arrived. Can your choice of caliber and bullet be counted on to put that bull on the ground? Photo Credit: Durwood Hollis

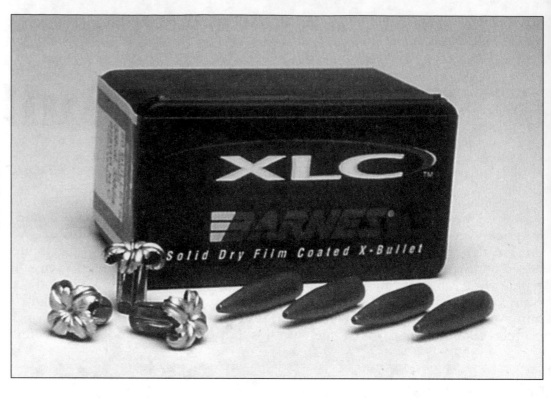

When cooking up elk loads, the handloader can't do any better than the premium Barnes X-Bullet. Photo Credit: Barnes Bullets

struck right behind the shoulder, took out the top of the heart, and tore through both lungs, making a clean exit. At the shot, the elk took off on a "dead" run and headed for some nearby timber. Several yards into the trees, a huge patch of blood marked the spot where he stumbled and fell. Amazingly, the bull managed to get up and travel even farther into the timber. Before the animal was down for good, he had covered more than 150 yards. Like I said, elk are tough!

Not only are they tenacious, elk are big animals. Even a diminutive Tule elk bull can weigh 500-pounds on the hoof. Rocky mountain elk and Roosevelt elk are larger still, tipping the scales at between 750 to more than 900 pounds respectively. In comparison, the live weight of the largest whitetail or mule deer seldom exceeds 250 to 300 pounds. Since any elk is two to three times as large (or larger) than the biggest deer, has a thicker hide and a substantially heavier skeletal structure, the need for caliber adequacy is more than well justified.

What are the best calibers for elk?

To cleanly take an elk, bullet velocity and weight, come into play. For example, a .270 Winchester, 150-grain bullet exits the muzzle at 2850 feet per second (fps), generating 2705 foot pounds (fp) of energy. However, at 300 yards, bullet velocity has dropped to 1886 fps, with only 1185 fp of energy remaining. At the other end of the spectrum, a 250-grain, .338 Winchester Magnum bullet produces slightly less velocity (2660 fps) at the muzzle than the .270 Win. load, yet it churns up over 1000 more foot pounds (3927 fp) of energy. At 300-yards, the same bullet is moving along at 2075 fps (slightly faster than the .270 Win. load), but retains more than double (2389 fp) the energy of the smaller, faster .270 Win. projectile.

The discussion of elk calibers doesn't end with velocity and energy alone. Two other factors, frontal impact (bullet diameter) and sustained projectile penetration (bullet construction), are also part of the equation. While it is possible to move a light, smaller diameter bullet fast enough to equal the energy of a larger projectile, the greater frontal impact of the bigger bullet transfers energy faster and opens a larger wound channel. Furthermore, the more weight a bullet retains after target contact, the deeper it penetrates.

The features to look for in an elk bullet are the ability to punch through muscle and bone without deflection, enhanced weight retention, and the production of a through-and-through wound channel. Federal, Remington, Winchester and other ammunition manufacturers all make fine products, and in selected calibers premium bullets like the Nosler Partition, Barnes X-Bullet, Swift A-Frame, and the Speer Grand Slam are often optional choices. Even production bullets like the Remington Cor-Loc, Remington Bronze Point, and the Winchester Power Point and Fail-Safe bullets can all provide excellent results on elk under a variety of conditions.

What are the best calibers for elk? The answer to that question is dependent on a number of elements, including: the nature of the hunting envi-

The Marlin lever-action (Model 1895M), chambered in .450 Marlin Magnum, is serious close cover elk medicine.
Photo Credit: Marlin Firearms

ronment (dark timber, mixed cover, or open parks), basic hunting methodology (still hunting on-foot, horseback spot-and-stalk or hunting from a stand), and personal recoil threshold. Most experienced hunters agree that elk hunting demands the use of the largest caliber rifle you can shoot accurately. However, overly large calibers and heavy bullets must never be considered substitutes for accurate shot placement.

A review of suitable elk calibers for close cover, mixed cover, and extended shooting presentations can provide greater understanding of both the bete noire and forte of each chambering.

Close Cover Elk Calibers: Whether it's the damp forests of the Pacific Northwest, Rocky Mountain black timber, or the juniper jungles of the Southwest, elk spend most of their daylight hours in heavy cover. In this hellishly thick vegetation, shots seldom exceed 50- to 75-yards. And it is not uncommon to push a bull out of his bed at near point-blank range. Furthermore, shot presentation is generally less than optimal. In such situations, a heavy-for-caliber bullet moving at a moderate velocity and capable of target penetration from nearly any angle, is just the ticket. Fast-handling, lever-action rifles, chambered in hard-hitting calibers like 348 Winchester, 405 Winchester, 444 Marlin, 450 Marlin, and .45-70 U. S. Government, are right at home in such environments.

348 Winchester: Long a well-respected woods and brush big game cartridge, this caliber made its commercial debut in 1936. A rimmed cartridge, it was developed by Winchester for their handy Model 71 lever-gun. Early on, 150-, 200-, and 250-grain bullets were factory loaded in this caliber. However, only the 200-grain round survived. The current .348 Winchester factory load features a 200-grain bullet exiting the muzzle at 2520 fps, producing 2820 fp of energy. Since the Model 71 lever-gun had a tubular magazine, the use of flat-nose bullets was a necessity. No doubt the inferior ballistic attributes of the stubby 150-grain load resulted in its demise. And I am sure that the substantial recoil generated by the 250-grain round wasn't easy to handle in a straight-stocked, lever-gun. Nevertheless, the 200-grain bullet in this caliber is fine elk medicine.

405 Winchester: Developed for the Winchester Model 1895 lever-gun, this rimmed cartridge has been out of production since the mid-1930s. At the dawn of the year 2000, Winchester announced that they would be offering a limited number of newly-produced Model 95 lever-guns in this caliber. Nearly as robust as the well-respected 375 H&H Magnum, this chambering pushes a 300-grain bullet out of the barrel at 2200 fps, with 3220 fp of energy. While the round-nose bullet sheds velocity at a rapid rate, the 300-grain is accurate enough to handle shots out to 150-yards. The Winchester Model 95 was a well-liked lever-gun that still garners attention among lever-gun enthusiasts. Available once again in the formidable 405 Winchester chambering, this rifle and caliber combination can be counted on to put a bull elk "down for the count."

444 Marlin: Generating energy comparable to the 348 Winchester, but in a larger caliber with more "knock-down" power, the 444 Marlin is a potent performer. Introduced by Marlin in their Model 336 lever-gun in 1964, this chambering has a lot to offer close cover elk hunters. The factory-loaded 240-grain bullet exits the barrel at 2350 fps, and produces 2942 fp of energy. While this round has a solid reputation on deer and black bear, for use on elk a handloaded 275- or 300-grain bullet would be the projectile of choice. Well suited for those who want to get up-close and personal with big bull elk, the 444 Marlin is a powerhouse within its performance envelope.

450 Marlin Magnum: Another year 2000 cartridge development, Marlin and Hornady Manufacturing have teamed up to come up with a potent new 45-caliber belted magnum chambering. Using a 350-grain bullet, this caliber generates 2100 fps of muzzle velocity, with over 3400 fp of energy. Available only in the Marlin Model 1895M, this caliber is a powerhouse of

The Browning BLR lever-action, chambered in .308 Win., or .358 Win., is a great rifle and caliber combination for mixed cover elk work. Photo Credit: Jim Matthews

an up close elk chambering in a lightweight, easy-handling lever-gun.

.45-70 U. S. Government: This venerable old-timer entered service as a U. S. military cartridge in the late 19th century. While it was replaced by the military with the newer .30-40 Krag chambering in 1892, it still remained a popular sporting round. Originally a blackpowder cartridge, the .45-70-405 (.45 caliber, 70 grains of blackpowder, 405-grain lead bullet) has never been commercially loaded to its full potential. Current factory ballistics are rather anemic, but handloaders can boost performance in this old warrior considerably. While the rainbow-like trajectory of the .45-70 prevents adequate shot placement much beyond 150 yards, nevertheless, it can still deliver enough power to be serious elk medicine. Currently available in lever-action rifles manufactured by Marlin and Winchester, and in single-shot rifles by Browning, New England Firearms, Remington, and Ruger, this chambering still has plenty of vitality as an elk cartridge after more than 120 years.

Mixed Cover Elk Calibers: While they spend a great deal of time in heavy cover, at the edge of day elk will seek out lush grassy openings to feed. It is here, in this mixture of timbered hillsides, scrub oak stands, juniper pockets, and open parks that most elk hunting is conducted. While target presentations will generally be less than 200-yards, the use of a caliber capable of handling the occasional longer shot is preferred. This is the arena where chamberings like 7mm-08 Remington, 280 Remington, 7mm Mauser, 284 Winchester, 300 Savage, 307 Winchester, 308 Winchester, 30-06 Springfield, 30-40 Krag, 8mm Mauser, 356 Winchester, 358 Winchester, 350 Remington Magnum, and the 35 Whelen are best suited.

7mm-08 Remington: This 1980 Remington introduction is one of a host of calibers based on the .308 Winchester cartridge case (.243 Win., 7mm-08 Rem., .358 Win.). Designed to work through short-action rifles, this round seems to have a measurable ballistic edge on its .308 and .358 diameter siblings. However,

> **While most elk are taken a moderate ranges, there are those occasions when a cross-canyon shot is the only option.**

the factory 120- and 140-grain loads, are too light for elk. Handloaded with a 175-grain bullet at 2600 fps, this chambering develops an impressive 2627 fp of energy. While principally a deer cartridge, with the right bullet the 7mm-08 is a suitable elk caliber—especially in a short-action rifle.

280 Remington: This chambering was introduced by Remington in 1957. Basically, it is nothing more than a .30-06 necked down to accept a 7mm diameter bullet. The heaviest factory load is a 165-grain bullet exiting the muzzle at 2820 fps, with 2913 fp of energy. While the 165-grain bullet is deadly accurate and offers extended-range performance, I would prefer to sacrifice some of that velocity and handload a 175-grain bullet. The heavier bullet certainly has enhanced sectional density, and that alone makes for a better elk load.

284 Winchester: This is another round specifically developed for use in lever-action designs. Brought out by Winchester in 1963 in their Model 88 lever-gun, the 284 has also been chambered in lever-actions made by Savage (Model 99) and Browning (BLR), as well as the discontinued Winchester Model 100 semi-auto. Interestingly, the 284 has a rim of smaller diameter (rebated or undercut) than the cartridge body. This offers increased powder capacity in a relatively abbreviated case, and provides performance comparable to the longer 280 Remington. At its inception, a single 150-grain factory load was offered. This bullet is a bit too light for elk, but handloaders can step up to a 175-grain pill. At the current time, no domestic gunmaker chambers this caliber. However, the discontinued Winchester, Savage, and Browning lever-guns are a dream to use in this chambering and you might be able to find a used gun for sale at a reasonable price. Given the right bullet and used judiciously, the .284 Winchester could put a bull elk in "a world of hurt."

300 Savage: A 1920 introduction specifically for the Savage Model 99 lever-gun, this chambering was designed to produce ballistics similar to the .30-06 Springfield. While short of the mark, the 180-grain

Elk Caliber Miscellanea: Several wildcat cartridges suitable for elk hunting deserve special mention. Two developments from the creative genus of gun writer Layne Simpson are paramount in this collection. The 7mm Shooting Times Westerner is based on a 8mm Rem. case necked-down to accept 7mm (.284") bullets. The 175-grain load leaves the barrel at 3110 fps, producing 3530 fp of energy. This wildcat has become so well-accepted by the shooting public that Remington and Winchester both chamber rifles and offer loaded ammunition in this caliber. Likewise, the .358 Shooting Times Alaskan also has serious elk potential. Beginning with the 8mm Rem. case, Simpson necked it to 35-caliber (.358), modified the body taper, and increased the shoulder angle to 35 degrees. Out of the muzzle, a 200-grain bullet has been clocked at 3305 fps, with 4845 fp of energy. While this wildcat hasn't yet reached the commercial market, it offers flat-shooting trajectory with heavy-for-caliber bullets.

A bullet for mixed cover elk hunting should be capable of sustained penetration and controlled expansion. This Nosler Partition is a prime example of superior bullet performance. Photo Credit: Nosler

load still exits the barrel at 2350 fps, and produces 2207 fp of energy. For many years, this was the caliber of choice for lever-gun aficionados. However, both the .307 Win. and the .308 Win. produce superior ballistics and have replaced this as a lever-gun chambering. Countless thousands of .300 Savage rifles are still kicking around, many of which see service every season in the hands of veteran elk hunters.

307 Winchester: For many decades lever-action enthusiasts have wanted a ballistic improvement on the old 30-30 Winchester chambering. In 1983, Winchester modified the design of the Model 94 lever-gun, allowing for the use of high intensity chamberings. In conjunction with these rifle modifications, the new 307 Winchester chambering was introduced. Essentially nothing more than a rimmed version of the .308 Winchester, this cartridge was introduced with factory-loaded 150- and 180-grain bullets. Of interest to elk hunters, the 180-grain pill exits the muzzle at 2510 fps, and produces 2519 fp of energy. With

Nothing clings to life with the tenacity of a wounded elk. Even with a fatal wound, an elk will cover a surprising distance on adrenalin alone.

approximately 6 percent less powder capacity than the rimless 308 Winchester, the new rimmed design loses 60 to 100 fps when comparisons are made. However, this slight loss of velocity is offset by the lightweight and easy handling characteristics of the Model 94. Furthermore, the 307 Winchester nearly duplicates the ballistics of the 308 out to 250 yards. For elk hunters, this new chambering in a familiar lever-gun design was a welcome improvement.

308 Winchester: Entering the commercial market in 1952, the 308 Winchester offers near 30-06 Springfield performance (approximately 100 fps less muzzle velocity) in all bullet weights. If the 30-06 is a suitable elk cartridge, then the 308 Winchester certainly joins that fraternity of chamberings. Elk stalkers will certainly appreciate the fact that the 308 Winchester moves a 180-grain bullet out of the muzzle at 2620 fps, generating 2743 fp of energy. Best of all, the shorter length of the 308 case allows its use in carbine-length rifle designs. Highly accurate and available in lightweight bolt-action, lever-action, and autoloading rifles, this caliber is an excellent choice for elk hunters who hunt on foot in the backcountry.

30-06 Springfield: Parent cartridge of the .270 Winchester, .280 Remington, and .35 Whelen, this chambering is the most versatile of all big game calibers. Worldwide, every rifle manufacturer offers one or more models chambered in the caliber. Bullet weights in this chambering of 180-, 200-, and 220-grains will be most attractive to elk hunters. The factory-loaded 180-grain projectile leaves the muzzle at 2700 fps, and manifests 2913 fp of energy. With more than adequate down-range performance to handle shots out to 250-yards (or even a tad farther), the 30-06 Springfield is a solid choice for the elk hunter.

30-40 Krag: With more than a century of experience under its belt, this old soldier seems to keep on going. Originally adopted in the 1800s by the U. S. military and chambered in the Winchester Model 95 lever-gun, it was replaced shortly after the start of the 20th century by the Springfield bolt-action service rifle chambered in .30-06. However, in recent years both Ruger (Model 3 single-shot) and Browning (Model 95 reproduction) have produced rifles for this chambering. The 180-grain load departs the muzzle at 2430 fps, producing 2360 fp of energy. While offering less whump than the .30-06 Springfield, nevertheless, the popularity of the Winchester Model 95 lever-action design has endeared this chambering to untold thousands of elk hunters.

356 Winchester: Introduced at the same time as the 307 Winchester, the 356 Winchester was also developed for the Winchester Model 94 XTR Angle-Eject lever-gun. In reality, this caliber is nothing more than

Even old-timers—like this Winchester Model 95 lever-gun in .30-40 Krag—can still do the job on elk. Photo Credit: Durwood Hollis

a rimmed version of the 358 Winchester. Both velocity and energy production are 6 to 7 percent less than the 358 Winchester, however, the 356 Winchester moves along fast enough to be an excellent mixed-cover elk cartridge. Both 200- and 250-grain bullets are factory-loaded in this caliber. The larger projectile lags well behind in both velocity and energy, making the 200-grain bullet at 2460 fps, with 2688 fp of energy the best choice in this caliber. Chambered in either a Marlin or Winchester lever-gun, the 356 Winchester can be a potent elk caliber in mixed cover.

358 Winchester: This useful caliber is nothing more than the 308 Winchester necked-up to accept a 35-caliber bullet. Introduced in the mid-1950s, it was initially offered in the Winchester Model 88 lever-gun. In recent years both the Savage Model 99, and the Browning BLR lever-action have been chambered in this caliber. However, no domestic firearms manufacturer currently produces a rifle in this caliber. Both 200- and 250-grain bullets have been factory-loaded for this chambering, however, the lighter bullet provides the best combination of velocity and energy. Exiting the muzzle at 2490 fps, with 2753 fp, the 200-grain load is more than adequate for elk at moderate ranges (up to 250-yards).

350 Remington Magnum: This chambering is one of several caliber and rifle innovations that Remington brought out in the mid-1960s. Interestingly, the .350 Remington Magnum has the same case capacity as the .30-06 Springfield. Out of a 20-inch barrel, the fat little 200-grain bullet leaves the muzzle at 2710 fps, and offers 3261 fp of energy. This chambering is a near ballistic twin to the larger .35 Whelen, and is an effective elk cartridge at most useful ranges. While this caliber isn't available in a current production rifle, Remington does offer it by special order from their custom shop. For those who desire the ultimate in a carbine-length elk rifle chambering, this is the caliber of choice.

35 Whelen: One of several calibers based on the .30-06 Springfield, this chambering is named for the late Col. Townsend Whelen. While Whelen had no role in the development of the cartridge, as a leading firearms authority of the period when this caliber was developed (1922), his name offered a level of respect to the new chambering. Made by necking up the 30-06 case to 35-caliber, this round didn't see the light of commercial production until 1987. Offered with 200- and 250-grain bullets, these loads produced 2675 fps and 2400 fps of muzzle velocity, with 3177 fp and 3197 fp of energy, respectively. While this caliber isn't a current factory chambering, you can order it from West Coast gunmaker, Charlie Merritt (American West, 5918 Temple City Blvd., Temple City, CA 91780, 626/285-9745). Merritt chambers the .35 Whelen in a Remington 700 action, with a 23-inch stainless steel Douglas barrel. The barreled action is combined with a rubber encapsulated Hogue stock, making it the ultimate in a near-magnum elk rifle. Extremely effective on big bulls within its performance envelope, this chambering offers enhanced frontal impact and bone-crushing sustained penetration without punishing recoil.

Extended-Range Elk Calibers: While most elk are taken at moderate ranges, there are those occasions when a cross-canyon shot is the only option. I've

The 35 Whelen, when handloaded with a 225-grain Nosler Ballistic Tip bullet, can easily handle a bull elk out to 250-yards, or even a tad farther.
Photo Credit: Nosler

always made it a practice to get as close to a bull elk as possible, but sometimes that isn't possible. It is here, at the very ragged edge of meaningful shot presentation that magnum caliber performance rules supreme. Calibers that are capable of handling such shots are: 7mm Remington Magnum, 300 Winchester Magnum, 300 H & H Magnum, 308 Norma Magnum, 300 Weatherby Magnum, 300 Remington Ultra-Mag, 8mm Remington Magnum, 338 Winchester Magnum, 340 Weatherby Magnum, 358 Norma Magnum, and the 375 Holland & Holland Magnum.

7mm Remington Magnum: A 1962 Remington innovation, the 7mm Remington Magnum is a fine long-range caliber. However, it does have a somewhat checkered reputation among elk guides. "Too many wounded elk," is the often repeated condemnation. Unfortunately, or fortunately (depending on your point of view), the 7mm Remington Magnum is available with a wide range (100- to 175-grains) of bullet weights. Since most hunters use the 140-grain bullet on deer and antelope, they are likely to use the same projectile on elk. When this happens, less than optimum performance can result. However, the 175-grain load exits the muzzle at 2860 fps, and produces 3178 fp of energy—more than enough for the biggest bull elk. Obviously, when used with the right bullet, this caliber can be a real powerhouse.

300 Winchester Magnum: This caliber saw its commercial birth in 1963. Since then, nearly every domestic and European rifle manufacturer has produced a firearm in this caliber. What this chambering offers is extended range capability with heavier 30-caliber bullets. The 180-grain bullet features a muzzle velocity of 2960 fps, with 3501 fp of energy. Likewise, the 200-grain load exits the muzzle at 2825, and produces 3544 fp of energy. Quite suitable at any range, even beyond the 300-yard mark, the .300 Winchester Magnum is the favorite of many elk hunters.

300 Holland & Holland Magnum: A mid-1920s introduction, the aging .300 H & H Magnum has been overshadowed by the new .300 Winchester Magnum. Nevertheless, the .300 H & H Magnum is a great all-around elk cartridge. The 180-grain bullet leaves the muzzle at 2880 fps, and develops 3316 fp of energy. With a strong reputation for accuracy, and dependable performance under all conditions, the .300 H & H Magnum is still right at home in elk camp.

308 Norma Magnum: While not well known in this country, the .308 Norma Magnum is chambered by several European firearms manufacturers. Norma makes ammunition for this caliber and the 180-grain load, with a muzzle velocity of 3100 fps and 3842 fp of energy, is quite an impressive elk load.

300 Weatherby Magnum: Brainchild of firearms developer, Roy Weatherby, the 300 is the best know, most popular, and possibly the best of his ultra-magnum creations. At one time, rifles and ammunition were only available from Weatherby. However, several firearms manufacturers now chamber for the caliber and loaded ammunition is available from Federal, PMC, Remington, Winchester, and Weatherby. Until recently, this caliber was the most powerful 30-caliber chambering available. However, it has been surpassed by the new 300 Remington Ultra-Mag. The 300 Weatherby spits out a 180-grain bullet out of the muzzle at 3120 fps, generating 3890 fp of energy. When it comes to serious elk medicine, this Weatherby offering is a potent pill!

300 Remington Ultra Mag: New for 1999, the .300 Remington Ultra Mag is a non-belted magnum cartridge. Based on English 404 Jeffery (Rimless Nitro Express) case necked down to accept 30-caliber bullets, the larger case capacity allows for the production of enhanced energy levels. When used with the same weight bullets, this new chambering has 6 percent more muzzle velocity and 10 percent more energy

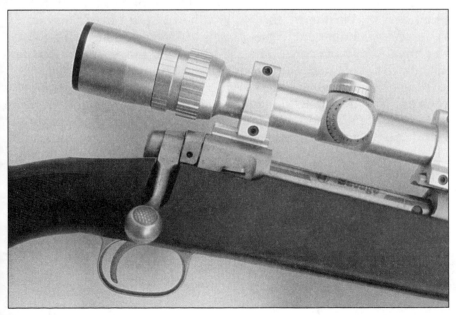

This stainless steel Savage bolt-gun, topped with a Bausch & Lomb variable scope and chambered in 7mm Rem. Mag., is just the right combination for the worst in elk hunting weather. Photo Credit: Durwood Hollis

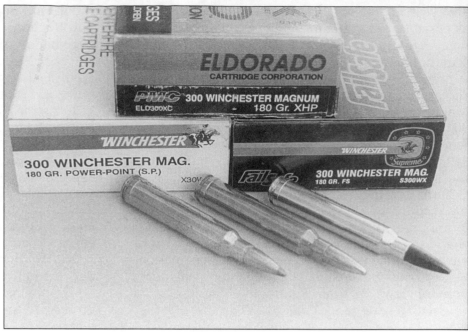

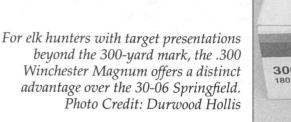

For elk hunters with target presentations beyond the 300-yard mark, the .300 Winchester Magnum offers a distinct advantage over the 30-06 Springfield. Photo Credit: Durwood Hollis

than the 300 Weatherby. Out of the muzzle, the 300 Remington Ultra Mag 180-grain bullet produces an impressive velocity of 3300 fps, with 4352 fp of energy. Even more interesting, if the 300 Ultra Mag is sighted-in 1.9 inches high at 100 yards, at 300-yards the bullet is only 2.8 below the mark. This is definitely an elk cartridge—and then some!

8mm Remington Magnum: Developed in 1978 by Remington, this chambering is based on the .375 H & H Magnum. You would have thought that this caliber would be a run-away best seller. However, it failed to interest gun writers and hunters alike. Part of this failure was no doubt the fact that Remington only offered 185- and 220-grain loads in this caliber. Even so, it is a magnificent elk caliber that offers excellent ballistic potential at all extended ranges. The 200-grain load produces 2900 fps of muzzle velocity, with 3734 fp of energy. Offering a definite edge over the 30-caliber magnums, the 8mm Remington Magnum is more than suitable for elk under any range conditions.

338 Winchester Magnum: If there was ever anything known as the "best of the best," when it comes to elk chamberings, then the .338 Winchester Magnum owns that title. Based on the 458 Winchester Magnum, this chambering was first introduced commercially in 1958. Two bullet weights—225- and 250-grain—offer the best balance of velocity and energy. The 225-grain load exits the muzzle at 2780 fps, and develops 3860 fp of energy. The 250-grain bullet is slightly slower at a muzzle velocity of 2660, with 3927 fp of energy. To be sure, this caliber carries a reputation for punishing recoil. However, if chambered in a rifle with an appropriate stock design, I've found recoil to be a negligible factor. The 338 Winchester Magnum is an elk cartridge with few peers,

and one that can be depended upon to put meat in the freezer.

338 Remington Ultra Mag: Building on the success of their first beltless magnum cartridge (300 Rem. Ultra Mag.), late in 1999 Remington unveiled a new addition to this cartridge family. This new big boomer has been named the 338 Remington Ultra Mag, and is also based on the rimless 404 Jeffery case. Firing a 250-grain Swift A-Frame bullet at a muzzle velocity of 2900 fps, developing 4668 fp of energy, this heavy-hitter nearly duplicates the performance of the 340 Weatherby. With a case capacity 25 percent greater than that of the 338 Win. Mag, the potential as an elk chambering is easily realized. However, the downside is increased recoil—something most shooters are hesitant to embrace.

340 Weatherby Magnum: Another hyper-velocity creation that can best be described as a 338 Winchester Magnum on steroids! Developed in 1962 by Roy Weatherby, the 340 Weatherby spits out a 200-grain bullet out of the muzzle at 3260 fps, generating 4719 fp of energy. The 250-grain load moves out of the barrel at 2980, and develops a whopping 4931 fp of energy. If the 338 Winchester Magnum is more than adequate for elk at extended ranges, then the 340 Weatherby Magnum is even more than that! For those who worship at the shrine of ultra-velocity elk loads, it doesn't get any better than this Weatherby offering.

358 Norma Magnum: Basically, the 358 Norma Magnum is a 338 Winchester Magnum necked-up to accept 35-caliber bullets. The Norma factory load offers a 250-grain bullet with a muzzle velocity of 2790 fps, producing 4322 fp of energy. The performance of this chambering is very similar to the .375 H & H Magnum and will be of interest to those who want maximum big-bullet performance at extended ranges.

Handloaded in the 8mm Rem. Mag., the new Nosler 180-grain Ballistic Tip bullet offers awesome velocity for flat trajectory. Photo Credit: Nosler

375 Holland & Holland Magnum: An old reliable British chambering dating to 1912, it has provided superior performance on a wide variety of game, including the dangerous variety, worldwide. A standard chambering with most American firearms manufacturers, Federal, Remington, and Winchester all produce ammunition for this caliber. Of note, the 270-grain factory load exits the muzzle at 2690 fps, generating 4337 fp of energy. Interestingly, the trajectory arc of this load nearly duplicates the flight path of the .30-06 Spfd., 180-grain load. An excellent caliber for those who prefer a slightly heavier bullet for elk out to the 300-yard mark (and beyond), the .375 H & H Magnum is an annual guest in many elk camps.

European Metric Calibers: A couple of European military chamberings are occasionally seen in elk camp. And some European sporting cartridges will also work quite well on elk.

7mm Mauser: Dating to the early 1890s, this caliber was originally designed as a military cartridge. There are several commercially-loaded bullet weights (140-, 145-, 154-, and 175-grains) available, but only the heaviest bullet should be used on elk. Factory ballistics list the 175-grain round with a

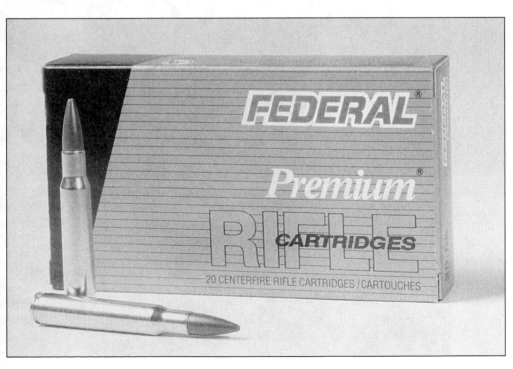

The right caliber, top-quality ammunition, and lots of practice will go a long ways toward putting elk steaks in the freezer and antlers on the wall. Photo Credit: Federal Ammunition

muzzle velocity of 2440 fps, and 2313 fp of energy. While this chambering has slightly less punch than the 280 Remington, handloaders can improve on factory ballistics.

8mm Mauser: More than a century old, this German military cartridge of World Wars I and II is still in sporting use on both sides of the Atlantic. The domestically-manufactured 170-grain load is a bit weak for use on elk. My choice for elk would be the European-loaded 198-grain bullet that is listed with a muzzle velocity of 2625 fps, and 3031 fp of energy. No doubt handloaders can get enhanced velocity and energy from 175-, 200-, and 220-grain bullets in this caliber.

8x64mm Brenneke: Another cartridge with a strong following, this creation of Wilhelm Brenneke dates to the beginning of the 20th century. The 185-grain load storms out of the barrel at 2890 fps, pro-ducing 3420 fp of muzzle energy. Quite similar to the .30-06 Spfd., this metric number has a lot going for it.

9.3x62mm Mauser: Nearly a century old, this German chambering is a robust big game caliber. Used successfully in Africa and Asia, it has gained some popularity here. The 232-grain factory load leaves the barrel at 2624 fps, developing 3548 fp of muzzle energy. Any elk hunter who acquires a new or used rifle in this caliber won't be disappointed.

The Dakota Cartridge Company also offers a quartet of proprietary chamberings—7mm Dakota, 300 Dakota, 330 Dakota, and the 375 Dakota—that have made some inroads with elk hunters. Dating to the early 1970s, this line of cartridges was designed by gunsmith Pete Grissel and stockmaker Don Allen. Based on the non-belted 404 Jeffery case (where have we seen this before?), these chamberings offer enhanced performance in standard-length rifle

This is what it's all about! An accurate rifle, the right bullet, and a careful stalk are all components of a successful elk hunt. Photo Credit: Bob Robb

actions. With Remington now using the 404 Jeffery case as the basis of its own Ultra Mag commercial cartridge family, it remains to be seen just how long Dakota keeps in the game. However, if you own a Dakota rifle in any one of these calibers, you have the right tool for the job.

The Last Shot: Several popular calibers are conspicuous in their absence, most notably the 270 Winchester. In spite of the fact that thousands of elk have been and will continue to be taken with this chambering, in my opinion the 130- and 150-grain loads are too light to offer reliable penetration. Likewise, comment on 243 Win., 6mm Rem., 25-06 Rem, 264 Win. Mag., 6x55 Swedish Mauser, and old warriors like 30-30 Winchester, 30 Remington, 32 Winchester Special, and the 35 Remington is also missing from this chapter. Simply put, all of these chamberings offer limited performance potential on elk. And why step off into the woods with something less than adequate?

If I've neglected to list one of your favorite elk calibers, then let me apologize for limiting my selection. In reality—it's not the rifle, the caliber, or even the bullet (okay, perhaps it's the bullet), that puts elk steaks in your freezer. The most important component in this equation is your own ability as a marksman. If you can't hit the target, then it's all academic!

Author's Note: The ballistic data contained within this chapter is reprinted from ballistic tables published by Federal Cartridge, Remington, Winchester Ammunition, Weatherby, RWS, Norma, and Cartridges of the World, Barnes, F. C., Ed., DBI Books, 1993.

Chapter 12

Downrange

It's all about bullet placement

Punching holes in paper may not be your thing, but the sighting-in process is absolutely necessary. Without undertaking this often tedious chore, you'll really never know with any certainty where your line-of-sight and your bullet's path intersect. And in the absence of this critical data, precise shot placement on an elk is simply a matter of luck.

For example, say that your bullet drop is about 8 inches at 300 yards. If the rifle is sighted-in so that the bullet strikes dead-on at 200 yards, it will theoretically hit approximately 4 inches high at 100 yards,

and 4 inches low at 300 yards. What you've actually done is to bisect the trajectory arc at 200 yards, making the bullet strike slightly higher and lower at either end of that arc.

All too often, shooters simply sight in their rifle for 100 yards. Given the trajectory arc cited in the preceding paragraph, this would mean at 200 yards, the bullet would strike 4 inches low, and at 300 yards it would strike 8 inches low. If you sighted in to be dead-on at 100 yards, it is entirely possible that a center-of-the-chest hold on an elk at 300 yards might

When sighting-in your rifle, a dead-steady rest is critical. Remember, you're trying to eliminate as much human error as possible.
Photo Credit: Durwood Hollis

This lever-gun, chambered in .356 Winchester, is shooting about right from an elevation standpoint. A few more clicks to the right, and it will be ready for opening day of elk season. Photo Credit: Durwood Hollis

result in a near miss just below the bottom of the rib cage. Given these facts, may I suggest that you sight in your rifle to strike somewhat higher than the line of sight at 100 yards. How much higher will depend on the individual cartridge trajectory.

Before you enter the field, most guides will make a carefully worded inquiry about the condition of your rifle. For sure, there will be at least one hunter in the group that will not have taken the time to sight-in. Worse yet, some hunters think that bore-sighting at the dealership where they purchased the rifle is all that's necessary. Sorry folks, it doesn't work like that! The sighting-in process takes time—range time.

While it's possible to prop some sort of target against a backstop almost anywhere shooting is allowed, serious sighting-in is best undertaken in a formalized setting. At a shooting range, there's usually access to shooting benches, stable target frames, and rental gear (spotting scope, sandbags, etc.) that can be of assistance in the sighting-in procedure. Also, the range offers a safe and controlled environment in which to evaluate your rifle, load, and sighting system.

Before you attempt to sight-in your rifle, disassemble it and clean it thoroughly. Check the attachment and adjustment of your sighting system (open sights or scope), so that repeated firing won't accidentally loosen any mounts, screws, or other sight components.

I suggest that you sight in your rifle to strike somewhat higher than the line of sight at 100 yards.

Probably the most important piece of work that can be performed, prior to initial sighting-in activities, is to adjust the trigger pull so it's crisp and reasonably light. Most rifles come with trigger pulls set too heavy (8 to 12 pounds) for accurate range work. Trigger work usually takes a competent gunsmith, but many rifles come with trigger adjustment instructions. Make sure you follow the instructions carefully.

Once you have your trigger pull set to where you want it, check the trigger safety. Make sure that the firearm is unloaded. Then, cock the firing mechanism, engage the safety, and pound the butt of the firearm on a carpeted surface to see if the hammer releases. Then, disengage the safety and repeat the procedure. If the hammer releases, then the sear engagement needs to be increased. Don't take any chances. If you find that there are problems with the trigger or the safety, take the rifle to a gunsmith.

Always use hearing protection at the range. I've met too many old time shooters who've suffered significant hearing loss. When I do any type of range work, I use plugs and hearing protectors that completely cover my ears. Your eyes also need protection. Don't use just any old pair of glasses. Whether the lenses are glass or plastic, make sure they're shatterproof.

Next, you'll need some kind of rest. It may be possible to rent some sand-filled bags at the range (in a pinch a couple of small pillows will do). Since there are several commercially manufactured rests available, I suggest squandering a few bucks in that direction. You needn't get too fancy, just select something that's simple to use. Anything is better than trying to sight in a rifle offhand (you'd need to be an Olympic-class rifleman to do it like that anyway).

Unless you're shooting at extremely short range (25 yards), bring along a spotting scope. If you don't own a spotting scope, you can probably rent one at the range for a nominal fee. The spotting scope enables you to see where you're hitting and allows you to adjust your sights accordingly. A pair of binoculars can do the job, but a spotting scope makes it a little easier.

Finally, you'll need a couple of rolls of target pasters (black and white) to cover bullet holes. Also, toss in some extra targets, several different sizes of stick-on blaze orange aiming points, and a note pad and pencil. Other amenities, like a padded shooting jacket, an assortment of gun-related tools (screwdrivers, Allen wrenches, etc.), materials to clean riflescope lenses, and gun cleaning gear will all come in handy at the range.

Always use hearing protection at the range.

Make certain that you sight-in with the same brand and bullet weight you expect to hunt with. It makes little sense to spend hard-earned dollars on a hunting trip after sighting in with bargain-basement ammunition. Review published ballistics, then select the bullet type and weight that best suits your needs. This should be your starting point in determining what works best in your particular gun.

Not all rifles shoot alike. In fact, two specimens of the very same model and caliber may exhibit considerable differences in their grouping ability. Sometimes finding out what kind of ammunition your rifle likes takes considerable experimentation with different bullet weights and brands. That's why range work is so important.

Much is said about rifles that can group three shots from the bench at 100 yards within 1 inch. You may be one of those fortunate individuals who owns one. But even if your favorite elk rifle can print three shots under 1-1/2 inches, it's still a winner. If you have problems, check your trigger squeeze, sight picture, and scope mounts (is everything tight?).

Before you take your first shot at the range, make sure that your rifle is bore-sighted. Most gunshops

Complete hearing and eye protection must never be overlooked when sighting-in your rifle. Photo Credit: Durwood Hollis

A perfect broadside target presentation. Is your rifle up to the job? Photo Credit: Derek Hanson/Rocky Mountain Elk Foundation

can quickly perform this chore, or if you have several different firearms you may want to purchase your own bore-sighting instrument. Either way, a bore-sighted firearm should print that first shot somewhere on the target at 100 yards, thus saving you considerable time and expense at the range.

Now, you're ready to get down to business. First, set up the target. If your range has a 25-yard target setting, then that's where to begin. If you first sight in at 25 yards, then at 100 yards, you'll only need to perform minor sighting adjustments. To adjust the point-of-impact on a rifle with metallic sights, move the rear sight in the direction you want the projectile to move. For example, if your point-of-impact is low and right, move the rear sight up and left. Scope adjustments are equally as easy. All scopes have two adjustment turrets, one for elevation (up and down), another for windage (left and right). To adjust the reticle, remove the adjustment turret cover cap and move the adjustment screw according to the inscribed directional arrow (don't forget to replace the turret cover caps when you're finished shooting).

When you're shooting from the bench, concentrate on squeezing the trigger. Most seasoned shooters recommend taking a couple of deep breaths, letting out half of the last breath, and then beginning the trigger squeeze. When it all comes together, you won't even anticipate the exact moment of the discharge. If you

Not all rifles shoot alike.

slap or jerk the trigger, then you'll anticipate the shot and the sight picture can shift at the last instant. Even the slightest movement of the sight picture will result in a significant point-of-impact change. You'll miss.

Should you be unable to produce a tight group, check your scope/mount setup carefully. All components should be tight. Next, make sure you're using the same type of ammunition. Finally, have someone watch you shoot to see if you're flinching. If corrections are in order, then take the necessary steps.

Flinching is probably the most common cause of poor shooting. Marksmanship takes practice, so don't expect to become an expert shot on your first trip to the range. Lots of folks have been shooting all of their lives and still can't put three shots inside of a bushel basket at 100 yards. The best cure for flinching is to start shooting all over again with a non-magnum or a smaller caliber rifle. The reduced recoil and lower noise level in a non-magnun or a smaller caliber often enhances shooting control. If you're having trouble shooting consistent groups, you might just be using too much rifle. Never forget, it's the bullet and where it's placed—not the caliber—that does the job!

Once you have your rifle shooting where you want it, don't just slip it into a gun case and forget about it until elk season. Try to spend some time at the range every month. This way your shooting skills will remain well-honed and you'll be ready on Opening Day.

Chapter 13

Elk Smoked With Black Powder

Taste and see

It's a thrilling experience to watch a bull elk, all slobbered up and ready to do combat, respond to an elk caller's challenge. That's just what happened to me one fine September afternoon in Arizona.

Hunting guide and longtime friend, Duwane Adams, and I had been trying to get a bull to come in all morning. The rut had been on for sometime, but the elk had been uncharacteristically silent. That is, until a bull opened up about 400-yards below us. From the sound, we could tell he was on the move and coming in our direction.

"Let's slip into that juniper and get ready," Duwane whispered excitedly.

Duwane's idea of slipping into a juniper was somewhat of a challenge. Trying our best to find an open shooting position, we squirmed and wiggled under some overhanging branches. It wasn't the best makeshift blind I'd ever used, but it did provide adequate concealment. Now, it was time to get serious.

Luckily we moved quickly, because the bull was coming "full-steam ahead." His bugling sounded like a roaring lion, and I could hear him rake a tree with his antlers. It was obvious that this big boy was intent on dealing with an intruder.

About 150-yards out, I could see antler tips moving through the trees. A few yards closer, the animal's buff-colored body could be seen drifting in and out of the junipers. Then, the bull came to an abrupt stop. Obviously, the hormonal urge of the rut hadn't made him entirely brain-dead.

"That old boy has decided it's time to be cautious. He wants to size up the competition," Adams said in a whispered hush.

Since most elk are taken at ranges well under 150-yards, blackpowder hunters face few obstacles to success. Photo Credit: Jim Matthews

Blackpowder hunters often enjoy special hunting seasons, which may take place when elk are in the rut.
Photo Credit: Wesley Hibner/Rocky Mountain Elk Foundation

Trying his best to sound like a raghorn bull, Duwane pleaded with his call like he was a teenager on his first date. For some reason, the elk fell silent. It was as if the bull had a "you want me, come and get me," attitude.

Again and again, Duwane tried to coax the animal closer, but the elk wasn't having any of it. "I can't get him to come any further. If this was bow season, we'd be out of luck," Duane whispered.

Fortunately, it wasn't bow season. I had taken advantage of a special black-powder elk hunting period and now the reality of that decision was clearly apparent. Indeed, I had just the right medicine for this situation in my hands. Taking care not to give our position away, I slowly eased the barrel of the Dixie Arms percussion rifle out of the tangle of juniper branches.

From our makeshift blind, I could watch the elk mill about behind a thin screen of junipers. Appar-

Keep all propellants away from an open flame. Never load, or store a loaded rifle (even uncapped) near a camp stove or heater.

ently, our calling efforts hadn't entirely convinced the bull, but his curiosity kept him glued to the spot. With open sights, and eyes that had seen well past more than four decades of living, it wasn't the easiest shot presentation. However, the bull was getting nervous and it was going to be now, or never.

Taking a careful rest, I sought to find an opening through which to place a bullet. Slowly, I thumbed the hammer back, set the trigger, and waited for just the right moment. When it came, the trigger squeeze was instinctual. However, instead of hearing the powder ignite, the only sound was a loud metallic snap! Obviously, the bull heard the noise, because he was gone in an instant.

"What happened," Duwane said with obvious frustration in his voice?

When I looked at the rifle, the answer was clearly apparent. In the excitement of the moment, I had forgotten to cap the nipple. Without a cap, the rifle would have never fired. Sheepishly, I admitted my failure. Duwane just laughed. I didn't think it was all that funny. In retrospect, it seemed that laughter was just a part of the experience. Because when it comes to black-powder hunting, if it can happen, it will. In my case, it cost me a heavy-antlered 5x6 bull elk.

If you haven't tried black-powder elk hunting, then you're missing a lot of great fun. Using black-powder gear is the ultimate "do-it-yourself" project. Unlike case-contained centerfire rifle ammunition, the black-powder bullet, propellant, and priming charge are all separate components. It's up to you to put it all together, and then make it work.

Special Seasons: The best aspects of black-powder hunting are special "black powder-only" hunting sea-

sons held in some states. Usually conducted right after bowhunters have had their opportunity in the field, and just before centerfire rifle hunters take to the woods, a black powder season is the best of all worlds. First, you catch the tail end of the rut. Second, you are able to use a rifle—albeit a single-shot, front-loader. And third, the effective range restriction of bowhunting doesn't have the same impact on shooting opportunities.

Your Choice: Muzzleloading rifles can be divided into two groupings—flintlocks and percussion—based on their manner of powder ignition. Flintlock rifles are beautifully made firearms, but the exposed flash pan is extremely sensitive to ambient moisture. Since big game hunting and wet weather seem to go

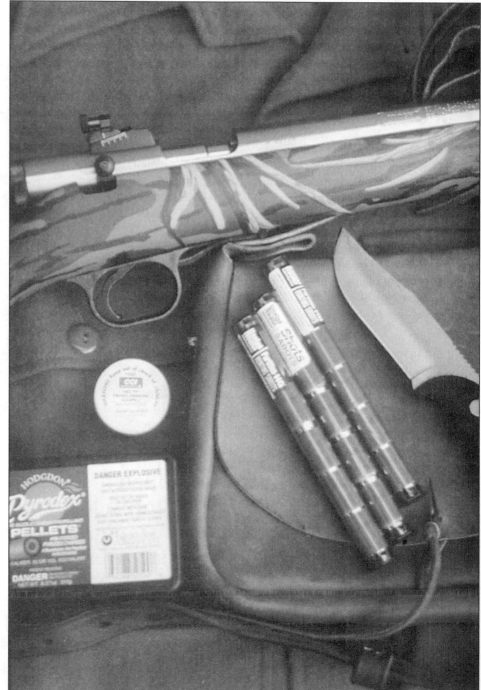

Modern technology—inline rifle, sabot bullet, pelletized powder, and reliable caps—provide the hunter with distinct advantages. Photo Credit: Durwood Hollis

together, the flintlock isn't always the best choice for an elk rifle.

A percussion rifle utilizes an exposed nipple that is threaded somewhere into the base of the barrel. A primer cap is slipped onto the nipple. When ignited by the hammer fall, the primer spark is fed through the nipple directly into the powder. This offers enhanced protection from wet weather and provides more reliable ignition under field conditions. Percussion rifles can be further divided into side-lock and in-line designs. The side-lock design features a side-mounted (right- or left-side of the trigger) hammer. While the in-line concept also features the use of an exposed nipple and a primer cap, the nipple is positioned at the breech of the barrel, directly in line with the bore. This provides for a direct in-line hammer strike, not unlike that of a centerfire rifle. The best features of this design are enhanced ignition protection from moisture, the use of

a spring-driven hammer (faster lock time), and a removable breech plug (easier barrel maintenance and load removal). Furthermore, the in-line concept fits nicely into a modern stock design.

I've used both side-lock and in-line percussion rifles. Either design can get the job done. However, an in-line rifle is easier to maintain on an extended hunt. If you want to unload a side-lock percussion rifle you must either shoot out, or pull out, the unused load. No matter which avenue you take, both necessitate a thorough barrel cleaning. Conversely, the in-line rifle can be unloaded without all of the hassle of shooting or pulling the load. Simply remove the threaded breech plug and use the ramrod to push the powder and bullet out of the barrel. Run a lightly oiled patch through the barrel, and you're done!

Traditionalists prefer side-lock designs and avoid in-line rifles like they were the plague. Most likely,

Lock, stock, and barrel—this traditionally-styled blackpowder percussion rifle is right at home in elk camp.
Photo Credit: Durwood Hollis

this grouping of black-powder shooters will select a Hawken rifle configuration. This is the rifle design most often used by mountain men, explorers, trappers of the 18th and early 19th centuries. However, crossover black-powder shooters (centerfire rifle hunters who also use black-powder rifles) are attracted to the in-line design because of its similarity to the modern centerfire rifle. Capitalizing on this market, the modern centerfire rifle manufacturers like Remington (870 Remington Dr., Madison, NC 27025, 800/243-9700), Marlin (100 Kenna Dr. North Haven, CT 06473, 203/239-5621), Mossberg (7 Grasso Ave., North Haven, CT 06473, 800/989-4867), and Ruger (200 Ruger Rd., Prescott, AZ 86301, 520/541-8820), all offer in-line rifles in addition to their centerfire rifle lines. Black-powder rifle manufacturers like Knight (21852 Highway J46, P. O. Box 130, Centerville, IA 52544, 515/856-2626) and Markesbery Muzzleloaders (7785 Foundation Dr., Suite 6, Florence, KY 41042, 606/342-5553) are also leaders in this field. And firms like, Dixie Gun Works (Gunpowder Lane, P. O. Box 130, Union City, TN 38281, 800/238-6785), Connecticut Valley Arms (5988 Peachtree Corners East, Norcross, GA 30071, 800/320-8767), Navy Arms (689 Bergen Blvd., Ridgefield, NJ 07657, 800/669-NAVY), Lyman (475 Smith St., Middletown, CT 06457, 860/632-2020), and Thompson/Center (P. O. Box 5002, Rochester, NH 03867, 603/332-2394), all offer both side-lock and in-line models.

Blued or Stainless Steel: Beyond the basic rifle ignition design, the choice of either blued or stainless steel firearm construction is another consideration. If you are committed to rifle maintenance, then a blue steel black-powder rifle doesn't present a problem. However, the barrel must be cleaned after every shooting session and exposed metal wiped daily with an oily rag. Maintenance with a stainless steel rifle is less demanding. I've left my stainless steel black-powder rifle dirty for several days after shooting, even a week or more, without any sign of rust. In elk camp, I am a lot more concerned about hunting, eating, and sleeping, than I am rifle maintenance.

Caliber choice: The selection of bore diameter—.50 or .54 caliber—for the black-powder elk hunter isn't really a problem. With the same weight bullet, the .50 offers a little better sectional density for penetration, and the .54 provides enhanced frontal impact with a larger wound channel. When used on elk, I haven't seen a lot of difference between either caliber. If you're convinced that the .54 is a better elk caliber, then go for it. Personally, I've had good success on elk with either one.

Bullets and Balls: When it comes to black-powder projectiles, the field is wide open. A broad selection of lead balls, cast lead and swagged lead conical bullets, and sabot-encased bullets are readily available. Lead balls must be patched and loading is a little slower than loading a conical or sabot-encased bullet. However, balls are lighter than bullets, offering greater muzzle velocity. Conversely, a ball sheds velocity faster and does not perform as well as a bullet after target contact. Many black-powder rifle manufacturers, like Connecticut Valley Arms, Thompson Center Arms, Remington Arms, and Traditions Performance Muzzleloading (1375 Boston Post Rd., P. O. Box 776, Old Saybrook, CT 06475, 860/388-4656), all offer their own brand of bullets. Black-powder projectile specialists, like Big Bore Express-Black Belt bullets (7154 W. State St., #200, Boise, ID 83703, 208/376-4010), Buffalo Bullet Company (12637 Los Nietos Rd., Suite A, Santa Fe Springs, CA, 90670, 562/944-0322), as well as other firms, also make fine products. Centerfire rifle bullet manufacturers, such as Barnes Bullets (750 North, 2600 West, American Fork, UT 84003, 800/574-9200), Hornady (3625 Old Potash Hwy., P. O. Box 1848, Grand Island, NE 68803, 308/382-1390), Nosler (P. O. Box 671, Bend, OR 97709, 541/382-3921), Remington, and Swift Bullet Company (201 Main St., P. O. Box 27, Quinter, KS 67752, 785-754-3959) also have black-powder projectiles in their respective product lines.

Conical bullets and sabot-encased bullets for use with black powder can be produced in hollow-point and jacketed designs, features that offer amplified accuracy and terminal performance. My choice for black-powder elk hunting is a heavy-for-caliber, solidly constructed conical, preferably in a hollow-point design. Beyond these suggestions, whatever bullet offers the best combination of accuracy and performance in your rifle should be the projectile of choice.

Real or Synthetic: Black powder comes in the form of loose granules and in several grades, from coarse to fine. The firms of Elephant Black Powder (7650 U. S. Highway 287, Suite 100, Arlington, TX 76001, 800/588-8282), and Goex Inc. (P. O. Box 659, Doyline, LA 71023, 318/382-9300) are both reputable black powder manufacturers. The Hodgdon Powder Company (6231 Robinson, P. O. Box 2932, Shawnee Mission, KS 66201, 913/362-9455) makes Pyrodex, a black powder substitute, that is available in loose granules or pelletized form. Pelletized Pyrodex comes in measured units that are quicker to load than loose powder. Furthermore, Pyrodex has a higher ignition threshold than black powder, making it safer to store.

> **Blackpowder rifles are all factory-equipped with open sights. Unless your eyes are as sharp as an eagle's, you'll find that such a sighting arrangement is less than optimal.**

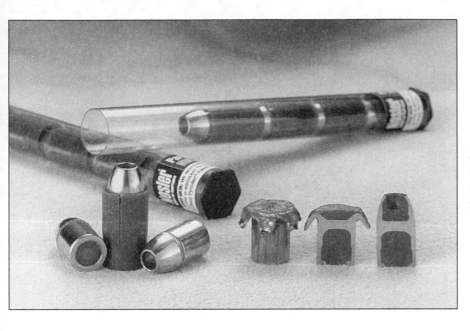

Sabot-encased blackpowder projectiles, like these .50 caliber Nosler 250-grain, Partition-HG bullets, offer the best in penetration and expansion. Photo Credit: Nosler

Keep Safe: The safe storage and use of black powder, or other types of propellants, should be a constant consideration. Keep all propellants away from an open flame. Never load, or store a loaded rifle (even uncapped) near a camp stove or heater. Furthermore, a loaded rifle has no place inside of a house, lodge, cabin, or tent. Load and unload your rifle outside. When loading, keep the muzzle pointed away from your person and in a safe direction. And never carry a loaded and capped rifle on horseback. Every time you return the rifle to the scabbard, always remove the cap and uncock the hammer.

Accessories: No matter what kind of propellant you select, problems with ignition can be encountered. This is particularly true during inclement weather. A replacement nipple, featuring a large-diameter priming path, can intensify primer flame presentation. Likewise, the use of a shotgun (209) primer, or a musket cap can produce a similar effect. Furthermore, all propellant should be stored in a dry environment at home, in camp, or when carried in the field. When I am hunting, I use plastic speed loaders that hold a measured powder charge, a bullet, and a couple of caps. Carried in this manner, the entire load is well protected from moisture. For additional protection, I cover the end of my rifle muzzle with a piece of plastic tape, and a square of rubber inner tubing is placed over the uncapped nipple and secured in place with the hammer.

"Starting" a projectile into the bore pathway can prove to be difficult. This is especially true of a patched round ball. After a shot or two, even a conical or sabot-encased bullet can be difficult to insert into a dirty bore. A short rod, or "starter," is the tool of choice for this assignment. The "starter" is used to insert the projectile a short distance into the bore, then the ramrod completes the chore.

Most black-powder rifles are equipped with wood or aluminum ramrods. If you're not careful, a ramrod can be bent or broken. If you have access to a blackpowder retailer, then it's an easy matter to obtain another. However, replacement ramrods are hard to find in elk camp. I solved this potential headache long ago by equipping my rifle with a fiberglass ramrod. The rod works as well as the original and can take a lot more punishment.

If you carry loose bullets, powder, and caps in the field, you'll need something in which to put them. A bullet bag, powder flask, and capper are made for just this purpose. There are lots of selections in this arena, including traditional leather bullet bags, brass powders flasks and cappers, as well as high-tech molded plastic containers and cappers. Quiet, dry containment, and total security are the features you want to look for in these accessories.

Black-powder cleaning accessories usually screw into the end of your rifle's ramrod. A cleaning jag, brass or stainless steel brush, and a bullet puller, along with bore patches, cleaning solvent, oil, and an gun wipes will be needed for cleaning and maintenance. After shooting, a blued steel rifle will need a thorough cleaning to prevent rust. A stainless steel rifle is less demanding, and usually only needs a daily wipe down. Also, a screwdriver with interchangeable bits to fit each screw on your rifle and sighting equipment can come in handy.

A compressed-air unloader is a great piece of gear that makes it a snap to unload a black-powder rifle. This little gadget uses a blast of compressed air to push the load out of the barrel. Simply place the nozzle over the open nipple, give it a blast, and the bullet and power are removed just as slick as a raccoon going down a hollow log. For side-lock rifle shooters, this eliminates shooting the load out, and then cleaning the rifle bore. Of course, it also eliminates the entire hassle associated with pulling the bullet and dumping out the powder. It even works well for in-

If you're a round ball blackpowder elk hunter, then these accessories, along with a possibles bag, will be part of your accouterment.
Photo Credit: Michael's of Oregon/Butler Creek

line shooters. Give it a try. I am sure you'll be surprised just how easy unloading can be.

Carrying a black-powder rifle in the field is easier if you use a sling. Some rifles are equipped with sling swivel mounting studs, and this makes it a simple matter to attach a carrying strap. Hawken style rifles, however, usually come without swivel mounting studs. You can either attach them, or use a slip-on or lace-on sling. Either way, the carrying convenience will make those hours in the field more comfortable.

Hauling all of your black-powder gear—powder, bullets, caps, patches, short starter, cleaning gear, and bullet puller—is a hassle. Rather than having all that stuff wearing a hole in your pocket or pack, most black-powder hunters use a possibles bag. Traditionally styled bags are made from leather and feature a broad "beaver tail" flap over the opening. Still, other bags are made from canvas or high-tech fabrics in various colors and designs. Zippered pockets might assault the historic sensibilities of some, but they make real sense when it comes to keeping all of your gear handy. The primary consideration with a possibles bag is safe containment and carrying convenience.

Iron Sights: Black-powder rifles are all factory-equipped with open sights. Unless your eyes are as sharp as an eagle's, you'll find that such a sighting arrangement is less than optimal. I would suggest you replace the rear sight with a large-aperture peep sight. The "ghost ring" effect of the rear sight will allow you to instinctively center the front sight and allow you to focus on the target. You might also consider using a light-gathering optic fiber front sight by HIVIZ (North Pass, Ltd., 1375 Ken Pratt Blvd., Suite A, Longmont, CO 80501, 800/589-4315), or Truglo Inc.

(P. O. Box 1612, McKinney, TX 75075, 972/774-0300). Under low-light conditions, the "light pipe" technology will make target acquisition much easier.

Scope it Out: In some jurisdictions, it is legal to mount a scope on your black-powder rifle. In low-light shooting situations—dark timber, early morning, and late evening—a scope will provide a better sighting image. While side-lock percussion rifles may look a little out of place wearing a scope, most in-line rifles come drilled and tapped for scope mounts. The firms of Burris (331 East 8th St., Greeley, CO 80631, 888/228-7747), Bushnell (9200 Cody, Overland Park, KS 66214, 913/752-3400), Leupold (14400 NW Greenbrier Pkwy., Beaverton, OR 97006, 503/646-9171), and Simmons (201 Plantation Oak Dr., Thomasville, GA 31792, 912/227-9053) all make rifle scopes especially for this purpose. Of course, it is possible to simply mount whatever scope you want on your favorite frontstuffer. I would suggest that you stick with a fixed-power scope in 2x, 3x, or 4x, or a low-power variable like a 1x-4x, or 1.5x - 5x. Anything with more magnification isn't really necessary.

What's the Difference?: Elk hunting with a black-powder rifle isn't all that different from using a centerfire rifle. The basic distinctions are two: range limitations and slower reloading. With open sights, most black-powder rifles have an effective sighting trajectory of about 100-yards. If local regulations allow the use of a scope, then with the right load it's possible to stretch that range out to 150-yards, or even a little farther. Since most elk are taken (even when a centerfire rifle is used) under 150-yards, a black-powder hunter has fewer range restrictions than one would assume.

Granted, reloading a black-powder rifle is slower than reloading a single-shot or repeating centerfire

Getting within effective blackpowder range will demand solid stalking skills.

rifle. Even a bowhunter can get a second arrow in the air more quickly than a black-powder shooter can seat a load. Shooting and reloading practice is the key. If you make the first shot count, then subsequent shots are unnecessary. Effective black-powder rifle use is dependent on staying well within the performance envelope of both rifle and shooter. The more time you spend at the range, the better you will understand the capabilities of your rifle and yourself.

Hunting Tips: Getting within effective black-powder range will demand solid stalking skills. Don't get in a hurry. If the elk aren't aware of your presence, then keep it that way. Go slowly, keep the wind in your favor, watch out for the cows, and focus on the bull. I hunt elk with my black-powder rifle just like I do with a bow. Camouflage clothing, scent cover and

a cow call are all part of my black-powder hunting accouterment.

When you finally have a bull in your sights, don't shoot off-hand. Wherever and whenever possible, rest your rifle on something. A rock, a tree branch, or even your hat can serve the purpose. If all else fails, drop to a kneeling or sitting position and rest the rifle on your knee(s). When the sight picture looks good, squeeze the trigger slowly. Assume that your bullet or ball went where it was aimed, and follow-up on every shot.

No matter whether the elk falls over, takes off on a dead run, or just stands there, reload your rifle immediately after shooting. If the bull goes down within sight, give things a few minutes to settle down—including your heart rate. I once watched a hunter

Your first shot, is your best shot. Take a rest and carefully squeeze that trigger.
Photo Credit: Jim Matthews

Called within blackpowder range using an elk grunt hose and a cow call, Jimmy Primos took this 7x7 monster bull with an inline muzzle-loader. Photo Credit: Bob Robb

shoot a bull squarely in the chest. The animal took off across a narrow meadow and fell just at the edge of a stand of timber. The excited hunter neglected to reload and quickly ran towards the fallen animal. To his surprise, the bull got to its feet and vanished into the trees. With an empty rifle, the only thing he could do was watch the elk disappear. It took hours to follow the scanty blood trail and another well-placed shot before the hunter tagged the bull. Like I said, reload your rifle before you do anything else.

Look for hair, blood, bone chips, or other evidence of a projectile strike. If you discover blood sign, follow to one side so as not to step on and disturb the

No matter whether the elk falls over, takes off on a dead run, of just stands there, reload your rifle immediately after shooting.

trail. In all likelihood, you will find the bull within 100-yards. If not, then keep looking. Should the animal still be on its feet, or have its head up—shoot again, then reload. When you're absolutely sure that the bull elk is down for the count, then, and only then, can you consider the matter concluded. Afterwards, you can unload your rifle and start in on the field dressing chores.

Shot Placement: No matter whether you use a bow and arrow, a centerfire rifle, or a black-powder rifle, your first shot at an elk is always your best opportunity. Subsequent target presentations are generally less than optimal and do not always produce the desired result.

SHOT PLACEMENT

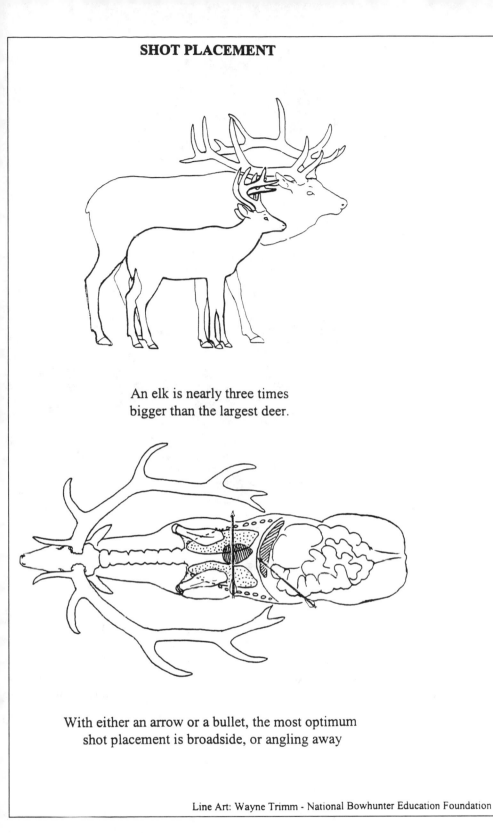

An elk is nearly three times
bigger than the largest deer.

With either an arrow or a bullet, the most optimum
shot placement is broadside, or angling away

Line Art: Wayne Trimm - National Bowhunter Education Foundation

The onus is on the hunter to accurately place the shot where it will be most effective.

The best place to shoot an elk is the lower portion of the heat-lung cavity. This target "pocket" is located just behind, and right below the point-of-the-shoulder. A projectile penetrating this area will damage the heart, major arteries of the heart, the lungs or all of these organs and structures simultaneously. The end result is will be major blood loss and a shut-down of the respiratory and circulatory systems. After the shot, the animal may run, but it won't go far. I've never had to track an elk that was hit in the heart-lung area any farther than a couple of hundred yards, and usually less than that.

A neck shot can produce near instant results, but it is possible to miss both the spine and major arteries to the brain. Likewise, a shot that breaks a leg, hits the paunch, or a hindquarter may only cause limited damage, making recovery difficult—if not impossible. No hunter wants to loose an elk because of poor shot placement, so effective placement of bullet or ball is essential.

Know the Law: Black-powder hunting regulations vary from state to state. In some jurisdictions, it is legal to use sabot-encased bullets and pelletized powder. In other areas, black-powder hunters may be restricted to the use of patched balls or conical bullets, and loose powder. Even such matters as propellant ignition, barrel length, and sights may not be the same in each bailiwick. The only way to understand these various statutes is to carefully read the regulations governing the use of black-powder firearms in the area you intent to hunt. If you have any questions, clear them up well ahead of time.

Game departments usually have an information officer designated to respond to public inquiries. Should any area within the law be unclear, use the telephone to get an answer. I would suggest that you document any telephone calls to game officials by writing a memorandum to yourself. Indicate the date, time, and name of the person who provided the answer(s). When your telephone bill arrives in the mail, find the line entry for your call and highlight it. Then staple the original telephone bill and your memorandum together. This might seem like a bother, but it can "save your bacon" should you ever be questioned by a game warden. If the matter goes before a magistrate, the

Sabot-encased bullets are the ultimate in frontloader projectile technology, but check local hunting regulations first to see if they are legal in your hunting area.
Photo Credit: Durwood Hollis

memorandum and attached telephone documentation will become evidence to support your position.

The Last Word: Many of us have walked the wild places where early frontiersmen and explorers once tread. In those lonely realms, the sights and sounds have changed little. Only time separates us from that period. Like a fictional time machine, the muzzleloading rifle is a transport mechanism to that era. If you want to know what elk hunting was really like when this country was new, then take up black-powder hunting. It will become a hunger that is not easily satisfied. Taste and see!

Chapter 14

Sticks And Strings

A Beginner's Guide to Bowhunting Elk

Bowhunting elk is just like hunting them with a rifle—only different! That, in a paradoxical nutshell, describes what bowhunting is all about. In both disciplines, the sportsman must research his hunting season, scout out potential hot spots, find a legal animal once the season opens and then maneuver into position for an effective shot. But that's where the similarity ends!

Getting and making that shot is much tougher with a bow than with a rifle. Furthermore, success rates are so low—in comparison to rifle hunting—that game managers actually believe that the current bowhunting harvest of elk has no real bearing on overall herd numbers. These same managers provide bowhunting opportunities for recreation, and they use the more effective gun seasons to control the elk population.

Why Bow Hunt? If bowhunting is such a low-success sport, then why is it the fastest-growing segment of the hunting business today? First, there is usually a special bow season in advance of muzzle loader or rifle seasons. In many areas, this season occurs during the September rut. During this period, elk forego much of their natural caution in a quest to reproduce the species. The primary interest of a bull elk is gathering and protecting his herd of cows. This makes it easier for a bowhunter to locate, call, and stalk a bull. Obviously, hunting during the rut offers significant advantages that cannot be equaled any other time of the year.

The reason many have moved over to the bow and arrow side of hunting are the challenges. Many rifle hunters have become efficient at bagging a bull elk each year. Elk hunting has become almost boring to them. They lose the fire that first excited them as hunting became too easy. Bowhunting, however, is anything but easy. When gun hunting, just seeing a bull elk often means he's in the bag. With a bow, spotting a bull is just the first step in a long process that, more times than not, ends with the hunter watching elk and hoping that a shot opportunity presents itself.

Bowhunting for elk is the best of all worlds—mild weather, better license odds, fewer hunters, and the opportunity to hunt bulls in the rut. Photo Credit: Bob Robb

This is every bowhunter's dream, but wait for a better arrow placement angle.
Photo Credit: J. Mark Higley

One Colorado bow season, I did nothing but watch elk day after day. Finding elk was easy. Even getting reasonably close wasn't all that difficult. However, getting within range of a bull was nearly impossible. Talk about frustration, it was the ultimate in heighten levels of anxiety. The problem was too many eyes watching me. Every move I made was the subject of scrutiny by cow elk. Just when things were coming together, some cow would get uncomfortable. Then the whole lot, bull included, would just wander off. I never really spooked the elk, they just knew something was amiss. On that trip I learned a lot about elk. However, it takes a lot more than knowledge to put a bull in the freezer.

If you're a bowhunter, then you aren't allowed mistakes. If I blunder into a bull during rifle season and

he bolts for cover, I can still usually make the shot. Likewise, if something alerts the bull during a stalk, I generally have time to send a bullet in his direction before he takes off. In other words, the rifle has erased my error. When bowhunting, such an error means the end of the game.

Because the ultimate bowhunting goal is to get a close-range shot at an undisturbed animal, shots at running animals should be avoided. One of the basic bowhunting rules is only attempt a clear shot at an elk that is broadside or angling slightly away, at ranges not exceeding 50-yards, (usually half of that distance). I've let more than one bull walk casually past me because I didn't have the right shot angle, or there was some intervening brush between us. Even

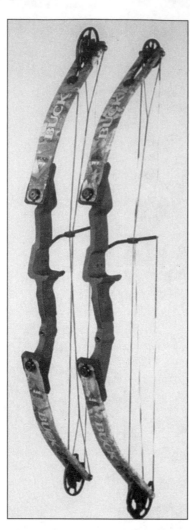

A modern bow, like these compound models from Buck Knives, can deliver flat-shooting performance in a short, lightweight, easy-to-handle configuration. Photo Credit: Buck Knives

when a bull hangs-up just outside the 50-yard mark, I make it a rule to never just fling an arrow in his direction. If you can't make the shot with a high degree of confidence in your arrow placement, then have the patience to just let it go. Like I said, bowhunting can be very frustrating.

Basic Bow Components: There are a couple of recommendations that any bowhunter ought to take to heart. Use a mechanical release aid to shoot with, rather than releasing the arrow with your fingers. If you can find a wrist strap-type release, all the better. The strap will keep help keep the release in place should you have move to quickly. When you use a mechanical release, you'll notice an improvement in your shooting over the use of a finger tab. However, carry an extra release in your pack just in case a mechanical foul-up happens. And I always stuff a shooting tab somewhere in my gear as a release aid of last resort.

There is a myriad of bow sight choices. When making a selection, simple is better than complex. The more parts, screws, and attachments, the greater the possibility that something can break, fall out, or fail to work properly. In their desire to keep things simple, many experienced bowhunters have gone to a one-pin sight. Sight pin visibility under failing light conditions is another consideration. Electronic sights that offer enhanced pin illumination, or fiber optic light gathering sight pins should be considered.

Getting Started: You'll need the right bowhunting equipment to get the most out of the sport. Bows that fail to fit, draw weights that are too heavy, or arrows that are the wrong length or weight, will result in poor performance and drive you absolutely crazy. Furthermore, all of the archery advertising hype is more than enough to confuse anyone.

If you have friends who are bowhunters, ask them about their equipment. They've probably tried lots of different gadgets and can give you solid advice on what works for them. Local archery clubs are another source of information. The best source, however, is a local pro shop that caters to bowhunters.

A pro shop is staffed by knowledgeable people, carries a full line of bows, arrows, and accessories, and can help you set up with the right gear. The guys behind the counter can help you tune your new bow, sight it in, and make sure that everything is in good working order before you walk out the door. If anything goes wrong, or you have questions later, it's easy to come back.

In today's budget-conscious world, many of us try to cut corners and purchase equipment from a large chain store or mail-order house. After you've become experienced in archery, that's not a bad idea—you can save money doing so. However, the personal attention and advice you'll receive at a pro shop are well worth the extra few dollars you'll spend. After bowhunting for many years, I still do most of my shopping at a full-service pro shop for just that reason.

While there are a lot of compound bows out there today (you should begin with a compound bow because it's much easier to shoot them accurately than a traditional longbow or recurve), most all of the major manufacturers produce outstanding models. The same is true with accessories. Just be sure that your equipment matches and gives the finished bow a balance that's easy to carry, hold, and shoot.

Most important, when choosing a bow, don't succumb to the notion that the harder it is to pull, the better everything will be. A pro shop will help you select the right draw weight. Keep in mind nothing is worse than having a bow you cannot easily draw and hold. More draw weight does not necessarily translate into faster arrow flight, since lighter bows shoot true with lighter arrows.

Correct range estimation is the critical factor in bowhunting, and a range finder can eliminate much of the guesswork. Photo Credit: Bob Robb

Another important sighting consideration is the use of a string-mounted peep sight, in conjunction with a limb-mounted bow sight. No one would consider accurate bullet placement possible from a rifle without both a front sight and a rear sight. Likewise, a string-mounted peep adds the same type of arrow placement precision. Compared with shooting without a peep sight, this sighting system will help your accuracy immensely.

A noisy arrow rest is often the source of more than one busted stalk. When you're close to a bull any little sound can blow your cover. When you bring your bow to full draw, the movement of the arrow across the rest can sound like fingernails on a chalk board. Even worse, the sound is amplified by the hollow arrow shaft. Simplicity in construction and silent function are the two factors to consider when selecting an arrow rest.

Next, use a bow-attached quiver instead of a hip or back-carry quiver. The quiver itself adds weight to your bow and acts as a stabilizer. This provides for a steady hold and dampens vibration during

Watch The Wind: Scent control is also critical in bowhunting. An elk 's first line of defense is its nose, and its ability to scent danger is incredible. Washing your hunting garments in scent-free detergent, storing them in a sealed plastic bag away from regular household or garage odors, and wearing rubber-soled shoes or boots will go a long way toward solving the scent problem. However, the most important thing is to always, always, hunt with the wind in your face. Even the slightest breeze will carry your scent to an elk that's downwind of you. If that happens, the party's over. Some bowhunters use a tiny piece of thread tied to the end of their bow as a wind detector. Still, others use a squirt of corn starch, unscented talcum powder, a pinch of down tossed in the air, or a lighter flame. Since there are wind currents that can't be easily felt, I recommend that you consider one of these methods for informed air current observation.

arrow release. More importantly, a bow-attached quiver provides enhanced arrow access without unnecessary movement.

You'll also want to invest in a quality bowhunting range finder. Misjudging the exact distance to the target is one of the biggest reasons for missing. The range finder will help you accurately measure bow-to-target yardage, while you develop a feel for eye-balling distances.

Most backcountry elk hunts involve horses. Carrying a bow in your hand, or slung over your shoulder in the saddle, can present problems. First of all, you may need both hands to control your horse and to stay aboard. Secondly, the bow may poke the horse in the flank or hindquarters at some inopportune moment. When that happens—hang on! If the best way to carry a rifle on horseback is a rifle scabbard, then the same is true for a bow. Take my advice and acquire a bow scabbard. You'll be money ahead in the long run.

Finally, an absolutely quiet bow is of paramount importance. When you're at eyeball-to-eyeball distance from a bull elk, any bowhunter-produced sound can blow hours of stalking. Make sure all of the wheels, pulleys, and any other moving part(s) associated with your bow are well-lubricated and sound-dampened. In extremely cold weather, graphite may need to be substituted for oil-based lubricants. Teflon-coated washers, heat-shrink tubing, and whatever else can be used to quiet down bow noise during the draw and release function should be employed. And don't forget silencers at either end of your bow string/cables.

Practice Makes Perfect: One of the ways bowhunting differs from gun hunting is the amount of practice required to become proficient. Most veteran rifle hunters can leave their guns in the rack all year, go to the local range two weeks before hunting season opens, shoot a box of shells at a target, and then be ready to go. It doesn't work that way in archery.

The best bowhunters I know are constantly practicing. They shoot all year around, tapering off to one or two sessions per week during the off-season, and increasing their practice time until they are shooting 20 to 50 arrows per day every day for two weeks to a month before opening day. Once the season opens, they shoot at least a dozen practice arrows every day to stay sharp.

Practice isn't as difficult as it sounds. For many of us, it's easy to set up a simple archery target in your backyard and shoot a few arrows after work every day. On weekends, an archery session lasting a couple of hours works wonders for your skill level. And that's plenty of time, because fatigue will set in after a few dozen shots. Several short practice sessions are much better than one long one. Practicing while tired only results in developing bad shooting habits.

Once the bow is sighted in and hunting season approaches, try to spend at least half your practice time away from hay bale-type targets set at known distances. Instead, begin practicing at targets set at unknown distances. Judging distance can be a challenge. Since the exact distance from bow to target is not predetermined, your ability to compute that distance accurately will begin to develop.

3-D target shoots—where life-sized animal targets are set at unmarked distances—are the best practice ever devised for bowhunters. Your local archery pro shop can help you find such shoots in your area. If such shoots aren't available, then invest in a 3-D elk target and set it up in your own backyard, an empty field, or at a local range. You'll be surprised at what a difference shooting at a life-size target will make in your level arrow placement confidence.

Lastly, before hunting season, begin practicing with broadheads, not field (or target) points. All arrows fly a little bit differently with broadheads than they do with field points, and you'll probably have to adjust your bow sight slightly to compensate for this difference.

Arrows and Broadheads: There are many choices in arrow shafts, but aluminum and carbon fiber get the nod from most bowhunters. Probably the most popular hunting shaft is the aluminum Gamegetter manufactured by Easton. However, carbon fiber shafts are continuing to grow in popularity. Part of this popularity is the fact that carbon shafts penetrate deeper and are a more rugged arrow. Both factors deserve some consideration when elk are part of the hunting picture. A dozen or so will probably set you back a couple of double sawbucks, but who's keeping track of small change? While arrows are expensive, don't be overly concerned about losing a few in the field. I know a bowhunter that thinks nothing of laying out several thousand dollars for a backcountry elk hunt, then spends hours looking for a lost arrow—go figure.

While arrows of an appropriate weight and spine are significant considerations, whatever broadhead you use is of paramount importance. Broadheads are available in fixed-blade, replaceable-blade, and mechanical models. All of them work (more or less), so the choice of design is one of personal preference. The most critical broadhead feature is blade edge integrity. To kill an elk with an arrow, the broadhead

> **In many areas, this season occurs during the September rut. During this period, elk forego much of their natural caution in a quest to reproduce the species.**

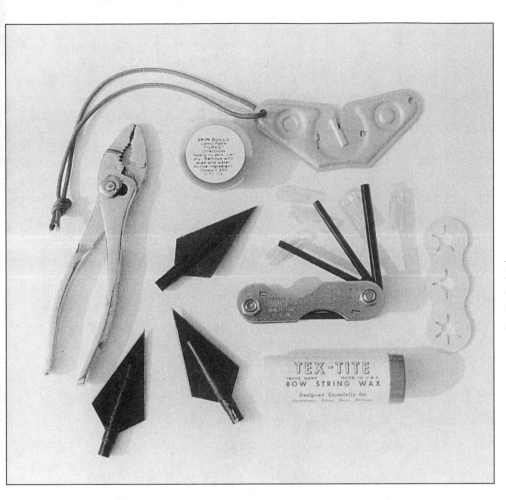

All the right stuff—spare broad-heads, nocks, string wax, camo cover-up, and a pair of pliers—can make or break an archery elk hunt. Photo Credit: Durwood Hollis

must be sharp enough to slice through the blood supply delivery system, not just push it aside. Moreover, thick elk hide and tough cartilage demands that broadheads have to be rugged as well as sharp. Buy the best broadhead you can afford and don't settle for second best.

Furthermore, the broadhead-arrow shaft link must provide the strongest attachment possible. If you don't want to be disappointed, forget about plastic ferrules and look for something in titanium. Like I've said before in these pages, elk are tough—really tough. You want your arrow to blow through both sides of an elk, or stay in the wound channel. Either way, you'll get a good blood trail. If the ferrule breaks, your arrow will separate from the broadhead and fall out. That means the wound closes and you get no blood trail—get the picture?

Silence is Golden: Silence and stealth are the keys to getting a controlled bow shot at an elk less than 35 yards (which in my mind is the ideal maximum distance). Think of yourself as a cat stalking a backyard bird. You have to begin to move slowly, thinking through each movement and step to be successful.

In addition to quieting your bow, silence is also an

The best bowhunters I know are constantly practicing. They shoot all year around.

important consideration when it comes to clothing (hat and gloves included), so forget nylon, denim and canvas—they're too scratchy and noisy. Synthetic outerwear material, like fleece, and wool are the quietest outerwear fabrics around and ideal for bowhunting.

Protection from inclement weather is always a consideration during elk season. Bowhunters should select rain gear that offers protection and is quiet in heavy cover. Avoid coated nylon and waxed cotton for actual hunting purposes. Both fabrics produce high levels of sound amplification and make stalking impossible. Several manufacturers combine a moisture-barrier lining with soft fleece or saddle cloth to produce outerwear that offers superior rain protection in an extremely quiet fabric. Just because a little rain is in the offing doesn't mean your hunting efforts have to be suspended until the storm passes. With the right gear, you can just keep on hunting.

Crepe-soled footwear is a good choice for stalking, however, it doesn't offer the same foot placement control as lug pattern or air bob soles. If the country you hunt in isn't too rugged, crepe-soled boots might be just the ticket. However, if shale-covered slopes, rocky outcroppings, or lots of straight up and down

In addition to silence and stealth, outdoor writer, Bob Robb, also had the right bow, arrow, and broadhead combination. Photo Credit Bob Robb

are part of your hunt environment, then a more aggressive sole pattern is best. This is where fleece boot covers come in handy during the final approach. Fleece boot covers silence movement during the final stalking approach and are another good investment. Many of the best bowhunters take off their boots and stalk in their bare feet (bad idea in snow), or stocking feet. I've tried both methods and have found fleece boot covers to be as quiet as stalking in your bare feet, or in socks, without all of the hassle associated with boot removal. Finally, knee-high rubber boots are recommended for tree-stand hunters. That's because the rubber will prevent your scent from getting on the ground as you walk to and from your tree stand. Leaving a trail of scent will spook elk you never knew were there.

Blend In: Complete camouflage is the order of the day for bowhunting. Choose a pattern that

> **When a bull responds to a call, he is looking for another elk. If he can't see what he's looking for, then his level of suspicion is aroused.**

matches the prevalent foliage in your area. The folks at Realtree (P. O. Box 9638, Columbus, GA 31908, 800/992-9968), Mossy Oak (Haas Outdoors, 200 E. Main St., West Point, MS 39773, 800/331-5624), and Trebark (3434 Buck Mountain Rd., Roanoke, VA 24014, 540/774-9248) all make camouflage patterns that work in a variety of environments. Also, remember to cover your shiny face with face paint or a mask. And don't forget to conceal your hands with drab or camo gloves.

More important than camouflage, is breaking up your outline using available foliage and remaining motionless. By using natural material to shield your body, you will blend into the surroundings like a shadow in bright sunlight. Never forget. A bull elk can pick up the slightest movement at close range.

Bowhunting Strategies: Not unlike riflemen during the general elk season, a bowhunter must find his quarry. An elk hunting axiom states: elk are where elk are, and not anyplace else. That is to say, elk are location-specific. Furthermore, such placement is dependent on adequate food, water, and protective cover. Elk, unlike deer that primarily consume weeds and browse, are chiefly grazers. Since timber country supports limited grassland, elk have to constantly move from one place to another in search of food. Even when open grassy slopes are found, elk will most likely only feed there under cover of darkness.

While elk generally have traditional movement patterns, they can be hard to find. This means that the bowhunter must cover ground—lots of ground. It's like the strategy many boxers use in the ring—stick and move. Move quickly from location to location, stopping only to glass and examine major game trails and crossing points. The more ground you can cover, the better. When you encounter fresh sign (tracks, droppings, recently used wallows, etc.), or elk, then it's time to slow down and start hunting.

You'll learn more about elk in a full season of bowhunting than you ever did in five years of hunting them with a rifle.

Stand hunting can also be effective bowhunting strategy. I would much rather have a bull come to me. Stands are especially deadly over wallows during the heat of the day. However, not every wallow is in use every day. When I encounter a wallow, I mark it on my map. If it has fresh mud scattered around, dripped on an approach trail, or left on nearby trees, then it's a hot prospect. If not, I pass it by and remember to check it again in a day or so. If the sign is fresh, then I make my stand somewhere along the most heavily used approach. Stand hunting in a ground blind or in a tree stand can get boring. Take a pocket book along (sometime it may take more than one before you see elk), and catch up on a little reading to pass the time. Be patient, and when the bull comes, take your best shot.

Elk Hunting Gear: One of the pieces of invaluable gear every bowhunter ought to carry in the field is a pair of binoculars. I use my binoculars both for distance glassing and close cover work in the timber.

Some gentle persuasion with a cow call was all it took to bring this enormous bull within range of Arizona elk guide, Frank Lopez. Photo Credit: Duwane Adams

While I have caught elk in the open, more frequently they are found at the edge of cover. How to glass and what to look for is discussed in depth in a subsequent chapter, so I won't spend a lot time with that aspect of elk hunting here. However, you can cover many times more ground with your binoculars than you can with boot leather. Don't just carry your binoculars around, use them!

Another piece of gear that really makes a difference, especially for bowhunters, is a cow elk call. If you use an elk bugle to locate bulls, they may, or may not respond. In fact, a bull may hear your bugle, remain silent and push his cows into the next drainage. Think about it; if you were a bull elk would you want to fight everyone in the neighborhood? Quite frankly, my experience bugling up elk has been a mixed bag. If the bull is heavy into rutting activities, he might come in all crazy-eyed, with his tongue hanging out and pumped up for a fight—or not. The rest of the time, it's hit or miss. Fortunately, a cow call seems to work all the time.

I remember how effectively outfitter/guide John Winter used his cow elk call during one September hunt in the Wyoming's Bridger-Teton Wilderness. I had spooked a bull off of a ridge into some heavy timber. John quickly pulled me behind a screen of cover and motioned for my hunting partner to do the same. Then he brought his cow call into play. After a few squeals and squeaks from the call, like a puppet on a string, the bull emerged from the timber. John continued coaxing the animal toward us until he was well within range. I didn't have a shot, but my hunting partner did. Apparently, the bull never winded us. After running off into the timber, he heard the cow call, became curious, and returned to see what the commotion was all about—bad mistake.

When a bull responds to a call, he is looking for another elk. If he can't see what he's looking for, then his level of suspicion is aroused. More than once, I've had a bull peer right through some intervening cover and look right at me. In such a situation, if you twitch the bull is history. The best approach is to give the bull what he wants.

Fellow outdoor writer and seasoned bowhunter, Bob Robb, often carries a single elk antler and uses it to attract an elk's attention. When a bull "hangs up" just outside bow range, Bob pokes the antler out of the brush and lets the elk see it. The twisting and

Outfitter Duwane Adams, and guide, Frank Lopez, put Keith Biggs on this huge Arizona bull. It takes stealth and the ability to blend into your surroundings to put an arrow in an elk of this caliber. Photo Credit: Duwane Adams

Every bull taken with a bow is a trophy!
Photo Credit: Jim Matthews

turning of the antler is sometimes all the convincing a bull needs. "It's a hassle carrying the antler all over the place, but it has turned the trick for me more than once," Robb told me.

Another approach to the same problem can be solved with an elk decoy. It can be difficult to find an elk decoy, but if you locate one— buy it! The faux elk might not fool you, but to a rut-blinded bull elk, it can be a real inducement. The whole concept is to focus the bull's attention on the decoy, not on the caller. Placed in an open shooting lane, an elk decoy can be used to your shot set-up advantage.

Cover scents for bowhunters are always a debatable subject. Some believe strongly in their effectiveness. Others eschew them entirely. However, nothing will substitute for keeping the wind in your favor. In addition to cow-in-rut (estrus) scent, another cover scent that I've used with considerable success in Arizona and New Mexico is skunk. Pungent and overpowering, the smell of the wood's kitten can mask a multitude of odors— including human. I've had elk look right at me, inhale a big whiff of skunk scent, and then return to feeding. If that isn't a testimony, then I don't know what is!

The Rewards of Bowhunting: It's hard to describe the feelings you get inside when bowhunting elk. You are forced to become a quieter, secretive individual as you strive to become part of the woods. You begin to see more of all that's about you—small animals, birds, foliage differences, and spider webs—things that you never even noticed while carrying a rifle.

Because it's so difficult to get a good shot at an elk with your bow, you'll spend much more time actually observing them, learning their habits, how they move, what they look for, and so on. You'll learn more about elk in a full season of bowhunting than you ever did in five years of hunting them with a rifle. Best of all, you'll learn about yourself.

When it finally all comes together and you harvest your first elk with a bow, the feeling of accomplishment is indescribable. There are no cheap, easy, or quick elk in bowhunting. Every single success is earned through weeks of preparation, practice and dues paid in the woods. Even a spike bull, a rag-horn or a cow is an animal to be proud of. Frankly, every elk taken with a bow is a trophy. And that's says a lot about bowhunting.

Chapter 15

Through The Looking Glass

An optical advantage is the key to elk hunting success!

While working on a magazine article several years ago, I had an opportunity to interview Arizona hunting guide, Duwane Adams. This man's reputation for success among big game hunters had become legendary. However, success didn't come easy for Duwane. He earned it through countless hours in the field.

Like most of us, Duwane's early days as a hunter didn't put any trophy heads in the record books. "I killed a lot of elk, but none of them were worth hanging on the wall! It seemed as if every decent bull I saw was hightailing it out of the country long before there was any possibility of a shot."

"At first," he continued, "it was hard to believe that a pair of binoculars could make that much difference. I'd used binoculars for years, but they hadn't been a particularly important part of my hunting gear. All that ever mattered to me was an accurate rifle, a handful of shells, a sharp knife, and a backpack. With that gear, I'd tagged more than my fair share of bulls. Of course, I hadn't ever taken what you'd call a trophy-quality elk. I'd seen a big bull or two over the years, but they always managed to slip away by the time I realized it. When I finally discovered the difference a pair of binoculars can make, it turned my hunting world upside-down. Now, if I can't glass it, I won't hunt it. If you really want to be a successful elk hunter, then learn how to glass."

After that interview with Adams, I began to appreciate the value of binoculars as a hunting tool. Realizing

The knowledgeable selection and use of binoculars can unlock the doorway to successful elk hunting. Photo Credit: Durwood Hollis

that my knowledge was minimal at best, I read everything I could lay my hands on about optics. It didn't take too long for me to realize that not all binoculars are created equal—or even alike.

Binoculars are nothing more than two separate monocular components which have been paired along a shared axis. The axis, or hinge, allows up and down rotation of each monocular to accommodate the viewer's eye positioning. Beyond this shared construction, there are differing prism positioning systems (porro prism and roof prism) and focusing systems (center-focus, monocular focus, and focus-free) used in the construction of binoculars. Each configuration provides certain features that offer enhanced utility for differing environments and requirements.

Porro Prism or Roof Prism: The traditional porro prism configuration is the familiar offset "z" shape of the joined monocular halves. Since the shape of the housing allows for wider prism mounting tolerances during manufacturing, less time is involved. Correspondingly, porro prism binoculars cost less to manufacture. Unlike the offset "z" shape of the porro prism configuration, the individual monocular halves of roof prism binoculars are completely straight tubes. Precise tolerances must be maintained when mounting the internal prisms, which adds time and cost to the manufacturing process. This increase in manufacturing cost is reflected in the retail price of roof prism binoculars. Also, the nature of prism placement in this configuration produces an overall reduction of light transmission, compared to a similar porro prism product, by 10 to 12 percent. However, the minor light loss and increased retail price are compensated for by lighter weight and a more compact instrument.

Binocular Magnification: Binoculars are described by a set of numbers, such as 7X35, 8X40, 10X50, which indicates both the magnification (first number), and

When it comes to serious glassing, nothing beats a pair of high-magnification, tripod-mounted binoculars. Used in this manner, the image remains steady.
Photo Credit: Durwood Hollis

Even in close cover, binoculars can give you an edge. Look for pieces of an elk, then put the puzzle together.
Photo Credit: Jim Matthews

the diameter of the objective lenses (second number). For example, 8X binoculars will magnify an image eight times larger than when the same image is viewed by the unaided eye. However, the greater the magnification, the smaller the field-of-view. For this reason, an increase in magnification should be accompanied with a corresponding increase in the diameter of the objective lenses. For mixed cover use, binoculars in the range of 6X, 7X, and 8X magnification will be the most useful. When glassing a wide expanse of elk country the increased magnification of 10X, 12X, and even 15X binoculars will come in handy.

Compact or Full-Size Binoculars: Over the last couple of decades, a movement toward smaller and leaner binoculars has emerged. However, reductions in binocular size and weight will result in a loss of field-of-view and light transmission. For the elk hunter, this means that shirt-pocket binoculars are of limited use for serious glassing and use during low-light conditions. However, compact binoculars still have a place in the scheme of things. I regularly carry a pair and use them frequently when making a stalk. It's just easier to reach into my shirt pocket when I am on my hands and knees, rather than dealing with a set of full-size binoculars.

However, if you really want to get serious about glassing, full-size binoculars are the way to go. Ten-power (10X) magnification is the bare minimum necessary to get into this game. Better yet, step up to 12X or 15X, with corresponding 50 or 60mm objective lenses.

The best way to glass is to sit down, grasp the instrument with both hands, and brace your elbows against your knees. When possible, shorten the neck strap and exert some pressure against it to help stabilize the binoculars. Settle into position quickly without excessive movement and noise. A piece of closed-cell foam under your rear end can help make extended glassing sessions a lot more tolerable. And consider tripod-mounting any pair of binoculars with magnification greater than 10X. This way, the weight of the binoculars rests on a stable platform and the image remains steady.

You may get a few "mill stone around your neck" comments from friends, but so what! If you want elk in the freezer and antlers on the wall, then get the right binoculars and learn how to put them to use.

Field-of-View: The horizontal distance of the area viewed through binoculars, expressed in feet at a given distance (in binoculars, this distance is usually 1,000 yards), is called the field-of-view. This viewing field narrows as the magnification of the binoculars increases. This can be compensated for by an increase in the size of the objective lenses, or by a specially configured wide-angle instrument. However, some binoculars that are advertised as "wide field" really don't have any wider field-of-view than other models. This just proves that an advertising claim is nothing more than an assertion that may, or may not, have any basis in fact.

Exit Pupil: The size of the exit pupil in a set of binoculars is determined by dividing the magnification (power) of the instrument into the diameter of the objective lenses. Thus, an 8X40 set of binoculars has an exit pupil of 5 millimeters. The larger the exit pupil, the greater the amount of light is transmitted through the instrument to the viewer's eyes. However, the eye has a limit to the amount of useable light that can enter therein. Unlike the binoculars, which have a constant exit pupil, the human eye can adjust to ambient light conditions. In full daylight, the pupil is smaller; at the edge of night, it expands. The normal range of the pupil is approximately 2 millimeters in full daylight, opening to a maximum of 7 millimeters in total darkness. At both dawn and dusk, the pupil opening is approximately 3-1/2 millimeters. Thus, the 5-millimeter exit pupil found in the 7X35, 8X40, and 10X50 binoculars is adequate for all usual light conditions.

Lens Coating: Image transmission through binoculars is critical under less than optimum light conditions. Since elk are most active early in the morning, and late in the evening, you need to select an instrument that offers the brightest viewing image possible. Most of us who use binoculars are under the impression that light passes through their instruments without

any degradation. Unfortunately, that is simply not true. After light rays enter the lens system, a significant amount is lost through reflection from one lens surface to another. The amount lost varies depending on the number of lens elements, but as a general rule light deprivation is about 5 percent at each lens surface. Since all binoculars have multiple lens elements, this reflective loss can impair visual acuity. To compensate, optics manufacturers coat their lens with a dielectric coating (usually magnesium fluoride) on each air-to-glass surface. This coating reduces the reflective light loss to about one-percent, and allows enhanced light transmission through the lens system.

Since lens coating drives up the cost of manufacturing, inexpensive binoculars generally only have the outside air-to-glass lens surfaces coated. This will result in a significant image degradation. Such products are usually advertised as having "coated lenses," but don't be fooled. Such wording is a dead giveaway that at least some lens system components are uncoated. More costly binoculars usually feature multi-layer exotic lens coating on all air-to-glass surfaces. This provides the ultimate in light transmission and image resolution. These upscale instruments will have the words, "fully coated lenses," or similar wording, in their descriptive material.

Focusing Systems: Center-focus binoculars feature a centrally-mounted focus wheel. This wheel connects to a worm gear that moves both eyepieces simultaneously. The in-and-out movement of the eyepieces allows the user to focus the instrument on objects viewed at varying distances. Additionally, one eyepiece usually features an individual plus or minus adjustment to make up for the slight image perception difference between the viewer's eyes. Individual focus binoculars lack the central focus wheel and instead provide focus adjustment on each monocular half (similar to the plus and minus adjustment usually found on one eyepiece of a central-focus design). Focus-free binoculars are focused during manufacture to provide distortion-free image resolution throughout the normal viewing range.

Carrying Binoculars: There are lots of ways to carry binoculars in the field. Some compact binoculars are small enough to slip into a breast pocket or into the front of your jacket. If the carrying strap is a bit too long, you can use a plastic cord-lock (obtainable at backpack shops) to shorten it. Medium-size binoculars are usually too large to fit into a shirt pocket. In this case, you might consider using some type of carrying system. Such systems utilize a restraint to keep the binoculars from pounding up and down on your chest. Larger binoculars must be carried in your pack, or they can be slung around the neck and carried under your arm. I've carried a pair of rather large 15X60 binoculars under my arm for many occasions without a problem. Supported in this manner, the instrument is out of the way, doesn't flop up and down, and is readily available when needed. Replacing the factory-supplied neck strap with one made from fabric-covered neoprene rubber will also enhance carrying comfort. The soft, resilient material spreads the weight of the binoculars over a wider surface and prevents the strap from cutting into the back of your neck. If you have trouble finding this accessory at your local hunting shop, try a camera dealer.

Successful elk hunters spend time—sometimes all day long—behind their binoculars. Photo Credit: Durwood Hollis

Binocular Applications: Binoculars can be used for occasional viewing or serious glassing, both of which are entirely distinct operations. Occasional viewing is how most elk hunters use binoculars. When you throw up your binoculars to quickly scan distant country or to identify an individual animal, the binoculars are put to short-term use as an adjunct to your own eyesight. On the other hand, serious glassing can be defined as extended usage that will enhance your hunting strategy. To be more specific, if you use your binoculars for a few moments to scan the countryside, that's occasional viewing. If you use your binoculars for an extended period of time (Duwane Adams has been known to sit behind a pair of tripod-mounted binoculars all day long) to pick apart the countryside in your search for game, that's serious glassing.

Occasional viewing is far less optically demanding than serious glassing. Thus, the size, magnification, focus system, and purchase price of occasional-use binoculars are usually different from those found in a serious, extended-use instrument. For occasional use, instruments providing 6X, 7X, and 8X magnification are usually selected. If the binoculars are used in full daylight conditions, then the need for a large exit pupil is not nearly so important as the overall size and weight of the instrument. For this reason, tiny roof prism binoculars with 20mm and 25mm objective lenses allow for an extremely compact package. However, if binoculars are used from dawn to dusk, then 35mm, 40mm, or 50mm objective lenses will offer greater light-gathering ability.

Central-focus binoculars are probably the easiest to use, but if you plan to hunt in the wet weather of the

Cost Does Make a Difference: An elk hunter needs the very best in optics. When it comes to binoculars and riflescopes, don't be a bargain shopper. There is always a nexus between manufacturing cost and retail price. An increase in production cost results in a corresponding increase in selling price. It is impossible for a manufacturer to assemble an optical instrument that offers both quality materials and quality construction at an inexpensive purchase price. Forget about the advertising hype and look carefully at the product specifications.

Pacific Northwest, Alaska, or parts of Canada, then individual focus binoculars offer better protection against moisture. When you're in the saddle, horses don't ever seem to stand still for more than a moment. By the time you're able to bring binoculars into play, whatever you wanted to view is long gone. If binoculars are used on horseback, then the nod goes to the focus-free variety. And if a four-wheeled vehicle serves as elk country transport (an approach used on many private ranches), the focus-free binoculars again warrant consideration.

How To Glass: Consistently finding game with binoculars, in a wide variety of terrain, is not as easy as it seems. Learning to use your binoculars the right way takes practice. First of all, select a glassing position that offers clear visibility for an extended distance. This enables you to maximize your viewing area without constantly changing position. At prime time (early morning and late evening), it's important that you get into position prior to first light, or before the sun sinks below the horizon.

Most hunters use binoculars to look at elk they have already seen with the unaided eye. Since elk have superior distance vision, they may already be aware of your presence. The use of binoculars should be centered on finding elk that are unaware of your proximity, not the other way around. Likewise, you won't find elk by using your binoculars like a kitchen broom. Attempting an optical sweep just won't get it. If binoculars are to be of any use at all, then optical scrutiny is the name of the game.

Begin glassing at the extreme edge of the instrument's viewing range. You'd be surprised just how many elk you can locate at a mile or more. As the day progresses, the sun's heat will create a mirage that inhibits distance viewing. In the first few hours after dawn, you'll be able to cover more ground with your binoculars, than on foot. Best of all, the elk you find will never know you're anywhere in the vicinity. It is possible to locate elk at such a distance that making an immediate approach may be out of the question. Simply store that optical data and plan an approach later in the day, or the following morning. Either way, you're ahead of the game.

When you glass, use a mental grid to section off your field of view into individual elements. The best description of this process is to imagine that you're looking for a particular person seated in the opposite bleachers at a football game. Begin at the top of the bleachers and glass along the entire length of each row. Once you've exhausted all of the visual data on one row, then shift your viewing efforts to the next bleacher down, and continue the process until you've found who you're looking for. Using this technique, it's possible to cover the entire area as thoroughly as a spy satellite would.

Since focus-adjustable binoculars have a very shallow depth-of-field, it is possible to use this to your advantage. When I am glassing, I try to peel the vegetation away—one layer at a time. To accomplish this, focus on the nearest line of trees or brush. Then, using the focus adjustment knob, move through subsequent layers of vegetation. When it comes to finding elk, you'd be surprised at just how effective this technique can be.

Even though you've glassed an area thoroughly without success, don't give up. Once, I spent more than hour glassing an isolated Alpine meadow. A short time before I arrived, my hunting companion had seen a couple elk feeding in the middle of that verdant utopia. However, by the time I got there, the elk had disappeared. We were situated on top of a cliff, well above the meadow. It appeared that everything would have been visible. Something was wrong. Elk just don't disappear that easily. What I didn't know was that the meadow had several benches, each one capable of hiding more than one animal. That fact became apparent when I watched a cow elk climb uphill directly from one-bench to another. In a few minutes, more elk made their appearance—including a fine 6x6 bull. Obviously, persistence has its own rewards. If I had given up early on, that particular bull would have escaped unseen. To my credit, a .338 Winchester Magnum bullet settled the matter—once, and for all.

Not all binoculars are created equal—or even alike.

Since elk are seldom standing out in the open, finding animals with your binoculars may present a challenge. However, there are certain optical clues to look for. Nearly everything in nature grows vertically, so anytime you see a horizontal shape, check it out. You'll never know when it might just turn out to be an elk.

Of course, any movement deserves a thorough evaluation. Even when bedded down during the heat of the day, elk will stand up and turn around, flick their ears, and move short distances. Also, any unusual reflected light seen with the binoculars may be the gleam of a set of antlers. Most of the time you'll look for parts of an elk rather than the whole animal. Other visual clues, like the "Y" formed at the ear and head junction of an elk, movements of animals in the brush, or even a puff of dust warrants more than a casual glance. Look for the pieces, they may turn out to be a whole elk.

Another visual tip-off is the characteristic creme-colored elk rump patch. Nothing else in the woods looks like it. When light hits this lightly pigmented hair, it almost shines. On a distant hillside, this lighter color can reflect light like a mirror. Likewise, the distinctive contrast between the dark hair on an elk's head and neck, and the buff-colored body is another visual give-away. I look for anything that's out of place, or off-color, and then try to turn it into an elk. Most of the time, it's nothing. The rest of the time, it's elk!

Close Cover Binocular Use: Binoculars have a place, even in dark timber. While you may only be able to glass a short distance, binoculars will enable you to peel back all but the heaviest cover. Like turning the pages of a magazine, layer by layer you can optically separate the seen from the unseen.

I once watched a good bull and handful of cows drift into some heavy timber from a distance of more than two miles. By the time I made my way to where the elk were last seen, the heat of the day was already starting to build. Reasoning that the animals had already bedded down for the afternoon, I began to formulate a hunting plan. The critical part of that plan was knowing where the elk were well before entering their security zone. Using my binoculars, I looked deep into the shadows until defined shapes came into view. Once I was assured that there were no elk in close proximity, I moved forward a few

yards. Stopping, I repeated the procedure. Glass and move, glass and move. The pattern was repeated until I found my first elk.

Because the elk were scattered across an area of about 25 square yards, it took some time to find the bull. Actually, I never really found the bull, he just sort of appeared. He was so well hidden, I looked past him repeatedly. What caught my attention was the top tine of an antler. It just looked out of place. At first, I didn't pay any attention to the antler. In fact, it just looked like a piece of a branch. Several different times the antler tine was in my field of view, but it appeared to me to be just more optical clutter. However, while glassing a solitary cow elk feeding in the shadows, I noticed the funny looking branch had changed position. Right then and there, I changed my optical focus. Using the binoculars to peer through the foliage, the shiny piece of branch became an elk antler. Sizing up the situation, I abandoned the binoculars and brought my riflescope into play. It took a little time to find the right opening through which to place a bullet, but that bull never

A high-end variable scope is a good match-up for a long-range bolt-action rifle. Photo Credit: Durwood Hollis

even knew what hit him. You see, binoculars are useful even in dark timber.

Carrying binoculars while you're stalking can present a dual challenge. Having ready access to binoculars can provide updated optical information during the stalk. However, just try crawling through knee-high sage brush while toting a pair of binoculars around your neck. When you're on your elbows and knees, the binoculars will probably drag on the ground. This can damage the surface of the optics, as well as coat the entire instrument with dust and debris. Compromise the focusing system with some grit and the instrument may fail to operate properly. Likewise, scratch the optical surfaces and you can degrade the viewed image. Furthermore, carrying anything that can drag, snag, or catch in the brush can turn a hushed stalk into a clamorous march. This is where a tiny pair of palm-size binoculars really comes in handy. Granted, small binoculars have a limited field of view and a less than optimal exit pupil. When used in full daylight situations, however, they can work for you even with these limitations.

Scope Sense: All of the optical science involved in the creation of binoculars also applies to riflescope construction. Features like instrument configuration (size), magnification (power), field-of-view, exit pupil, and lens coating all apply equally to scopes. Furthermore, the stabilization of the instrument's internal atmosphere by replacing the oxygen with nitrogen eliminates fogging on the lenses. Keep these matters in mind while we discuss riflescopes and their applications.

Many times, elk hunters fail to realize that the selection of an appropriate riflescope is paramount to shooting success. The two major scope configurations are fixed-power and variable-power. Fixed-power scopes have pre-set magnification (power), contain fewer optical components than a variable, and are less costly to manufacture. If you're on a limited budget, these instruments are a better value than a low-priced variable. Variable scopes offer a user-adjustable range of magnification. A low-power variable (1-4X, or 1-4.5X) provides a better sight picture than open sights in close cover, and does so without compromising its optical ability on long shots. Variable scopes offering greater upper end magnification (2-7X, 3-9X, or 2.5-10X) are best suited to mixed cover work or extended range presentations. While the variable allows the hunter to adjust the magnification to each individual shooting situation, scope selection should still be appropriate to the caliber.

Instrument Size: Like binoculars, riflescopes are also available in both full-size and compact configurations. The differences between the two include overall length, weight, and field-of-view. Tailoring the scope to the length and weight of an individual rifle can be a significant consideration. While the full-size scope is the preferred selection for rifles with full- or magnum-length actions, such an instrument may simply be too large for carbine-length rifles.

Reticles: Within each scope, a reticle has been placed to facilitate precise shot placement. The reticle may be a simple free-floating dot or circle, a pair of crosshairs, an upright tapered post and crosshair, or other similar arrangement. Scopes for big game hunting usually contain a set of crosshairs—the most popular being the plex type. The plex reticle is a pair of coarse crosshairs tapering or dropping down to fine crosshairs at the point of intersection. The coarse crosshairs provide instant target bracketing and the thinner middle sections allow precise bullet placement. Usually, the scope manufacturer will indicate—in degrees or inches—the area that the fine crosshairs cover at 100 yards. This allows the shooter to utilize the scopes for rough range estimation.

Electronic Amplified Sighting Instruments: These optical sighting devices feature an adjustable aiming point that is projected within the instrument body and serves the same purpose as a reticle. This battery-powered, illuminated dot can be adjusted to remain visible under all lighting conditions. While most of these instruments are non-magnifying, some manufacturers offer an attachment that can provide limited image magnification. The illuminated dot instantly

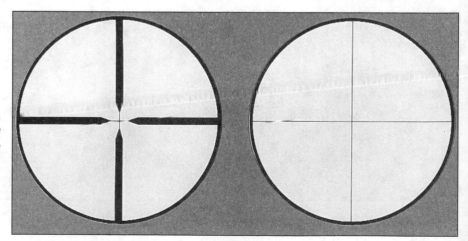

A duplex style reticle (left) is easier to pick up in low light conditions than the standard crosshairs (right). Photo Credit: Bushnell

Scope mounts are the critical component in a sighting system. Many shifts in bullet impact blamed on the scope are actually due to improper mounting. Photo Credit: Redfield

draws your eye to the target, making these sights extremely useful in dark timber and on running game. There is no need for precise target acquisition or concern about rifle positioning, where the dot hits the target is where your bullet will go.

Scope Mounting: Most scope problems can be traced to loose mounts. If there's even the slightest movement of the scope or mounting system, accuracy will suffer. Most mounts consist of a base(s) and rings. However, some rifles—such as the Ruger Model 77—have an integral base machined into the receiver. This eliminates the need for a separate base and provides for the direct attachment of the scope rings to the receiver.

Even with the optical advantage of a rifle-scope, there is no substitute for a solid rest. Photo Credit: Durwood Hollis

Since all modern rifles (and some blackpowder models) come from the factory pre-drilled and tapped for scope mounting, you'll first need to remove the plug screws. Next, position the scope base(s) in its (their) relative position(s). Apply a small amount of Loc-Tite or clear nail polish to the mounting screws and attach the base(s). Make sure the mount screws are tight, but not overly so. Using a drop of thread fixative on each screw, attach the lower halves of the scope rings to the base(s) following the manufacturer's instructions. Place the scope in the lower halves of the rings and loosely attach the top halves. Place the scope so that the elevation (up-and-down) adjustment turret is on top, and the windage (left-to-right) turret is on the right side of the scope. Place the rifle on a flat surface, or into a padded vise, and rotate the scope in the rings until the verticle crosshair is straight up-and-down. Next, slide the scope back-and-forth to provide adequate distance from your eye to the eyepiece. When you have the scope in position, apply a small amount of thread fixative to each ring screw and tighten.

Even though you've glassed an area thoroughly without success, don't give up.

Scope Usage: Where shots seldom exceed 100 yards (dark timber), I would put a 3X fixed-power scope—with a post-and-crosshair reticle—on my rifle. As a close cover alternative, a 1-4X, 1-4.5X, or 1-6X variable would merit consideration. For mixed cover elk hunting, a 4X fixed, or a 2-7X, 3-9X, or 2.5-10X variable would be my choice. Interestingly, both the 4X fixed-power and the 2-7X variable are approximately the same size and weight in their full-size configurations. Since there's heavy competition between manufacturers in the fixed-power arena, the 4X is cheaper. However, the 2-7X offers enhanced flexibility for a variety of sighting situations.

The Optical Advantage: Binoculars and riflescopes are two of the best tools an elk hunter can use. Selected intelligently, binoculars can make the difference between elk hunting success or failure. Likewise, when you have the bull of a lifetime in your scope, you are able to take full advantage of your rifle's ballistic capabilities.

Chapter 16

A Roaring Good Time

Elk calling—the sound of success

A book on elk hunting wouldn't be complete without some commentary on artificial elk vocalization. Unfortunately, elk calling is a mixed bag of tricks—sometimes it works. Other times it doesn't. During the height of the rut, an elk bugle can work wonders. However, this period is highly variable and an elk bugle isn't a magic wand. The bugle, which can draw a bull like a magnet one day, can also send him packing the next. Furthermore, many bulls simply remain silent no matter what the vocal provocation. Even if you arouse a quiet bull, you'll never know. Either he'll slip in when you least expect him, or you'll give up after a couple bugles and leave. In each instance, the call failed to produce the desired results.

The Call: There are principally four types of elk calls: internal diaphragm, external diaphragm, reed, and calls based on a tube design. The internal diaphragm call is made to fit inside of your mouth, against the hard palate. This type of call uses a thin latex reed that produces the actual sound. Such calls may employ one, two, or even three reeds to produce different tones. While the internal diaphragm call leaves your hands free, it isn't for everyone. You'll need lots of practice to become proficient with this type of call, and some folks just can't seem to use it at all. The external diaphragm call uses the same latex reed material, but the call is configured in such a way that you can produce the same sound without having to place the diaphragm inside of your mouth. Reed-type calls use a metal, plastic, or rubber (a rubber band) reed, set in a hand-held fixture, to produce vari-

The forest is an elk caller's music hall. His hidden audience may, or may not, appreciate the sound of his horn. Photo Credit: Bob Robb

The roar of a bull elk is the most distinctive sound in the woods. Photo Credit: Randall Cooley/Rocky Mountain Elk Foundation

ous sounds. While not as flexible as either the internal or external diaphragm call, this type of call is still a solid choice. Elk calls based on a tube design are one of the oldest of elk calling devices. Despite the advent of newer call technology, a tube call still can work. I've used a tube call made by P. S. Olt (12662 Fifth St., P. O. Box 550, Pekin, IL 61554, 309/348-3633) for many seasons. The call, designed to produce the squeal of a spike bull, has drawn response when nothing else worked.

Elk Vocalizations: Elk are real talkers. Bulls can bugle, squeal, grunt, gunk, bark, chirp, and mew like a cat. Cows also can make a lot of noise, but cow talk is generally restricted to barks, chirps, and soft mews. Most elk callers would be best served keeping their efforts restricted to bugling, grunting, creating cow chirps and mews. If you try to imitate the entire range of elk vocalizations, you're bound to make a mistake somewhere.

Nonverbal Communication: Elk also often direct their sexual frustration toward a convenient bush or tree. These mock attacks can become quite loud and will be heard for a considerable distance. You can imitate the sound of a bull raking a tree by using a stick and scraping it up and down a nearby tree. As an alternative, use the stick to beat a small bush or tree.

> **Calling down slope seems to work better than calling uphill. And when you're on top you can cover more country with less effort.**

The tree scraping sound carries quite a long way and should be used when the bull is some distance off. Bush beating or trashing is a more subtle means of communication and should be used when the bull is in close proximity.

The sound of antler contact is also quite distinctive. How well elk respond to antler rattling hasn't been well established. No doubt the inconvenience of carrying a set of overly large antlers to the field, as well as manually attempting to produce fighting sounds, has proven to be difficult. Nevertheless, elk rattling does have its adherents in some quarters.

Get Started: Many hunters are just too embarrassed to use their call. Calling elk is a learning experience. Everyone who has used a call went through the initial stage of sounding like a goose with hemorrhoids. You'll never learn how to use your call correctly if you don't try. Since they are the easiest call to master, I would suggest that you start out with an external diaphragm or reed bugle. Then after you've become proficient with that call, give the internal diaphragm call a try. Initially, most folks struggle with an internal diaphragm elk call. Be prepared. It will take time and practice to master the internal diaphragm. However, once you are able to replicate the sound of an elk bugle—it will seem

The Best Time To Call: Judging from bull response, late afternoon and early evening seems to be the best time to call. However, early morning can also be productive. I've even had bulls respond during midday. You just never know when a bull is going to sound-off in response to your calling efforts. For this reason, both bugling and resonant cow calling can be effective locator calls all day long.

This 5x4 satellite bull came to a cow call like a puppet on a string. Photo Credit: Durwood Hollis

easy. Best of all, you'll have your hands free to bring your bow or rifle into play.

Can He Hear You And Can You Hear Him?: How far away your call can be heard will depend on your position and prevailing winds. Sound travels in a straight line in all directions simultaneously. If there are barriers—terrain, vegetation, or prevailing winds—these barriers will inhibit the distance that your calling can be heard. Likewise, the same barriers can prevent you from hearing a response. I am convinced that an elk can hear sound at much greater distance than a human. There have been times when a bull has been bugling loudly, but I couldn't hear him. Only when I moved my position, the bull changed location, or the wind shifted, was I able to detect his reply. For these reasons, I like to give each calling location at least 15 to 20 minutes before moving. This provides enough time for the bull to move closer, where his reply is more audible, or for the prevailing wind to bring his call to my ears.

Calling down slope seems to work better than calling uphill. And when you're on top you can cover more country with less effort. I like to follow a ridge line or plateau top, bugling down into each canyon as I go. If I get a reply, or hear a bull bugling on his own, then the real hunt begins.

If I don't hear anything after a couple of tries on my bugle, then I like to switch to a cow call. You'd be surprised at how many times a bull never replied to my bugle, but sounded off loudly when I switched to a cow call. When the cow call is used as a locator call, pump up the volume as much as possible. If a bull replies, then tone things down a bit. It's all about locating elk. Once you know there's a bull in the immediate area, then it's time to get busy.

What Now?: If a bull responds to your calling, three things can happen. First, he can move in the opposite direction. In that case, his bugle will begin to get fainter and fainter. If you want to catch up with this bull, you better get on the move—and now! Second, the bull can continue to respond without changing his location. He may not want to leave his cows, or he perceives that the bull he hears (you) isn't a

Okay. You've got his attention, now what? Photo Credit: Bob Robb

threat. In either case, you need to press him. This can be accomplished by increasing the pitch and tempo of your calls, or by closing the gap between you and the bull, or both. The third thing that can happen is that the bull may quit bugling entirely. This bull has probably already been fooled by a call, so now he's being more cautious. Since he has already given away his position, you can try to move closer.

A word of caution—if the bull sees you, it's all over. When you move, use whatever cover is available. Try to blend into the surroundings and avoid exposing yourself to full sunlight. Move into the wind and be aware of any cow elk in the immediate area. Use your cow call to cover any inadvertent noise. When you think you're close enough, try shocking the bull into action by bugling. He might just think that a rival has moved in on his territory. In this case, he may just come running. As an alternative, get on your cow call and try to sound lost, lonely, and receptive.

A word of caution—if the bull sees you, it's all over.

Be Prepared: When you call, realize that a bull elk could appear at any time. Satellite bulls are always on the move, and they often come right into the call without a sound. These bulls aren't big enough to do serious combat, but they are still curious. After getting their behinds kicked a few times, they are reluctant to give away their presence. If they think a herd bull is busy with a rival, they will try to sneak in and get some action going with an available cow. When they come, it's usually without a sound. Even a larger bull, or the herd bull, can respond silently. If you're not ready, then the opportunity may be lost.

On one occasion, while I was bugling down into in a deep canyon, a nice 6x6 bull bailed out of a tiny draw right behind me at less than 50 yards. Of course, this was the last thing I expected. To say the least, I was completely unprepared for such a situation. The elk, on the other hand, was ready to do battle. It was a completely unplanned and unprepared shooting opportunity. Almost instinctively, the rifle came to my shoulder and I slapped the trigger. A certain degree of good fortune is part of any hunt, and this was one of those times. The bullet went where it was intended and the bull was mine. However, I learned something about elk calling. If it can happen, it will. When it does happen, it will occur when you least expect it. After that experience, I never use an elk call without making adequate preparations.

Cow Calling: When you use a cow elk call, you're really not calling cow elk. What you're trying to do is sound like a cow elk. You would be surprised just how far a cow call can be heard. With every elk hunter in the woods blowing an elk bugle, a cow call may be the only sound a bull will come to. In addition to using the call as a locator, I also have used it to calm a bull down after I've accidentally blundered into him in close cover. You may be skeptical, but believe me, a cow elk call works. In fact, I've almost completely abandoned bugling in favor of cow calling. Calls made by Quaker Boy (5455 Webster Rd., Orchard Park, NY 14127, 800/544-1600), and Sceery Game Calls (P. O. Box 6520, Santa Fe, NM 87502, 800/327-4322), are my personal favorites.

Mix It Up: Successful elk callers learn to alternate calling strategies. Don't be afraid to use an elk bugle

Bowhunter, Merritt Pride has learned to expect the unexpected. This is reason enough to get into position for a shot before the elk bulge is brought into play. Photo Credit: Bob Robb

Sometime you have to abandon the new-fangled calls and use an old favorite. Photo Credit: Durwood Hollis

A Roaring Good Time

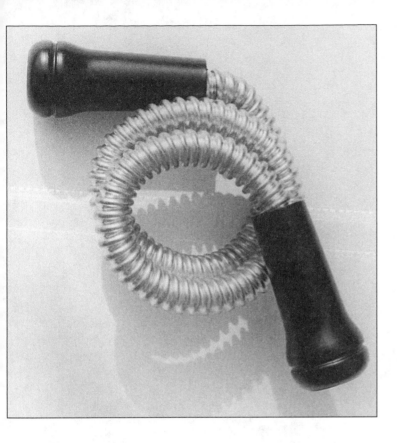

Not the same old sound! When a modern diaphragm or reed call fails to produce the desired response, an old gas pipe elk bugle might just do the job. Photo Credit: Durwood Hollis

and a cow call at the same location. Each call has its own tone, so switching from a diaphragm to a reed can produce an entirely unique sound. Experiment and change both the pitch and tempo of your calling efforts. Just calling to a bull won't get it, talk to him like you mean it.

Elk calling is a game of challenge and seduction. There are no hard and fast rules. Good elk callers are made. That process takes time and lots of practice.

Chapter 17

After The Shot

Game Care Basics

Every hunting season, tons of prime elk venison are wasted by hunters who simply aren't prepared to handle field dressing and skinning duties. Unfortunately, most elk hunters focus on the hunt, rather than the harvest. However, once your hunting activities have met with success, all knowledge of guns and hunting techniques will be of little use in the vital area of game care.

My own interest in big-game hunting didn't come to fruition until I was an adult. While dad had taught me how to field dress all manner of fish, fowl, and small game, the mysteries of big-game field care weren't revealed until my first deer hunt.

Since the process shared many facets with small-game field dressing, I didn't think it was going to be any big deal. Filled with the confidence of a tyro (and theoretical field care knowledge), I shouldered a rifle and entered the woods. Before that weekend was over, I found myself elbow deep into a game care assignment. Without anyone to guide me, I somehow managed to successfully field dress a forked-horn mule deer buck. I do remember that the procedure

The bull is down. Now the real work begins. Photo Credit: Bob Robb

took almost an hour and my clothing ended up covered with blood and other unpleasant material.

Feeling confident, I'd grabbed the nearest antler tine and began the arduous process of transport. I had been smart enough to figure out that the animal would have to be moved from kill site to camp. A couple of hours later, the ultimate reality of big-game hunting had become obvious, even to me.

After I'd arrived at camp with my prize, my hunting companion indicated that we would have to skin, quarter, and cover the meat. Somewhere along the line, the deer had changed from animal to meat, all in the matter of a few hours.

"First, we'll have to hang this deer in the shade," he advised. Not wanting to seem completely ignorant, I agreed. Using the hoist and a sturdy limb of a nearby oak tree as a hoisting point, we managed to pull the buck up off of the ground. Grabbing the plastic bag and a canteen of water, my companion added, "Let's hike back to where you made the kill and see if we can't retrieve what you left up there."

Still somewhat confused about what seemed to be a needless effort, I tagged along obediently. It took the better part of an hour to reach the place where the forked-horn had fallen. The weather was cool and abandoned viscera seemed unmolested by insects, birds, or other animals. Using his knife, my friend bent down and cut both the heart and liver free from the gut pile. Next, he washed both organs carefully and placed them in the bag. My hunting companion felt that the liver and heart were gourmet quality. Unfortunately, I hadn't even thought about them when I initially field dressed the animal. I now realize that organ meats receive rave reviews from some folks.

"Now, let's get back to camp and finish working on your deer," my coach said, as he bagged both items.

Next on the agenda was skinning. Following the lead of my instructor, I carefully separated skin from muscle with a combination of knife work and hide manipulation. When we reached the juncture of the head and neck, we severed the head from the body with a quick twist. Next, I stood out of the way to watch my companion cut through the spinal column with a bone saw, effectively splitting the carcass into halves. As a final act, we covered the two carcass portions with a cloth bag to prevent insect intrusion.

"Now the job is done right. The only thing that's left is to clean up the knives and the saw, salt the hide,

Somewhere along the line, the deer had changed from animal to meat, all in the matter of a few hours.

dispose of the head and feet," said my instructor with a smile. "Then," he added, "I can fill my tag."

While I cut my field care teeth on that little buck, the process is no different with a bull elk. The basic concept of field care is to inhibit spoilage and preserve the meat until it can be refrigerated. This is accomplished by removing all internal organs, dissipating the contained body heat, protecting the meat from insect and animal damage, and keeping the carcass cool and dry. Of course, consideration should be given to organ meats, trophy caping, and hide retention, but those issues are really secondary to meat preservation.

Since elk are considerably larger than deer, dragging a bull back to camp by yourself and hoisting the carcass up into a tree is generally out of the question. Even with three or four men, it's tough dragging an elk anywhere. And if you were to hoist a field-dressed elk off of the ground, the carcass would be so high that you'd need a step ladder to work on it. Because of the size of the animal, most elk field care work is done on the ground. Once you have the carcass cut up and hauled back to camp, you can hang an individual quarter to make it easier to work on.

Whatever you do, don't try to use your knife to cut an elk's throat as a means of hastening death. Even a mortally wounded animal will resist such an effort with every ounce of life left in it. Just approaching a mortally wounded animal can be dangerous. I once watched as a hunter grabbed the antler of a near-dead bull elk. With surprising strength, the elk pitched the astonished nimrod into the air. The only thing that saved the hunter from more serious injury was the fact that the elk expired seconds later. Neck cutting is a complete waste of energy. If the animal is still alive, such an act is shear folly. If the animal is dead, it serves no purpose other than ruining a perfectly good head skin cape.

If you believe the animal to be dead, then approach carefully (preferably from uphill) and use the tip of an arrow, the end of your rifle barrel, or a stick to touch the surface of the eyeball. If the animal blinks, back off immediately. Once out of the way of potential harm, you can make whatever decision is necessary to humanely terminate all signs of life.

Don't Forget: When all signs of life from the elk have ceased, unload your firearm and put it in a safe place. If you're a bowhunter, return the nocked arrow

Use Caution: Once you've located a downed elk, make sure all signs of life have ceased. If you're a bowhunter, the best thing to do is to step back and wait for the combination of blood loss and shock to take effect. This may sound cruel, but the animal feels little pain and really doesn't know what's happening. A rifle hunter can simply use a carefully placed bullet to accomplish the job.

Approach any downed bull with caution. Be prepared, because anything can happen. Photo Credit: Bob Robb

to the quiver and set your bow out of the way. Next, mark, sign, notch, or otherwise validate your elk license or tag. Unless state regulations demand immediate attachment to the carcass, put the license or tag into your wallet and secure the wallet. If you must attach the license or tag directly to the elk, then slip it into a plastic sandwich bag and duct tape it to an antler or a leg. This way, you are less likely to lose the legal documentation of hunting success. If you don't believe this is important, just try explaining away the missing document to a game warden.

Get In Position: If possible, move the elk to a position where you can work on the carcass easily. Try to turn the animal on its back. You may have to use rocks, a length of tree branch, or rope to secure the carcass in place. I once shot an elk on a steep hillside. Before we could even begin field dressing, the antlers

had to be tied to a tree to keep the elk from sliding down the slope. Then we tied each of the four feet to other trees. This was necessary to keep the carcass in a position to facilitate the field dressing. Once you have the animal where you want it, take out your knife and sharpening tool and get ready to go to work.

Basic Field Dressing: Field dressing can be a little messy so remove your jacket or coat, roll up your sleeves, and take off your watch (if you don't, you'll have a devil of a time getting elk blood out of an expandable watch band). The use of elbow-length protective plastic gloves is a good idea. The gloves keep the mess on your hands to a minimum, as well as making clean-up a lot easier. If you have a pair of field dressing gloves with you, put them on.

The first step in gutting an elk is to free the terminal end of the digestive system (that's a delicate way

Disposable field dressing gloves can keep you from becoming part of the mess.
Photo Credit: D&H Products

of expressing a rather distasteful act). Accomplish this by cutting completely around the external margin of the anus to the depth of your knife blade (2 or 3 inches deep should do it). If the animal is a cow, include the external genitalia within the circumference of this incision.

Next, make an incision that runs lengthwise from the top of the male sex organ to the bottom of the rib cage. Use care not to puncture the underlying viscera. The stomach and intestines may billow out of the initial opening, just push them aside and continue cutting. You will notice that a wall of muscle tissue, the diaphragm, separates the abdominal cavity from the chest cavity. Use your knife to cut through the diaphragm on both sides of the carcass, all the way down to the spine.

Now you're ready to detach the leading end of the digestive system. Push the heart and lungs out of the way and reach forward to grab the windpipe (a ribbed tube leading from the mouth to the lungs and stomach). Once you have the windpipe in hand, reach forward with your knife hand (be careful not to cut yourself) and cut the windpipe in half.

Still holding on to the windpipe, pull down and out to remove the heart and lungs from the chest cavity. You will have to cut through several ligaments that attach these structures to the spine. Using your knife carefully, you should be able to free these organs easily. With the lungs and heart free, the stomach and intestines will follow. Once everything is out of the chest and abdominal cavities, grab hold of the lower end of the intestine where it disappears into the pelvic cavity. If you made a thorough initial incision, the urine bladder, the remainder of the intestines, and the anus should come free. If not, use

Special Considerations: Since a skinned carcass will dry out faster than one with the hide left intact, in cold weather it might be more practical to delay the skinning process until just before the trip home. Should the ambient daytime temperature begin to warm, you can cover the meat with a tarp as insulation. The tarp, in conjunction with the intact hide, will help keep the meat cool during the heat of day. If you want to tan the pieces of the skin, spread the hide out on a flat surface (hair-side down) and remove as much residual meat as possible. Salt the hide thoroughly (at least five pounds of table salt per hide piece) and continue to apply salt on the hide to accelerate the drying process. When the hide is nearly dry—but still flexible—roll (skin-side in). Upon your return to civilization, you can make tanning arrangements through your taxidermist, or a tanning house.

After field dressing, an axe or a saw is the right tool for opening up the carcass. Photo Credit: Durwood Hollis

your knife blade to cut points of attachment, including any ligaments and the urethra (urine tube). Take care not to puncture the bladder. However, if it happens, the blood pooled in the abdominal cavity can be used to flush the area clean.

At this point, the entire internal viscera should be free from the carcass. Use your hand to sweep any remaining blood, tissue, digestive material, or fecal material out of the eviscerated animal. If you want to save the heart or liver, remove both organs before they hit the ground. Then, pull the gut pile well away from the carcass. Should scavengers or predators discover the elk in your absence, they will most likely feed on the viscera and leave the carcass alone.

You will note I make no mention of cutting through the rib cage, or the pelvic bone. However, if you don't plan on mounting the head, then cutting through the rib cage will make access to the chest cavity easier. Cut-

> **Field dressing an elk can result in considerable mess. Anything you can do to keep blood, digestive fluids, and visceral contents off of your hands and clothes is a step in the right direction.**

ting through the pelvic bone isn't really necessary to field dress the animal. If you decide to do so, use a saw rather then trying to pound your knife through the pelvic suture (a good way to break the knife blade in half).

Most likely, you'll have to return to camp for help with meat transport (usually mules or a couple of pack horses). Before leaving the area, check around and make sure you have all of your gear. Finally, prop the elk carcass open with a stick. This way the residual body heat will dissipate faster. If there isn't anyone to help, and you plan on packing the meat out alone, you've got a lot more work ahead of you.

Skinning: Separating hide from underlying muscle tissue isn't all that difficult. Most guides prefer to leave the hide on the carcass and do all of the skinning back at camp. This is done to protect the meat as the quarters are hauled in saddle panniers. If you're going to mount the entire head skin, you'll have to cape the front shoulders and the

Skinning out a bull take patience,
a sharp knife, and a deft hand.
Photo Credit: Durwood Hollis

head. This will be discussed in a subsequent paragraph, so let's move on to carcass skinning.

First of all, remove each one of the four lower legs. With your hand, locate the hock joint (the first major joint above the hoof). These joints will look like elbow and knee joints, but they are actually wrist and ankle joints. You will note that there is an upper and a lower protrusion at both sides of each joint. Make a circular cut around the lower protrusion. Once this cut has been made, bend the lower leg backwards, and twist. If you cut through hide and tendons correctly, the lower hock should come free. If you have trouble, there's no harm in using an axe or saw to finish the job.

After you have removed the lower hocks, the next step is to make all the preparatory skinning incisions. Starting with the rear legs, slit the hide from

hock to anus along the rear of both legs. Next, make a cut from the anus to the bottom of the abdominal cavity. Move to the front legs and slit the hide along the rear of each leg. Extend this cut across the side of the chest to the bottom of the sternum. Beginning with one rear hock, use a combination of discreet knife work and pulling the hide to remove the skin. I would suggest that you skin one side of the carcass all the way down to the spinal column. When you have finished skinning one side of the animal, spread the hide out flat on the ground. When you roll the carcass over to finish the job, this will provide protection for the half you've already skinned. Once the hide has been completely removed, the carcass can be quartered and individually covered with a protective bag.

Once the carcass has been split into pieces, it's easier to skin each individual quarter. Photo Credit: Bob Robb

Field Butchering: Meat removal from kill site to base camp, or another location, will necessitate cutting the carcass into manageable pieces. When using mules or pack horses as meat transport, all you'll need to do is to cut the carcass into four quarters. If you're packing the meat out on your back, then skin the carcass, bone out the meat, cover each portion with a protective cloth bag, and leave the heavy hide in the field. Skinned or with the hide left on, you can cut the animal into four quarters by inserting your knife in between the second and third rib. Cut all the way down on both sides of the carcass, from the abdominal incision to the spinal column. Then use a saw or an ax to sever the spine. Now, split each half by cutting through the spinal column lengthwise. Remove the head at the junction of the top vertebrae and skull, cut out the antlers, and the job is done.

If you're going to bone-out the carcass, more than half of the total carcass weight will be eliminated. Who wants to pack out anything other than meat, a set of antlers, and a head cape skin anyway? You don't have to be a butcher to undertake this assignment. Just get in there with your knife and cut the major muscle groups off of the skeletal structure the best way possible. Place each piece of meat into a breathable cloth quarter bag (you did remember to bring the elk quarter bags, didn't you?).

Depending on the elk species and gender, an average carcass will yield about 150-350 pounds of pure meat. Most adult males, in reasonable physical condition, can carry 50-70 pounds on a packframe. If the country is extremely rough, the amount of weight that can be carried will decrease. Generally, it will take one individual about six trips from kill site to camp to retrieve all of the useable meat. Add an additional trip to pack out the capeskin and the antlers, and you can understand why equine assistance is an elk hunting necessity. Two men can cut the work in half. And if you are able to use a wheeled game cart, then the whole project is a lot easier. No matter what you do, you'll still have your work cut out for you.

Meat Storage: In the northern part of the Rocky Mountains, elk country is bear country. Bears like meat. Bears eat elk. So, you'll have to protect the meat from possible ursine marauders. The only way to insure absolute protection is to store the meat in an above-ground cache, or suspend individual quarters by rope in between two trees. The meat should be stored at least 10-feet off of the ground, and well away from intervening trees. Furthermore, all meat should be stored in deep shade, and covered to protect it from rain. If daytime temperatures rise much over 50-degrees for an extended period of time, then transport the meat to refrigerated containment as soon as practical.

Trophy Work: If you decide to have your elk head mounted, make sure you provide enough cape skin to make the taxidermist's work easier. Since most hunters are unfamiliar with a total caping procedure, the most practical approach is to free the cape from the shoulders, front legs, brisket, and neck and leave the skull and antlers intact for final caping by the taxidermist. Remember, a headskin cape includes the hide covering the entire shoulder area and the front legs. I would suggest that you remove the headskin cape before you skin the rest of the carcass.

Begin caping by cutting through the hide all the way around the deer's body well behind the front shoulders. Next, make an incision that runs from each front leg hock, along the rear margin of the leg to join the initial caping incision that circles the body behind

Storing meat, antlers, and capes in an elevated bear-proof cache is essential in the backcountry. Photo Credit: Durwood Hollis

Heavy-duty elk quarter bags will keep meat from drying out, provide protection from insects, and are reusable. Photo Credit: McCoy Industries

the shoulders. Finally, make an incision that begins between the shoulders and runs forward along the spine to the base of the skull.

Working carefully with your knife, skin the hide forward and down over the shoulders, front legs, brisket, and neck until you reach the juncture of the skull and the spinal column. Sever the head from the spine by cutting through the neck at the base of the skull. At this point you can roll the cape up (skin side in) and transport the head and its attached cape directly to your taxidermist.

Game Care Gear: The following items—knives (general purpose, skinning, and boning), knife sharpening tools, bone saw or axe, carcass bag, and disposable gloves—are essential game care components. Since knives, knife sharpening, and butchering tools are covered in the following chapter, I'll defer comment on those issues at this time. Nevertheless, meat protection from environmental invectives and personal protection from the mess associated with field dressing does deserve some mention.

Nothing protects skinned elk meat any better than a breathable cloth bag. For my money, the best choice in protection are heavy-weight cotton quarter bags. After use, you can soak the bags in cold water, wash them, and then use them over and over again. Best of all, the heavier material offers enhanced protection from meat-eating bees, dirt, and wind-blown debris. I've had good luck with game bags manufactured by Alaska Game Bag (P. O. Box 21025, Anchorage, AK 99521, 907/337-9538), and McCoy Industries (15093 Marquette St., Moorpark, CA 93021, 805/523-0722). While more expensive than one-time use bags, a set of reusable, heavy-duty elk quarter bags will provide many years of game care service.

Protective gloves are another good idea. Field dressing an elk can result in considerable mess. Anything you can do to keep blood, digestive fluids, and

Elk meat goes well in many recipes. Best of all, it's lower in fat and calories than beef. Photo Credit: Durwood Hollis

visceral contents off of your hands and clothes is a step in the right direction. I even watched as one successful elk hunter tied on a plastic apron before he began the field dressing procedure. While I don't advocate going to such extremes, the use of protective gloves will make clean-up a lot easier.

In The Freezer: When cutting elk for the freezer, I suggest removing all of the fat, gristle, and bone. The loin and major muscle groups from the hindquarters can be cut into steaks (chops). Meat from the front shoulder, lower legs, as well as all of the trimming can be turned into ground meat. To enhance the taste, a small amount of ground beef or pork sausage can be added. The meat should be sealed in freezer bags (Zip-Loc, One Zip, etc.), or wrapped in plastic-backed freezer paper for long term storage. Frozen, elk meat has a useable life of approximately one-year.

On The Table: Properly cared for, elk meat makes for some excellent table fare. Most hunters report that elk favorably compares to beef—and that's saying a lot! To my palate, the meat has far less of a wild game taste than deer venison. No matter how you serve it, the addition of a gravy side dish will bring out the flavor of the meat. Elk meat also lends itself to inclusion in casseroles, stews, soups and a host of other hearty dishes. Even on the bar-b-que, the meat will remain moist and flavorful. No matter what you use it in, or how it's prepared, the taste is always superb.

From the days of the Pilgrims, across the Great Plains with the pioneers, and into the western wilderness with the mountain men, elk meat was one of the dietary mainstays of those who built this country. Even today, on urban dinner tables, it is still a gourmet treat to savor.

Packaged properly for long-term freezer storage, elk meat will keep up to one year, or more. Photo Credit: Durwood Hollis

Chapter 18

The Elk Hunter's Edge

Select the right knife for the job

The telephone call came to my office late Friday afternoon. The voice on the other end of the line spoke with authority.

"The elk are down on the ranch. You better hurry and get here. There's only a couple of days left in the season," the voice proclaimed.

I recognized the voice as that of a rancher who lived in a neighboring state. Quite frankly, I had been waiting for this telephone call all season. Now, the hunt invitation had come at the last minute. No matter, with an invitation like that you don't hesitate. I thanked the rancher for his generosity, hung up the telephone, and started things in motion.

First, I made a quick call home and asked my eldest teenage son to throw my gear together. Then, I beat it out of the office as quickly as possible. Arriving home, I didn't even take time to change my clothes. It was going to be an all-night drive to the ranch and there wasn't any time to spare. In short order, I tossed down a sandwich, grabbed my hunting gear, and piled into the truck.

Driving most of the night without any sleep can be grueling, but somehow an internal shot of hunting adrenaline kept me wide awake. By the time I turned off the pavement onto the ranch access road, it was well-past midnight. And it took another hour of tough four-wheeling, to make it to the solitary cabin that served as ranch headquarters. As expected, the place was empty. The rancher lived in town and he had already filled his elk license.

With no time to waste, I scrambled inside the cabin, dumped my gear on the single bed, and began to get ready for the coming day. After changing my clothes and pulling on boots, I couldn't seem to find a knife anywhere. Apparently, my son had forgotten to put it in my bag. Left with few options, I searched the cabin for a replacement. After rummaging around in the meager supply of kitchen utensils, I managed to come up with a dull paring knife. It would have to do. A flat rock outside of the cabin and lots of elbow grease produced a passable edge. A piece of folded and taped cardboard turned into a functional sheath. Before the morning was over, I dressed out a nice bull with that same humble paring knife.

After your bullet or broadhead has produced the desired effect, every bit of hunting strategy, equip-

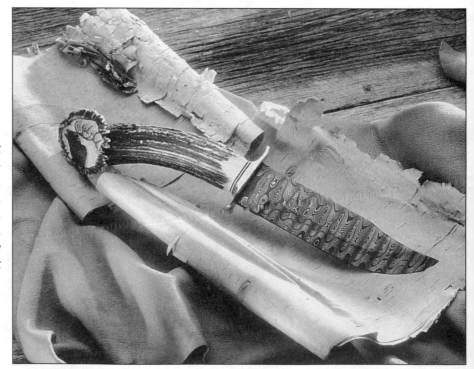

Commissioned by the Rocky Mountain Elk Foundation in 1999, this custom fixed-blade elk knife, by Loyd Thomsen (Horsehead Creek Knives, HCR 46, Box 19, Oe richs, SD 57763, 605/535-6162), features a Damascus blade, brass guard, and carved natural slug handle Photo Credit: Kevin Elbeck

ment, and skill are meaningless without a knife. This primary game care tool is absolutely the most important component of a successful elk hunt. Unfortunately, many hunters give little thought to game care cutlery. Faced with the chore of handling an elk, too late they realize that the edged tools they've selected are inadequate for the job. If you don't believe me, then leave your knife at home. Just see how well you do field dressing a bull elk without it. Been there, done that!

Knives can be divided into two groups—fixed-blade and folding. Each style has its own benefits and drawbacks.

Folding knives can be further subdivided into those with locking and non-locking blades. This categorization also must consider blade and handle material, knife configuration, and cutting function. Beyond knives, there are heavy-duty cutting tools for game butchering. In all, the scope of a sharp edge for the elk hunter deserves more than just a casual glance.

Fixed-blade: A fixed-blade knife incorporates the blade and handle into one continuous rigid unit. To protect the user from accidental injury, the knife is carried in a sheath that covers the exposed blade edge. Because the blade is not housed in the handle (as is the case with a folding knife) an endless array of blade shapes can be engineered into a fixed-blade design. And a fixed-blade knife with a full-length tang (extension of the blade completely through the handle) offers blade strength that cannot be equaled by a folding design. Quite frankly, the farther from camp I find myself, the more I like a fixed-blade knife.

Folder: Folding knives generally (some folders have sliding blades) feature a blade that is hinged at some point in the knife frame. When closed, the blade rests inside of, or along the handle frame. To open the knife, the blade is rotated 180-degrees to align with the handle, forming a rigid unit. The addition of a locking mechanism prevents the blade from closing unintentionally and causing injury to the user. While not essential, a blade lock is a desired feature on an outdoor knife. To facilitate blade opening, a nail nick is cut into the back of the blade. In this manner, the edge of a finger nail can be used to extract the blade

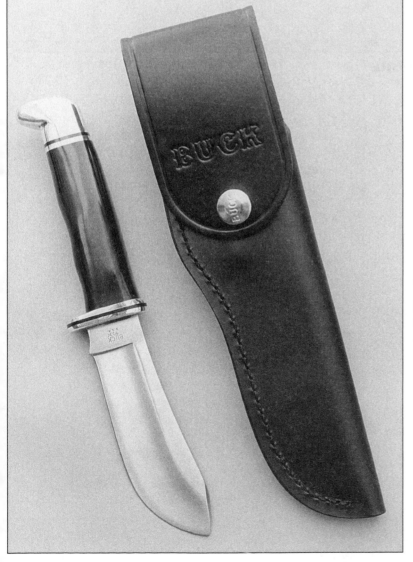

The broad sweeping blade belly and somewhat blunt point of the Buck fixed-blade Skinner makes it ideally suited for separating hide from carcass.
Photo Credit: Buck Knives

from its resting place within the knife handle. As an alternative, an opening hole in the blade back can be engaged with the pad of the thumb to affect the same process. As well, other blade opening methods and mechanisms are also used. More of a hassle to open and close in cold weather and definitely difficult to keep clean, the folder only offers carrying convenience—nothing more. That's not to say that I dislike the folding knife for elk work. On the contrary, a large folder is just the ticket much of the time. It's just that I am fond of both types of knife designs.

Blade Material: A knife blade can be made out of anything—wood, bone, stone, glass, metal, steel, or ceramic. Early man used fire-hardened wood, pieces of sharpened bone, and chipped stone for his butchering implements. Fortunately, the evolution of society included the development of steel, an alloy of iron with no more than 2 percent carbon. Various other elements can be combined in this mixture to produce selected properties. Throw a little chromium in the mix and you have rust-resistant, or stainless steel.

Despite the recent entry of ceramic and other exotic materials into the knife arena, steel still remains the preeminent blade material. Various formulations of carbon steel have been, and continue to be used as blade materials. However, carbon steel rusts quickly in the face of environmental invectives. For this reason, stainless steel is usually the blade material of choice for outdoors folk. The presence or absence of elements within the steel (carbon, chromium, cobalt, copper, manganese, molybdenum, nickel, phosphorous, silicon, sulfur, tungsten, and vanadium), are indicated by a particular numbering designation. Popular stainless steels for use in the manufacture of hunting knives are 440A, 440B, 440C, 425 modified, 154CM, ATS 34, ATS-55, AUS-6, AUS-8, AUS-10, CPM 420V, and CPM 440V. Other stainless formulations can be used, but those listed above are often seen in both production and custom knife offerings.

Once the knife maker selects a particular type of steel for his cutlery, then specific procedures are used to bring out the performance qualities of that steel. This is done through a heat-treating process. The heat dissolves the carbon and other trace metal into the iron. Using a combination of repeated heating, quenching, and forging, the actual lattice structure of the steel is reduced to a fine grain. Internal stress is reduced through tempering (a slight softening of the steel) which produces a blade material that is able to resist impact, deformation, and breakage.

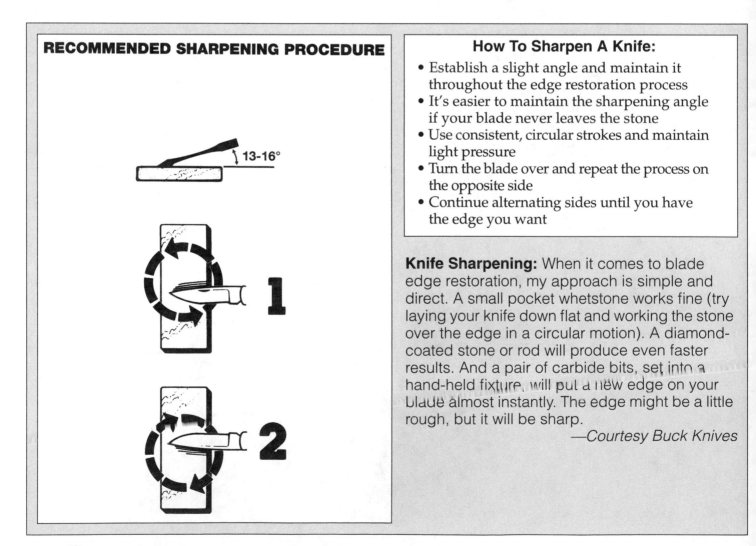

RECOMMENDED SHARPENING PROCEDURE

13-16°

1

2

How To Sharpen A Knife:

- Establish a slight angle and maintain it throughout the edge restoration process
- It's easier to maintain the sharpening angle if your blade never leaves the stone
- Use consistent, circular strokes and maintain light pressure
- Turn the blade over and repeat the process on the opposite side
- Continue alternating sides until you have the edge you want

Knife Sharpening: When it comes to blade edge restoration, my approach is simple and direct. A small pocket whetstone works fine (try laying your knife down flat and working the stone over the edge in a circular motion). A diamond-coated stone or rod will produce even faster results. And a pair of carbide bits, set into a hand-held fixture, will put a new edge on your blade almost instantly. The edge might be a little rough, but it will be sharp.

—*Courtesy Buck Knives*

BASIC STEPS IN MANUFACTURING A KNIFE

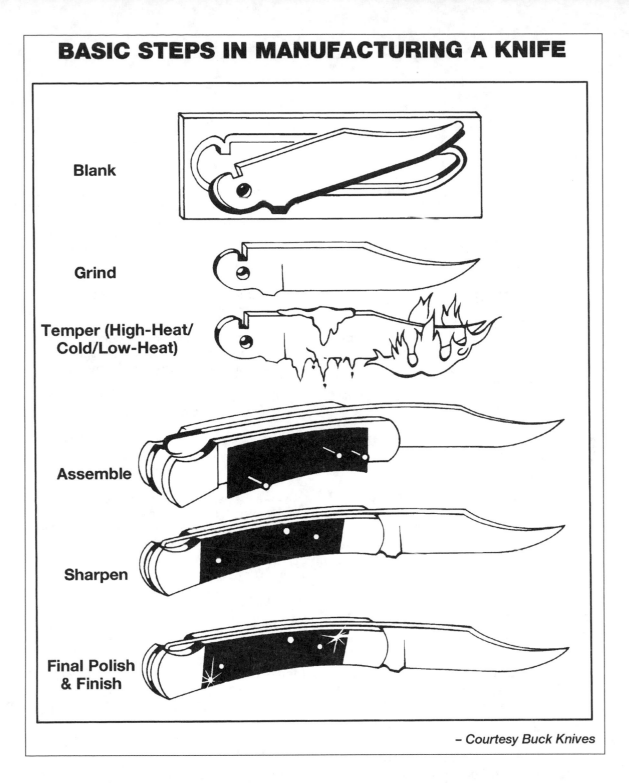

Blank

Grind

Temper (High-Heat/ Cold/Low-Heat)

Assemble

Sharpen

Final Polish & Finish

– Courtesy Buck Knives

The measurement of the steel hardness is determined by using a Rockwell testing machine. This process measures the resistance against a diamond-tipped cone impressed, under constant pressure, into the blade itself. The Rockwell measurement is expressed by the letters, "Rc," followed by a number. Blades testing in the range of Rc 52-55 are relatively soft, will sharpen easily, but offer limited edge life. At the other extreme, blades measuring Rc 60-62 are extremely hard, will present considerable sharpening difficulty, but provide extended edge usage. At the midpoint, Rc 56-59, a blade offers the best combina-

tion of edge retention and ease of sharpening. Most knife manufacturers produce outdoor cutlery with blades testing in this mid-range of hardness.

Blade Shape: Three blade shapes—clip-point, drop-point, and skinning—are useful in elk field care. The first two are multi-functional. The last one is a more specialized pattern. The back spine of a clip-point blade features the tip "clipped" away in a straight or concave manner. This blade shape offers an extremely fine point for precise incisions. As well, the clip-point blade belly usually provides a sweeping curve that also makes it useful in skinning chores.

BASIC BLADE SHAPES

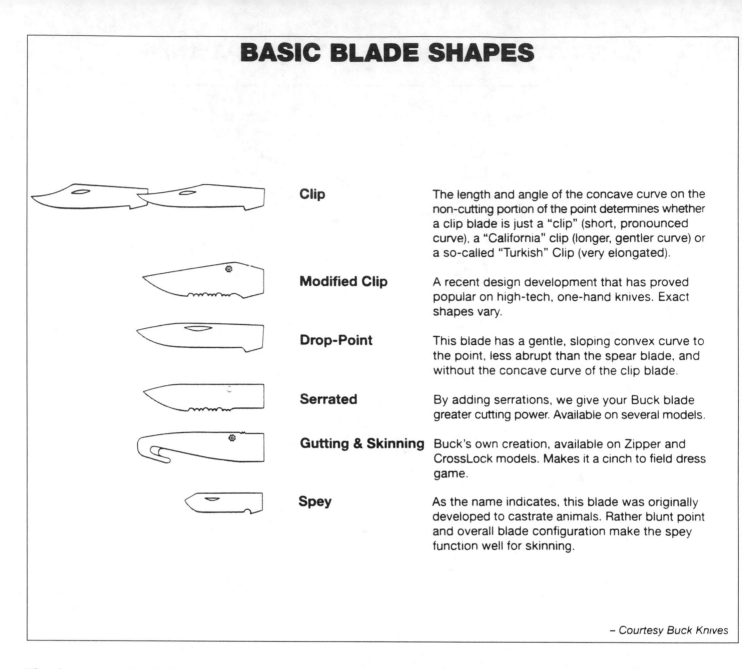

Clip
The length and angle of the concave curve on the non-cutting portion of the point determines whether a clip blade is just a "clip" (short, pronounced curve), a "California" clip (longer, gentler curve) or a so-called "Turkish" Clip (very elongated).

Modified Clip
A recent design development that has proved popular on high-tech, one-hand knives. Exact shapes vary.

Drop-Point
This blade has a gentle, sloping convex curve to the point, less abrupt than the spear blade, and without the concave curve of the clip blade.

Serrated
By adding serrations, we give your Buck blade greater cutting power. Available on several models.

Gutting & Skinning
Buck's own creation, available on Zipper and CrossLock models. Makes it a cinch to field dress game.

Spey
As the name indicates, this blade was originally developed to castrate animals. Rather blunt point and overall blade configuration make the spey function well for skinning.

– Courtesy Buck Knives

The drop-point blade features a convex curve on the back edge of the blade tip. This enhances the strength of the blade tip, which many hunters prefer. Like the clip, the drop-point also features a broad sweeping blade belly for skinning. The skinning pattern can feature a blade tip that rises above (trailing-point) the blade spine, or with an abrupt clip-point. Extremely useful when separating the hide from underlying muscle tissue, the skinning blade design is an important game care tool.

Particular mention should be made of the gut-hook blade design. This is nothing more than a sharpened hook for hide slitting to facilitate skinning. The gut-hook may be engineered into the back of the leading edge of the blade, or it may be an individualized blade all by itself. The European-style gut-hook is simply a blunt-nosed blade that cuts only after the hide rides up onto the blade edge. More familiar to American elk hunters are the hook-style gut-hook

blades typified by the Buck CrossLock Hunter (Buck Knives, 1900 Weld Bl., El Cajon, CA 92020, 800/326-2825), and the Remington Rattler folder (870 Remington Dr., Madison, NC 27025, 800/243-9700). I like a gut-hook because it's like having a built-in zipper in the hide. There's never any worry about slitting open underlying viscera or muscle tissue. If you skin very many elk, the strength of the gut-hook design will quickly become manifest.

Blade Length: If all you ever hunt are deer and antelope, then you can field dress and skin either species with nothing more than a medium-size pocket knife. On the other hand, a bull elk is a lot bigger than a buck deer or antelope. A 2- or 3-inch blade is all right on smaller animals. However, when used on an elk, the abbreviated blade length will draw you into the work. This fosters a situation where the knife works you, rather than the other way around. My own preference for elk is a blade in the 4- to 6-inch

This fixed-blade Jim Zumbo signature elk knife from Schrade features both a bone saw and a guthook on the blade spine. Photo Credit: Schrade Cutlery

range. The longer length allows me to control knife movements without undue discomfort or strain. Most writers will tell you that the mark of a novice hunter is an overly large knife. If that's true, than the elk knife designed by outdoor writer Jim Zumbo for Schrade Cutlery (7 Schrade Ct., Ellenville, NY 12428, 800/351-9658) is definitely an anomaly. The 6-inch blade on the knife is just about the right length. In addition, the gut-hook tip and the saw-edge blade spine make this knife the quintessential edged game care tool.

Handles: The purpose of a knife handle is simply blade control. Knife handles can be made of synthetic (rubber, laminates, plastic, etc.). Likewise, natural materials (bone, horn, antler, wood, etc.) are also used. The primary handle considerations are: comfort, control, and durability. Heat-molded thermo-rubber/plastic materials (Kraton, Sermollan,

> **The knife you carry is as important as any other single piece of hunting gear. Without it, you're out of business.**

etc.), which have a resilient "tacky" feel, offer enhanced user comfort, control, and durability. Other synthetics, like Micarta, carbon fiber, and the tough G-10 handle material provide lightweight and high tensile strength. However, if the handle is smooth, it may prove to be difficult to grasp when wet. Natural handle materials, like chipped bone and stag offer magnificent beauty and a wonderful gripping surface. Unfortunately, bone and stag can chip or break if the knife is dropped on a hard surface. Stacked leather washers are another possibility. The drawback here is that the leather is usually polished smooth and provides a less than adequate gripping surface. Also, leather doesn't hold up well when placed in contact with moisture (blood, digestive fluids), and if neglected it can dry out and become brittle. Wood can also be used for a knife handle, but unless it is epoxy-impregnated, it will

Caping a bull elk can be tedious work. A steady hand and a sharp knife are necessary prerequisites. Photo Credit: Durwood Hollis

When it comes to skinning elk quarters, a sharp knife is your best friend. Photo Credit: Bob Robb

Working in conjunction with outdoor writer, Jim Zumbo, Schrade Cutlery developed this lockblade folder especially for elk hunters. Photo Credit: Schrade Cutlery

demand continual care. My personal choice for an elk knife handle is either stag or thermo-rubber/plastic. Basically, it's a choice between warm and lovely, and cold and ugly—you decide!

Carrying Containment: There are four ways to carry a knife: in a sheath, with a clip, in your pocket, or in your pack. Knife sheaths can be crafted out of many materials—leather, fabric, or molded synthetic are common. As much thought needs to be put into sheath construction as the design of the knife itself. Unfortunately, some cutlery makers seem to regard the sheath as an afterthought. Fixed-blade knife sheaths can be made from top-grade leather, nylon webbing, or a molded synthetic material and feature a snap strap/flap, or other type of security containment device. The features to look for in a fixed-blade knife sheath are safety, security, durability, and carrying comfort. Folding knives can also be carried in a sheath or pouch. Made from leather or woven material (nylon webbing, Cordura, or fabric), containment is provided by means of a snap flap or hook/loop clo-

sure. Carrying clips on folding knives are a recent innovation. Pioneered by Spyderco (2091 Golden Gate Canyon Rd., Golden, CO 80403, 800/525-7770) in the 1980s, clothing clips can now be found on many manufacturer's folding knives. Easily attached to any edge—pocket, belt, or boot—the clip does away with the traditional knife sheath and facilitates knife accessibility. Of course, you can always slip a knife into your pocket or pack. It's all up to you.

Game Care Kits: A couple of game care kits deserve special mention. United Cutlery (1425 United Blvd., Sevierville, TN 37876, 423/428-2532) markets a Big Game Field Kit (Model CU1117) that contains all of the tools necessary to field dress, skin, and butcher an elk. The molded plastic carrying case holds a butcher knife, boning knife, skinning knife, bone saw (with two replacement blades), sharpening steel, and one-dozen pair of disposable field dressing gloves. Likewise, Wildlife Enterprises (22 Laurel Wy., Kerrville, TX 78028, 210/257-4538) also makes a Big Game Processing Kit. This grouping of tools includes a bone

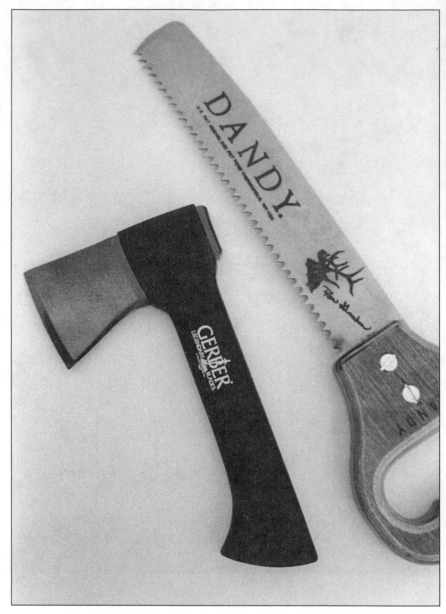

When it comes to heavy-duty cutting chores, an axe or a saw are the tools of choice.
Photo Credit: Durwood Hollis

saw, sharpening steel, boning knife, and a skinning knife. Best of all, all of the tools are contained in a rugged Cordura nylon carrying case which folds flat to conveniently fit into pack or saddle bags.

Rough Cutters: In addition to a knife, you'll need either an axe or a saw to cut through bone (pelvic arch, spinal column, etc.) and cartilage (rib cage, leg joints, etc.). An axe cuts a little faster than a saw, but you have to have room to swing it and there are more safety considerations. The best in this category is Buck Knives' Hunter's Axe, or the Gerber Back Paxe™ (14200 SW 72nd Ave., Portland, OR 97281, 800/950-6161). The Buck axe is crafted from stainless steel, and the thin head is especially designed for working on big game. The Gerber axe is a more general purpose tool, but it can also be used on game. Both Remington and Camillus Cutlery (Western Cutlery line) also market game axes that can make short work of cutting through

heavy bone. When it comes to saws for use on big game, it doesn't get any better than the Dandy Saw (Robertson Enterprises, P. O. Box 1711, Cody, WY 82414, 800/548-5748). Made from Swedish bandsaw steel, this is a "get-serious" saw. The oversized laminated wood handle won't blister your hand, and the non-clog teeth cut like crazy. Available in 12-, 18-, and 24-inch blade lengths, this saw has "elk" written all over it. I also like the Gerber and Browning (One Browning Place, Morgan, UT 84050, 801/876-2711)folding saws. Both products are lightweight, take up little space, and are hard-working tools.

The knife you carry is as important as any other single piece of hunting gear. Without it, you're out of business. With it, you have the best primary game care tool ever designed. Select your elk knife carefully, use it knowledgeably, keep it sharp, and whatever you do—don't leave home without it!

Chapter 19

Elk In The New Millennium

Where do we go from here?

Prior to European contact, an estimated 10 million elk of various species roamed North America. By the beginning of the last century, with the loss of critical habitat and unregulated hunting, this population had been decimated, dropping to less than 100,000 animals. Beginning with the establishment of Yellowstone and Grand Teton National Parks and the creation of the National Elk Refuge in Jackson Hole, Wyoming, elk have slowly made their way back from the brink of endangerment. At the beginning of the new millennium, Canada and the United States together can boast of a total elk population reaching nearly one million animals.

The reemergence of elk on this continent is a game management success unsurpassed in its scope and magnitude. Even as these words are written, throughout the West specific elk population objectives are being met and in some areas—exceeded. In the Midwest and East, where elk have been reintroduced to historic ranges, these populations are steadily increasing. Similar introductions, in areas where suitable habitats and the cooperation of local agencies exist, are already in the planning stages. Even so, the total North American elk population exists at only about 10 percent of its estimated historic numbers. And as long as environmental, biological, and political threats to this species are still manifest, the work remains unfinished.

Over the years, several different membership-based wildlife conservation organizations have been formed.

Elk have emerged from the shadows of unregulated hunting and habitat destruction to where game managers are now seeing population objectives being met and exceeded throughout the west. Photo Credit: Bob Robb

Each of these groups had their own special interests—waterfowl (Ducks Unlimited), quail (Quail Unlimited), pheasants (Pheasants Forever), wild turkeys, wild sheep, deer, bass, trout, as well as others. In the main, hunters and anglers have been the formative and driving forces in these organizations.

In 1984, four dedicated Montana elk hunters joined together to form the Rocky Mountain Elk Foundation (RMEF). The mission statement of this group is, "... to ensure the future of elk, other wildlife, and their habitat." From this humble inception, the RMEF has grown to more than 110,000 members in 50 states and 31 foreign countries. The phenomenal success of this organization is derived from its members, who organize annual fundraising events in their own communities. The monies garnered from these events go toward wildlife projects in specific areas. The U. S. Forest Service, Bureau of Land Management, state and provincial wildlife agencies, and private entities are often involved as cooperators in these efforts.

Many of these efforts are designed to enhance existing elk habitats. Such projects have involved the creation of water sources, the development of prescribed burns to remove decadent vegetation, the planning and implementation of fence removal, the transplantation of elk into suitable areas, and the funding of various wildlife research projects. Through these efforts, more than 2.8 million acres have been conserved and enhanced since the inception of the RMEF. Furthermore, the organization has spent $900 million on various conservation projects in 47 states and eight Canadian provinces.

RMEF's President and Chief Executive Officer, Gary J. Wolfe, is the leading proponent for elk in this country. From the very beginning, his love of the outdoors and wildlife determined his life's work. As a

President and Chief Executive Officer of the Rocky Mountain Elk Foundation, Gary J. Wolfe, has dedicated his life's work to ensuring that elk maintain a firm foothold in the new millennium.
Photo Credit: Rocky Mountain Elk Foundation

young man, he graduated from the University of New Mexico with two Bachelors' degrees, one in biology and the other in chemistry. Subsequently, he also obtained both a Master of Science and Doctor of Philosophy degrees in wildlife biology from Colorado State University.

During his college years, Gary spent four summers as a backcountry/climbing ranger at Mount Rainer National Park, in Washington state. He also spent an extended season as a ranger at Big Bend National Park, Texas. His professional career as a wildlife biologist began at Pennzoil Company's, 500,000-acre Vermejo Park Ranch, in New Mexico. Here, he was responsible for managing one of the southwest's largest elk herds, and directed North America's preeminent private land elk hunting operation. Gary's career at Vermejo Park spanned a total of 12 years, the last three as vice president and general manager.

Gary Wolfe joined the RMEF team in 1986 as the organization's second field director. He has held several other positions during his term of employment. In 1998, he became the foundation's president and chief executive officer. He is a professional member of the Boone and Crockett Club, a life member of RMEF and the National Wildlife Federation, a member of Trout Unlimited, The Wildlife Society, and the National Eagle Scout Association. He has served on the boards of several nonprofit conservation organizations, and is currently a member of the Wildlife Habitat Council's national board of directors—serving on the national Blue Ribbon Committee for the Campaign for Rock Creek. In 1978, Gary Wolfe received the New Mexico Wildlife Federation's "Conservationist of the Year" award. In 1983, he garnered the Northwest Section of the Wildlife Society's "Wildlife Administrator of the Year" award.

In a recent conversation with Gary, several issues surrounding elk and elk hunting in the new millennium were discussed. Paramount among those issues are the following: habitat conservation and management; conflicts between wildlife and human development; the changing pattern of land ownership; the insidious threats that game ranching presents to wild elk populations, and what each of us can do to insure

Habitat improvement projects between the Rocky Mountain Elk Foundation, public agencies, and private land owners, help improve the quantity and quality of forage on elk winter range. Photo Credit: Penny Kaphake/Rocky Mountain Elk Foundation

Unrestrained movement through traditional migration corridors and access to secure wintering grounds are essential to elk herd stability. Photo Credit: Edward Michalski/Rocky Mountain Elk Foundation

the future for elk and elk hunting. The following paragraphs summarize the thoughts that were shared in this discussion.

Habitat Conservation and Management: During the early part of the 20th century, major fires played a significant role in improving elk habitat. With the exception of the Yellowstone fire, there really hasn't been any significant timber fire in the west until very recently, and the effects of those fires won't be known for a year or more. Where fires have occurred, the U. S. Forest Service and local agencies have made every effort to quickly control the extent of the burn. All too often this fire control strategy was based primarily on timber protection. Fire of any origin was seen in a negative light and suppressed on the grounds of the protection of life and private property. This message was strongly preached to the public through educational programs. Unfortunately, such fire control efforts have allowed the forest canopy to close in, blocking out sunlight and destroying plant communities that are valuable food sources for elk and other wildlife. Many fires are nothing more than a naturally occurring events. If these events are prematurely curtailed through overly -

aggressive suppression efforts, it can have a negative effect on wildlife. Efforts must continue to educate the public to the fact that fire can be beneficial to the entire forest ecosystem—including elk.

Conflict with Man: Where elk come into contact with man, conflicts occur. This is particularly true when development occurs along elk migration routes, or on historic wintering grounds. Simply put, elk tear up fences, damage crops, and conflict with domestic stock. When this happens, it presents a serious challenge for the private land owner. Without any alternative recourse (financial compensation, land exchanges, etc.), or other type of incentive, the land owner is often forced into making difficult choices. Invariably, these choices negatively impact elk. There is a very real need to develop a partnership between private land owners, game officials and sportsmen so that the land owner is able to see monetary gain by allowing elk on his property. Management tools like private land permits, enhanced public hunting access, and monetary reimbursement for damage, provides tangible benefits to all parties—including the elk.

Elk are wild creatures, not domestic animals. When captive elk are breed like farm animals, the potential for the spread of disease to wild elk is a distinct threat. Photo Credit: Bruce Richards/Rocky Mountain Elk Foundation

Community Planning: Wildlife management should play a part in the development of any community, large or small. Throughout the West, there is a growing need to plan growth so that it minimizes the impact on wildlife. Community planners must begin to focus on strategies to work with private land owners, developers, and game officials to provide enhanced wildlife protection in all areas. This is true in areas where elk traditionally are found, and in non-traditional areas.

Changing Patterns of Land Ownership: Large ranches are being bought up by those interested primarily in personal recreation. This will be a key factor in elk management for the future. Many of these new owners are looking for ways to manage the wildlife on their property. The Rocky Mountain Elk Foundation, along with state game officials have an opportu-

nity to influence this thinking. This strategy should include encouraging habitat protection and public hunting access.

Game Ranching: The most insidious threat to a healthy elk population is commercial game ranching. When elk are fenced in and raised like livestock, a serious risk for disease introduction and transmission is present. Already we have seen the emergence of bovine tuberculosis and chronic wasting disease (CWD). Captive elk can and have escaped, which presents a threat to wild elk populations. We have seen a move by ranchers to take such operations away from the control of game officials and transfer that responsibility to agriculture authorities. This would remove many of the restrictions now in place, and open the door to the exploitation of these animals purely for profit. State legislators have the ability to make

The future of elk hunting is in our hands. Quality bulls, like this Arizona giant, will become a fleeting memory if we all don't get involved. Photo Credit: Duwane Adams

changes in the laws governing commercial game ranching. To protect the integrity of wild elk herds, the future expansion of these operations must be limited, and where possible—phased out over time.

Get Involved: Hunters need to get involved politically. If you can't find the time to participate individually, then contribute your support to groups like the RMEF, the NRA, and other similar organizations. Currently, there are 190 million acres of National Forest lands on which we need to insure continued public access. There is a resurgence of the movement to return public lands to the individual states. Should this occur, states have a proven track record of converting public land to private ownership. This would spell disaster for wildlife in general, and elk specifically. This is a complex issue with no simple answers. Unfortunately, sportsmen tend to be apathetic about these matters. The time for apathy is over. We need to be actively involved in the planning of public policy issues with regards to forests, parks, and community

development. The best way to get involved is to join an organization that will work for you.

What Does the Future Hold?: Public perceptions of hunting will determine its future. As our population grows, we need to do a better job of presenting a positive image of hunting and hunters. Shot-up road signs, poaching and other selfish and lawless actions only strengthen the anti-hunting position. Hunters are less than 7 percent of the total population. If we don't take steps to influence public opinion in a positive manner, then hunting may not be accepted as a legitimate recreational activity. Without that acceptance, everyone loses—hunters and wildlife alike.

What can we do? The answer to that question is easy. Avoid getting into arguments about the efficacy of hunting. No matter how well you present your position, you can end up in a "no-win" situation. An old adage states, "a person convinced against his will, is of the same mind still." Don't try to convert anti-hunters. You'll fail at every turn. Even worse, you may push

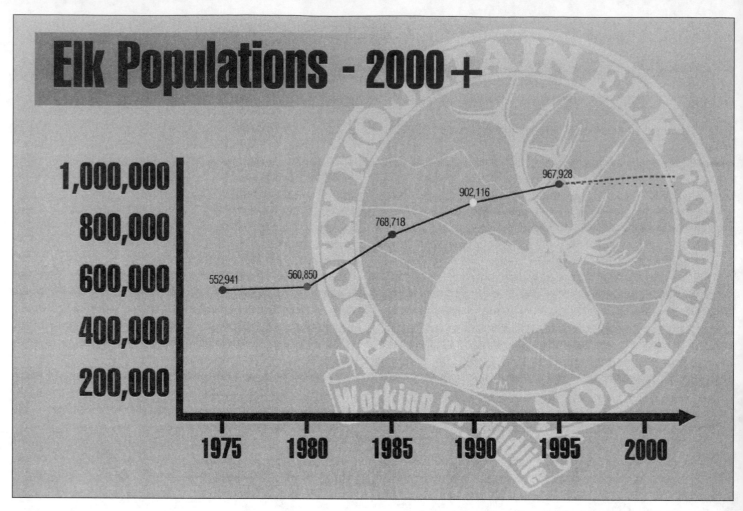

Elk Populations - 2000 +

1,000,000
800,000
600,000
400,000
200,000

552,941   560,850   768,718   902,116   967,928

1975   1980   1985   1990   1995   2000

—Courtesy Rocky Mountain Elk Foundation

them into a more rigid stance. The very concept of hunting has emotional overtones. Try as you will, you cannot overcome emotion with logic. Simply endeavor to get others to accept hunting as part of the total recreation picture, no different from skiing, snowmobiling, hiking, fishing and other outdoor sports. Raise that acceptance barrier and then collectively come together on the same side of the issue.

One of the final statements during our conversation summed up the challenge for hunters in the new millennium. Gary said, "We must make sure that public land continues to remain truly open to the entire public for a variety of public uses—including big game hunting." Thankfully, men like Gary Wolfe and the RMEF are in the midst of the battle. Hopefully, we'll win the war.

Afterword

It had been a long day in Wyoming's Bridger-Teton Wilderness. Earlier, in the darkness that preceded the dawn, Wyoming outfitter and guide, John Winter, and I had ridden up the winding trail to the top of Two-Ocean Plateau. Other than a solitary bugle just after daylight, the elk remained hidden in the verdant cover that blanketed the lower slopes. To say the day was disappointing wouldn't be accurate. Just plain boring was more like it.

As the afternoon wore on, we worked our way east along the plateau. Other than a covey of blue grouse, we really hadn't seen any game. To be sure, we'd sat over an elk wallow for a couple hours, stalked through some thin timber, and hunted along a stand of fire-ravaged pines. It was just one of those days when nothing seemed to work.

The sun had long passed its zenith when we arose from an afternoon nap. John rounded up the hobbled horses and we prepared for the evening hunt. In the midst of all of this activity, he stopped suddenly and turned a listening ear to the wind. I hadn't heard anything, but apparently something audible had piqued his interest. Tying the horses to a stunted pine, he walked to the edge of a nearby rim and listened again. This time he turned and smiled. It didn't take a genius to know what that smile meant—elk!

"There's a bull bugling somewhere on that far rim," John said.

With the binoculars it was easy to put the bugle and the bull together. John found the bull—a smallish five-point—standing right in the open. Not that the animal was impressive, but where there was one elk, there could be others. Without a word we were in the saddle and riding laterally along the edge of the scarp searching for the most direct route to the bull. With little sunlight left, and a major storm approaching, time wasn't a luxury we could afford.

It took us an hour to ride from where we heard the first bugle, to a point within stalking distance of the bull. Pulling up at the edge of a heavy stand of timber, we dismounted, tied up the horses, and cautiously moved down the slope toward the steady bugling. It was then that we realized that more than one bull was sounding off. In fact, there were several different bulls, each calling out its own unique challenge to the others. Motioning for me to follow, John led the way down the ridge. With every step, the bugling rose with thundering intensity until it roared in our ears.

John pointed to a thin stand of burned-out timber below and said, "get ready, there's a group of elk working across the slope below us." At first, I couldn't see what he was pointing at. Then a solitary cow elk moved through the dead pines like a gray ghost. In short order, another, and then another cow followed in rapid succession. At that moment, the bull roared again, and again, each time with deep-throated fervor. This definitely wasn't the same bull we'd heard earlier.

"The bull is in the rear," John whispered.

Taking a sitting position, I draped the Winchester Model 70 across my knees and found the animal in my scope. The elk were less than 100 yards away, moving in a straight line through the trees. Waiting for a clear shot, I placed the crosshairs low and just behind bull's shoulder, and squeezed the trigger.

Without missing a stride, the antlered giant kept on moving. Thinking that I'd missed, I chambered a fresh cartridge. Hurriedly, I shot again only to see my bullet strike the trunk of a dead tree that the bull passed behind. As I worked the bolt for a third time, the excitement of the moment was building as each second passed.

"Take it easy. You hit him good the first time. Put another bullet right where the first one went and it'll be game over," John's reassuring voice came to my ears.

This time there was no mistaking target contact. When I sent the bullet on its way, a distinct whack came to my ears. The bull bugled for the last time, missed his footing, pitched forward and then started to roll down the slope. Fortunately, his antlers hung up on some blowdown timber. Indeed, it was game over!

Now, the problem was getting to the animal. We slid and scrambled our way down the ridge, picking our way through a maze of burned stumps and dead trees. When we reached the downed warrior, his size was overwhelming. The antlers were thick and wide, with bases nearly a foot in diameter and six long tines on each side. Indeed, this was a bull of marvelous proportions.

Hurriedly, the business of field dressing was undertaken in the failing light. When we were finished, I realized that there would never be an end to the challenge of elk hunting. Intoxicated with success, my thoughts pressed forward to the next time. And as I watched as the darkness gradually cloaked the land, all that remained was the search for answers to questions only the stars could ask.

Game Departments

Western States and Alaska

Alaska Dept. of Fish and Game P. O. Box 25526 Juneau, AK 99802 telephone: 907/465-4112 www.state.ak.us/local/akpages/FISH.GAME	Nevada Div. of Wildlife P. O. Box 10678 Reno, NV 89520 telephone: 775/688-1500 www.state.nv.us/cnr/nvwildlife
Arizona Game and Fish Dept. 2222 W. Greenway Rd. Phoenix, AZ 85023 telephone: 602/942-3000 www.gf.state.az.us	New Mexico Game and Fish Dept. State Capitol, Villagra Bldg. Santa Fe, NM 87503 telephone: 505/827-7911 www.gmfsh.state.nm.us
California Dept. of Fish and Game 1416 Ninth St. Sacramento, CA 94244 telephone: 916/227-2244 www.dfg.ca.gov	Oregon Dept. of Fish and Wildlife P. O. Box 59 Portland, OR 97207 telephone: 503/872-5268 www.dfw.state.or.us
Colorado Div. Of Wildlife 6060 Broadway Denver, CO 80216 telephone: 303/291-7299 www.dnr.state.co.us/wildlife	Utah Div. of Wildlife Resources 1594 W. North Temple Salt Lake City, UT 84114 telephone: 801/538-4700 www.nr.state.ut.us/dwr/homeypg.htm
Idaho Dept. of Fish and Game P. O. Box 25 Boise, ID 83707 telephone: 208/334-3700 www.state.id.us/fishgame	Washington Dept. of Fish and Wildlife 600 Capitol Way N. Olympia, WA 98501 telephone: 360/902-2200 www.wa.gov/wdfw
Montana Dept. of Fish, Wildlife and Parks 1420 E. Sixth Ave. Helena, MT 59620 telephone: 406/444-2535 http://fwp.state.mt.us	Wyoming Game and Fish Dept. 5400 Bishop Blvd. Cheyenne, WY 82206 telephone: 307/777-4600 http://gf.state.wy.us

Selected American Elk Rifle Cartridge Ballistics

Caliber	Bullet Weight (grains)	Muzzle Velocity (feet per second)	Muzzle Energy (foot pounds)
7mm-08*	175	2600	2627
.280 Rem.	175	2650	2730
.284 Win.*	175	2600	2627
.300 Savage	180	2350	2207
.30-40 Krag	180	2430	2360
.307 Win.	180	2510	2519
.308 Win.	180	2620	2743
.30-06 Spfd.	180	2700	2913
.30-06 Spfd.	220	2410	2837
.300 H&H Mag.	180	2800	3315
.300 H&H Mag.	220	2550	3167
.300 Win. Mag.	180	2960	3501
.300 Win. Mag	220	2680	3508
8mm Rem. Mag.	185	3080	3896
8mm Rem. Mag.	220	2830	3912
.338 Win. Mag.	200	2960	3890
.338 Win. Mag.	210	2830	3735
.338 Win. Mag.	225	2785	3871
.338 Win. Mag.	250	2660	3927
.348 Win.	200	2520	2820
.356 Win.	200	2460	2688
.356 Win.	250	2160	2591
.358 Win.	200	2490	2753
.358 Win.	250	2250	2810
.350 Rem. Mag.	200	2710	3261
.35 Whelen	200	2675	3177
.35 Whelen	250	2400	3197
.444 Marlin	240	2350	2942
.444 Marlin	265	2120	2644
.405 Win.	300	2200	3220
.45-70 Govt.	300	1810	2182
.45-70 Govt.	405	1330	1590

* Non-commercial handload, Barnes, F. C., *Cartridges of the World*, 7th Edition, DBI Books, 1993
Remington Centerfire Ballistics Table, Remington Firearms Catalog ,2000

Selected European Elk Rifle Cartridge Ballistics

Caliber	Bullet Weight (grains)	Muzzle Velocity (feet per second)	Muzzle Energy (foot pounds)
308 Norma Mag.	180	3100	3842
.358 Norma Mag.	250	2790	4322
7mm Mauser	175	2440	2313
8mm Mauser	170	2360	2100
8mm Mauser	196	2526	2778
8mm Mauser	198	2625	3031
8mm Mauser	200	2320	2390
8mm Mauser	227	2330	2737
8x64 Brenneke	185	2890	3420
8x64 Brenneke	227	2578	3347
9.3x62mm Mauser	232	2624	3548
9.3x62mm Mauser	256	2560	3726
9.3x62mm Mauser	286	2360	3544
9.3x62mm Mauser	293	2430	3842

Selected British Elk Rifle Cartridge Ballistics

Caliber	Bullet Weight (grains)	Muzzle Velocity (feet per second)	Muzzle Energy (foot pounds)
.375 H&H Mag.	270	2690	4340
.375 H&H Mag.	300	2530	4265

Selected Weatherby Elk Rifle Cartridge Ballistics

Caliber	Bullet Weight (grains)	Muzzle Velocity (feet per second)	Muzzle Energy (foot pounds)
7mm Wby. Mag.	175	3070	3662
.300 Wby. Mag.	180	3300	4352
.300 Wby. Mag.	190	3030	3873
.300 Wby. Mag.	220	2905	4122
.340 Wby. Mag.	200	3260	4719
.340 Wby. Mag.	210	3250	4924
.340 Wby. Mag.	250	2980	4931
.378 Wby. Mag.	270	3180	6062
.378 Wby. Mag.	300	2925	5701

Barnes, F. C., *Cartridges of the World*, 7th Edition, DBI Books, 1993

BIG BOOKS FOR BIG HUNTING SUCCESS

The Complete Guide to Hunting Knives
by Durwood Hollis
Once you bring your game home, the next part of the hunt (utilization) begins. Knowing which knife to use to get the job done quickly and safely is a paramount concern. This text details information on construction, materials, characteristics, handles, sheaths, and blades as well as care and maintenance. Knives for big game, small game, upland and waterfowl, camping and filleting are covered.

Softcover • 8-1/2 x 11 • 224 pages
225 b&w photos • 16-page color section
Item# BHKN • $19.95

Big Bucks the Benoit Way
Secrets from America's First Family of Whitetail Hunting
by Bryce Towsley
Finally, the long-awaited second book on the tried-and-true hunting strategies of the legendary Benoit family. Although tracking and woodsmanship are emphasized, hunters of all ages, no matter where they hunt, will gain the knowledge needed to bag trophy bucks.

Hardcover • 8-1/2 x 11 • 208 pages
150 b&w photos • 16-page color section
Item# HBB • $24.95

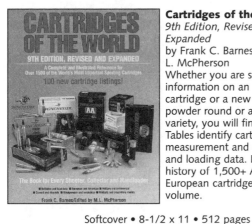

Cartridges of the World
9th Edition, Revised and Expanded
by Frank C. Barnes, Edited by M. L. McPherson
Whether you are searching for information on an obsolete cartridge or a new wildcat, a black powder round or a smokeless variety, you will find it here. Tables identify cartridges by measurement and offer ballistics and loading data. Learn the history of 1,500+ American and European cartridges in this single volume.

Softcover • 8-1/2 x 11 • 512 pages
627 b&w photos
Item# COW9 • $27.95

Gun Digest® 2001
55th Annual Edition
edited by Ken Ramage
This edition of an annual favorite incorporates the best writing on arms history, technical development and use. Specifications and pricing for more than 3,000 firearms are included in the illustrated catalog, plus detailed specifications and pricing for scopes, ammunition, iron sights and reloading presses. Updated directories of the firearms industry, arms books, periodicals and shooting associations round out this information-packed volume. Bonus! Buy this edition to receive a free trial subscription to Gun List or Blade magazine.

Softcover • 8-1/2 x 11 • 544 pages
2,000+ b&w photos
Item# GD2001 • $24.95

Hunting Mature Bucks
by Larry Weishuhn
Special focus on the awesome old buck and incredible tips from North America's top whitetail deer authorities sets the pace for hunting those big, elusive bucks. Learn about proven hunting methods and herd management techniques.

Softcover • 6 x 9 • 213 pages
80 b&w photos
Item# HMB01 • $14.95

Mule Deer:
Hunting Today's Trophies
by Tom Carpenter and Jim Van Norman
Monster mule deer lead hunters into the toughest territory around, but this book shows you how to bring back "one for the wall." From the art of spotting mule deer before they spot you to the delicate job of stalking for the perfect shot, this book puts you right in the middle of mule deer action.

Softcover • 8-1/2 x 11 • 256 pages
150 b&w photos
16-page color section
Item# HTMD • $19.95

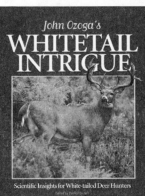
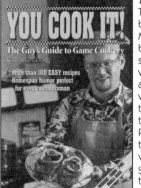